CW01508923

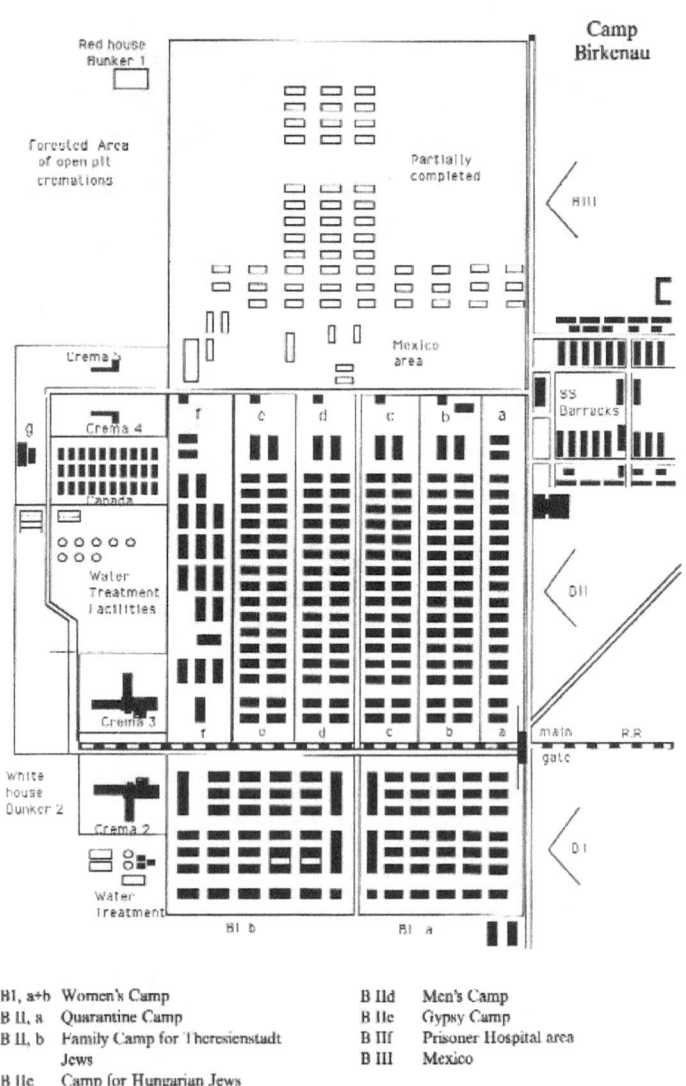

Camp Birkenau

Red house Bunker 1

Forested Area of open pit cremations

Partially completed

B III

Crema 5

Crema 4

Canada

Mexico area

SS Barracks

g

Water Treatment Facilities

f   e   d   c   b   a

D II

Crema 3

f   e   d   c   b   a

main gate   R.R

white house Bunker 2

Crema 2

D I

Water Treatment

Bl b   Bl a

B I, a+b   Women's Camp
B II, a   Quarantine Camp
B II, b   Family Camp for Theresienstadt Jews
B IIc   Camp for Hungarian Jews

B IId   Men's Camp
B IIe   Gypsy Camp
B IIf   Prisoner Hospital area
B III   Mexico

Layout of Auschwitz

The Master of Auschwitz

by

Rudolf Höss

Kommandant 𝕊𝕊

Together with His Nürnberg Interviews

Stephen R. Pastore, ed.

Gunther Hart, translator

American Bibliographic Press

2017

The Master of Auschwitz

Together with the Nürnberg Interviews

Edited by Stephen R. Pastore

Translated by Gunther Hart

American Bibliographical Press

New York, New York

Copyright © 2017 by American Bibliographical Press

Published by American Bibliographical Press
New York, New York

Library of Congress Cataloging-in-Publication Data
Höss, Rudolf..

The Master of Auschwitz

    p.   cm.

Includes bibliographical references and index.
ISBN 978-1-937727-67-3
1. Höss, Rudolf, 1901-1947-Years as commandant of Auschwitz.

DD247.SRP281913 2017 1043.6'2100037'092—dc37 [B] 17-3737886

First Edition
1 3 5 7 9 8 6 4 2
Printed in the United States of America on acid-free paper

The
Master
of
Auschwitz

Upper Left:: SS-Sturmbannführer Rudolf Höß (actual German spelling)

Upper Right: Höss on trial at the Polish Supreme Tribunal for War Crimes

Lower Middle: Höss on the scaffold at Auschwitz

The SS Camp Street

Above: A transport of Hungarian Jews arrives at Auschwitz–Birkenau in the spring/early summer of 1944. The twin chimneys of crematoria 2 and 3 can just be seen in the background to the left and right of the train.

Above: Auschwitz prisoners digging drainage ditches at Birkenau—one of the most life-sapping tasks in the camp.

Introduction

I have been studying the Third Reich for nearly three decades, commencing with my interest in the artwork of Adolf Hitler. As a student of art history and a collector of certain renown, I tried to find in Hitler's paintings the seeds of the future dictator. I found none. But the search led to the life of the young man who painted so avidly, the young man who gave up his life to pursue art. It is a story common to many artists, great and small. But no other artist also possessed within himself the dormant power of a dictator. Vincent Van Gogh had a background similar to Hitler's: a loving mother and a disapproving father; an obsession with art above all other things including food and shelter. Both failed miserably. Both ended in suicide. But it would be absurd to wonder what would have happened had Van Gogh risen to the same positon of absolute power that Hitler attained.

Needless to say, innumerable historians have wrestled with the problem that Hitler poses: how could an uneducated, failed artist living in a homeless shelter in 1914 become Chancellor of Germany in 1933? The answer I believe in part, evolves from the memoir of Rudolf Höss, the one-time commandant of Auschwitz. Written when he was awaiting execution for his role in the Holocaust, Höss says many things. Often he attempts to hold his wife and family blameless because of their supposed lack of knowledge as to what went on beyond the garden wall of the commandant's residence in Auschwitz, the striped uniforms of his domestic help, the comings and goings of SS personnel at all hours of the day and night, the incessant trains delivering what? the ever present stench and smoke. No reasonable person would blame him for obfuscating in an attempt to keep his family at a distance from his crimes.

He discusses the theory and practice of Hell at Auschwitz in a clinical voice that is genuine and forthright; he denies nothing about his involvement and only in a cursory manner does he dwell on the "just following orders" rationale that permeated the Nürnberg trials. In fact, he admits that he feels, even awaiting the noose, that he was doing the right thing. I had been in a district attorney's office handling felony prosecutions after my stint in law school and in every instance without fail, the accused either flatly denied the allegations or blamed someone else for his criminal acts. Höss does not so indulge. Why?

The answer comes out of his own words as you will see. He truly believed the propaganda not only of the Third Reich but of centuries of such theories preceding the Third Reich, that Judaism and the peoples of eastern Europe posed a mortal threat to his homeland. What else could a patriot do but defend his family, his neighbors and his nation against an enemy hell-bent on their destruction. World War I, the Treaty of Versailles and the impact of foreign investment in Germany all proved the point. Unlike most Populism which tends to appeal mostly to the undereducated, Hitler's doctrines appealed across the intellectual spectrum from brick-layers to brain surgeons. How far away was the "Red Scare" of the McCarthy era in the mid-1950s in the United States were the beginnings of the Nürnberg Laws? How far from depriving the perceived threat of the means to make a living to segregating the enemy within? And then, what to do with them? And what men in the street would rise to their defense?

The memoirs of Rudolf Höss shed light on the questions raised about the often-condemned and frustrated allegations that there was a unique flaw in the German character that allowed the Nazis to unleash their fury on the world, that it could happen nowhere else in the First World. I will let the reader decide if this is so.

Crematorium V Door

An Operating Table from the Infirmary

Höss's Desk and Chair

Prisoner Bunks

The SS Garrison

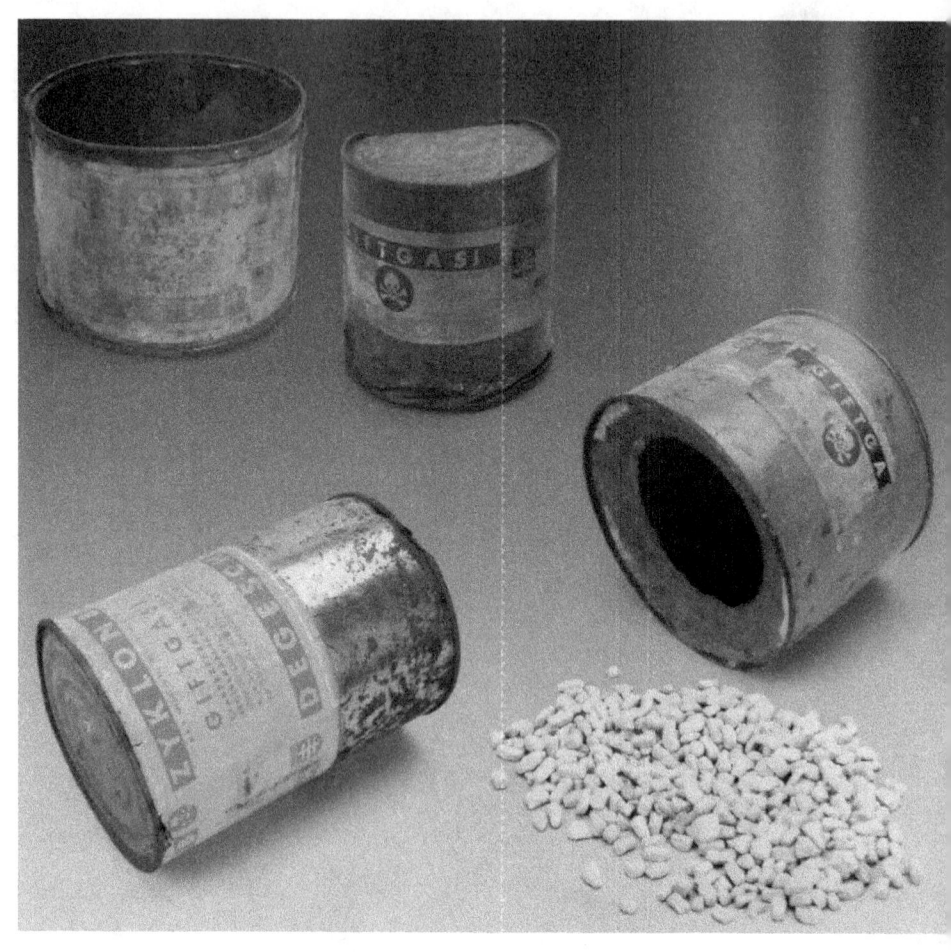

Zyclon B

Crematorium IV

Experimental drugs for use on inmates.

Eyeglasses of the dead to be sent back for German civilians to use.

Inmate art.

I

The Final Solution of the Jewish Question in Concentration Camp Auschwitz

In the summer of 1941, I am unable to recall the exact date, I was suddenly ordered by Himmler's adjutant to report directly to the Reichsführer SS in Berlin. Contrary to his usual custom, his adjutant was not in the room. Himmler greeted me with the following: "The Führer has ordered the Final Solution of the Jewish question. We the SS have to carry out this order. The existing extermination sites in the East- are not in a position to carry out these intended operations on a large scale. I have, therefore, chosen Auschwitz for this purpose. First of all, because of the advantageous transport facilities, and secondly, because it allows this area to be easily isolated and disguised. I had first thought of choosing a higher-ranking SS officer for this job so as to avoid any difficulties with someone who doesn't have the competence to deal with such a difficult assignment. You now have to carry out this assignment. It is to remain between the two of us. It is a hard and difficult job which requires your complete commitment, regardless of the difficulties which may arise. You will learn the further details through Major [Adolf] Eichmann of the RSHA [Reich Security Headquarters], who will soon visit you. The administrative departments involved will be notified by me at the appropriate time. You are sworn to the strictest silence regarding this order. Not even your superiors are allowed to know about this. After your meeting with Eichmann I want you to immediately send me the plans of the intended installations.

"The Jews are the eternal enemies of the German people and must be exterminated. All the Jews within our reach must be annihilated during this war. If we do not succeed in destroying the biological foundation of Jewry now, then one day the Jews will destroy the German people."

After receiving this far-reaching order, I returned to Auschwitz immediately without reporting to my superiors at Oranienburg.

A short time after that Eichmann came to see me at Auschwitz. He revealed the secret plans of the police roundups in the individual countries. I cannot recall the exact sequence anymore. The Jews in eastern Upper Silesia were to be first, then the neighboring areas of the General Government [the southern part of Poland]. At the same time and according to their location, the Jews from Germany and Czechoslovakia, and finallyfrom the West, France, Belgium, and Holland, were to be sent to Auschwitz. He also mentioned to me the approximate numbers anticipated to be transported, but I don't recall the exact figures. We further discussed how the mass annihilation was to be carried out. Only gas was suitable since killing by shooting the huge numbers expected would be absolutely impossible and would also be a tremendous strain on the SS soldiers who would have to carry out the order as far as the women and children were concerned.

Eichmann told me about the killings by engine exhaust gas in the gas vans! and how they had been used in the East up until now. But this method was not suitable in view of the expected mass transports to Auschwitz. We also discussed killing by carbon monoxide through the shower heads in the shower rooms; but this would also create a problem because too many intricate installations would be needed. The killing of the mentally ill was carried out in various places in Germany using this method. But the production of such great quantities of gas for such large numbers of people would be a problem. We didn't reach any decision about this. Eichmann wanted to find a gas that was easy to produce and one that would require no special installations; he then would report back to me." We drove around the Auschwitz area to locate a suitable place. We thought the farmhouse at the northwest comer of Birkenau near planned Section III would be suitable," The house had been abandoned, and it was hidden from view by the surrounding trees and bushes and not too far from the railroad. The bodies could be buried in long, deep pits in the nearby meadows. We didn't think about burning them at this time. We calculated that in the space available in the farmhouse [later called Bunker 1], approximately eight hundred people could be killed using a suitable gas after the building was made airtight. We later found this to be the actual capacity. Eichmann was unable to tell me the precise starting time of the operation because everything was still being planned, and Himmler had not yet given the order to begin.

Eichmann returned to Berlin to report our meeting to Himmler. Several days later I sent a courier to Himmler with a detailed layout and an exact description of the designed installations. I never received a reply or a decision. Later on, Eichmann told me that Himmler agreed with my plan. At the end of November there was an official conference in Eichmann's Berlin office about the overall Jewish operation to which I was also invited. Eichmann's deputies reported the status of the police actions in the individual countries and about the difficulties that interfered with the execution of these operations: how those who were arrested were housed, the preparation of the transport trains, scheduling difficulties, and so on. I was not yet able to find out when the operation would begin. Eichmann still had not found a suitable gas.

In the fall of 1941 a special secret order was issued to the POW camps by which the Russian politruks, commissars, and other political functionaries were selected by the Gestapo and moved to the nearest concentration camp to be killed. Small transports of this kind were continuously arriving at Auschwitz. They were shot in the gravel pits at the Monopol Factory or in the courtyard of Block 11. While I was away on camp-related business, Captain Fritzsch, on his own initiative, employed a gas for the killing of these Russian POWs. He crammed the Russians into the individual cells in the basement [of Block 11] and while using gasmasks he threw the Zyclon B gas into the cells, thereby causing their immediate death.! The gas called Zyclon B was supplied by the firm of Tesch and Stabenow and was used constantly for insect and rodent control. We always had a large supply of gas canisters available. At first only the employees of the firm of Tesch and Stabenow handled this poison gas, a prussic acid preparation, under the strictest safety measures. Later on some members of the Medical Corp S9 were trained at the firm to carry out disinfection procedures, and it was these medics who then carried out disinfection and pest control. During Eichmann's next visit I reported all this to him, about how the Zyclon B was used, and we decided that for the future mass annihilations we would use this gas.

The killing of the above-mentioned Russian POWs using Zyclon B was continued, but no longer in Block 11 because it took at least two days to air out the building. We therefore used the morgue of the crematory as the gassing facility. 10 The doors were made airtight, and we knocked some holes in the ceiling through which we could throw in the gas crystals.

But I remember only one transport of nine hundred Russian POWs who were gassed there. It took several days to burn their bodies.

23

No Russians were ever gassed in the above-mentioned farmhouse [Bunker 1], which now had been prepared for the extermination of the Jews.

I am unable to recall when the destruction of the Jews began-probably in September 1941, or perhaps not until January 1942. At first we dealt with the Jews from Upper Silesia. These Jews were arrested by the Gestapo from Katowice and transported via the Auschwitz-Dziediez railroad and unloaded there. As far as I can recall, these transports never numbered more than a thousand persons.

A detachment of SS from the camp took charge of them at the railroad ramp, and the officer in charge marched them to the bunker in two groups. This is what we called the extermination installation.

Their luggage remained on the ramp and was later brought between the DAW [German Armaments Works]and the railroad station.

The Jews had to undress at the bunker and were told that they would have to go into the delousing rooms. All of the rooms-there were five of them-were filled at the same time. The airtight doors were screwed tight, and the contents of the gas crystal canisters emptied into the rooms through special hatches.

After half an hour the doors were opened and the bodies were pulled out. Each room had two doors. They were then moved using small carts on special tracks to the ditches. The clothing was brought by trucks to the sorting place. All of the work was done by a special contingent of Jews [the Sonderkommando]. They had to help those who were about to die with the undressing, the filling up of the bunkers, the clearing of the bunkers, removal of the bodies, as well as digging the mass graves and, finally, covering the graves with earth. These Jews were housed separately from the other prisoners and, according to Eichmann's orders. they themselves were to be killed after each large extermination action.

After the first transports Eichmann brought an order from Himmler which specified that the gold teeth were to be pulled from the mouths of the bodies, and the hair was to be cut from the dead women.This work was also carried out by special groups of Jews. Supervising the extermination at that time was the camp commander [Captain Hans Aumeier] or the duty officer [Master Sergeant Gerhard Palitzsch].

The sick who could not be brought to the gassing rooms were simply killed with small-caliber weapons by shooting them in the back of the neck. An SS doctor also had to be present. The gas was administered by trained medics.

During the spring of 1942 we were still dealing with small police actions. But during the summer the transports became more numerous and we were forced to build another extermination site. The farm area west of Crematories IV and V, which were built later, was chosen and prepared. Five barracks were built, two near Bunker I and three near Bunker II. Bunker II was the larger one. It held about 1,200 people. As late as the summer of 1942 the bodies were still buried in mass graves. Not until the end of the summer of 1942 did we start burning them. At first we put two thousand bodies on a large pile of wood. Then we opened up the mass graves and burned the new bodies on top of the old ones from the earlier burials. At first we poured waste oil over the bodies. Later on we used methanol. The burning went on continuously-all day and all night. By the end of November all the mass graves were cleared. The number of buried bodies in the mass graves was 107,000. This number contains not only the first Jewish transports which were gassed when we started the burnings, but also the bodies of the prisoners who died in the main Auschwitz camp during the winter of 1941-42 because the crematory was out of order. The prisoners who died at Birkenau [Auschwitz II] are included in that number.

During his visit in the summer of 1942, Himmler very carefully observed the entire process of annihilation. He began with the unloading at the ramps and completed the inspection as Bunker II was being cleared of the bodies. At that time there were no open-pit burnings. He did not complain about anything, but he didn't say anything about it either. Accompanying him were District Leader Bracht and SS General Schmauser. Shortly after Himmler's visit, SS Colonel Blobel from Eichmann's office arrived and brought Himmler's order, which stated that all the mass graves were to be opened and all the bodies cremated. It further stated that all the ashes were to be disposed of in such a way that later on there would be no way to determine the number of those cremated.

Blobel had already conducted various experiments in Kulmhof [Chelmno], which tried to bum the bodies in various ways. He was ordered by Eichmann to show me the installations. I drove with Hossler to Chelmno for an inspection. Blobel had different auxiliary ovens built and used wood and leftover gasoline for the burnings. He also tried using dynamite to blow up the corpses, but he had very little success with this method. After the bones were ground up into dust in the bone mills, the ashes were scattered in nearby wooded areas.

SS Colonel Blobel had a standing order to find the location of all mass graves in the Eastern Sector and to eliminate them. His staff was working under a disguised designation called 1005. The actual work was done by a unit of Jews who were shot after completing their jobs. Concentration Camp Auschwitz had to constantly supply Jews for the 1005 unit.

During my visit to Chelmno I also saw the airtight trucks used to kill prisoners with carbon monoxide gas [exhaust gas from the truck engine]. The officer in charge of that unit, however, described this method as unreliable. The gas supply was erratic and often not enough to kill. I could not learn how many bodies were in the mass graves at Chelmno, or how many had already been cremated.

Blobel had a fairly accurate knowledge of the number of mass graves in the eastern districts, but he was sworn to the greatest secrecy in the matter.

Originally, all the Jews transported to Auschwitz by the authority of Eichmann's office were to be destroyed without exception, according to Himmler's orders. This also applied to the Jews from Upper Silesia. But during the arrival of the first transports of German Jews, the order was given that all able-bodied men and women. were to be separated and put to work in the arms factories. This occurred before the construction of the women's camps since the need for a women's camp in Auschwitz only arose as a result of this order.

Because of the steadily growing arms industry, which was developing extensively in the camps, and also because of the recent use of prisoners in the arms factories outside the camps, a serious shortage of prisoners suddenly made its impact on us. This was something new because before this Kommandants had to think of ways to keep their prisoners occupied.

The Jews, however, were only to be employed in the Auschwitz camp.

Auschwitz-Birkenau was to become a Jewish camp exclusively. Prisoners of all other nationalities were to be transferred to other camps. This order was never completely carried out, and later Jews even worked in the arms factories outside the camp because of a shortage of workers.

The selection of the able-bodied Jews was supposed to be made by SS doctors, but it often happened that officers of the protective custody camp and of the Labor Department themselves selected the prisoners without my knowledge or even my approval. This was the cause of constant friction between the SS doctors and the officers in the Labor Department. Differing opinions developed among the officers in Auschwitz and were further inflamed by the contradictory interpretations of Himmler's orders by the headquarters in Berlin. For security reasons the Gestapo headquarters had the greatest interest in the destruction of as many Jews as possible. The Reichsartz [medical section] SS established the policy of selection and believed that only Jews who were completely fit and able to work should be selected. The weak, the old, and those who were relatively healthy would soon become incapable of work, which would cause a further deterioration in the general standard and an unnecessary increase in the hospital accommodations, requiring further medical personnel and medicines, and all for no purpose, since they would all be killed in the end.

The Economic Administration Headquarters [Pohl and Maurer] was only interested in gathering the largest possible labor force to be employed in the arms factories, regardless of the fact that these people would later become incapable of working. This conflict of interest was further sharpened by the immensely increased demands for prisoner labor made by the Ministry of Supply and the Todt Organization [ministry of armaments]. Himmler was always promising both of these departments numbers which could never be supplied. [Colonel] Maurer was in the difficult position of being able to only partially fulfill the insistent demands of the departments referred to and therefore was perpetually harassing the labor office to provide him with the greatest possible number of workers.

It was impossible to get Himmler to make a definite decision on this matter.

I believed that only the strong and healthy Jews should be selected to work.

The sorting process went as follows: The railway cars were unloaded one after another. After depositing their baggage, the Jews had to individually pass in front of an SS doctor, who decided on their physical fitness as they marched past him. Those who were considered able-bodied were immediately escorted into the camp in small groups.

On average in all transports between 25 and 30 percent were found fit for work, but this figure fluctuated considerably. The figure for Greek Jews, for example, was only 15 percent, while there were transports from Slovakia with a fitness rate of 100 percent. Jewish doctors and administrative personnel were taken into the camp without exception.

It became apparent during the first cremations in the open air that in the long run it would not be possible to continue in that manner. During bad weather or when a strong wind was blowing, the stench of burning flesh was carried for many miles and caused the entire area to talk about the burning of Jews, despite official counter-propaganda. It is true that all members of the SS detailed for the extermination were bound to secrecy, but even the most severe punishment was unable to stop their love of gossip.

The antiaircraft defenses protested against the fires because they could be seen from great distances at night. Nevertheless, the burnings had to continue, even at night, unless further transports were to be refused. The schedule of individual operations which was set at a conference of the Ministry of Communications had to be rigidly adhered to in order to avoid congestion and confusion with military rail transports. It was for these reasons that the energetic planning and construction of the two large crematories [II and III] and the building of the two smaller crematories [IV and V] were completed in 1943. Another crematory was planned which would have exceeded the others in size, but it was never completed because in the fall of 1944 Himmler called an immediate halt to the extermination of the Jews.

The two large crematories were built in the winter of 1942-43 and brought into service in the spring of 1943. Each had five ovens with three doors [retorts] per oven and could cremate about two thousand bodies in less than twenty-four hours. Technical difficulties made it impossible to increase the capacity. Attempts to do this caused severe damage to the installations and on several occasions they were unable to function. Crematories [II and III] both had underground undressing rooms and underground gas chambers in which the air could be completely ventilated. The bodies were taken to the ovens on the floor above by an elevator. The [two] gas chambers could hold three thousand people, but this number was never achieved, since the individual transports were never that large.

The two smaller crematories [IV and V] were capable of burning about 1,500 bodies in twenty-four hours, according to the calculations made by the construction company called Topf of Erfurt. Because of the wartime shortage of materials, the builders were forced to economize during the construction of Crematories [IV and V]. They were built above ground and the ovens were not as solidly constructed. It soon became apparent, however, that the poor construction of these two ovens, each with four retorts, did not meet the requirements. Crematory [IV] failed completely after a short time and later was not used at all. Crematory [V] had to be repeatedly shut down, since after its fires had been burning for four to six weeks the ovens or the chimneys burned out. The gassed bodies were mostly burned in pits behind Crematory [V].

The provisional building [the red farmhouse] was demolished when work began on building section [B] III in Birkenau.

[Gas Chamber] II [the white farmhouse], later designated Bunker V, was used up until the last and was also kept as a standby when breakdowns occurred in Crematories [II or III]. When larger numbers of transports were received, the gassing was carried out by day in Crematory V, while Crematories I to IV were used for the transports that arrived during the night. There was no limit to the number of bodies that could be burned at [the white farmhouse] as long as the cremations could be carried out both day and night. Because of enemy air raids, no further cremations were allowed during the night after 1944. The highest total figure of people gassed and cremated in twenty-four hours was slightly more than nine thousand. This figure was reached in the summer of 1944, during the action in Hungary using all the installations except Crematory [IV]. On that day five trains arrived because of delays on the rail lines, instead of three, as was expected, and in addition the railroad cars were more crowded than usual.

The crematories were built at the end of the two main roads in the Birkenau camp. First of all, this was done so as not to increase the area of the camp and with it all the safety precautions required, and secondly, so that they would not be too far from the camp since there were plans to use the gas chambers and undressing rooms as bathhouses when the extermination program was completed.

29

The buildings were to be screened from view by a wall or hedges, but lack of material prevented this from being done. As a temporary measure, all extermination buildings were hidden under camouflage nets.

The three railway tracks between Sectors [B] I and [B] II in Birkenau were supposed to be rebuilt as a railroad station with a roof. The railroad was to be extended to Crematories [IV] and [V], so that the unloading process would also be hidden from the eyes of unauthorized people. Again the shortage of materials prevented this plan from being completed.

Because of Himmler's increasing insistence about the employment of prisoners in the arms factories, [SS General] Pohl found himself compelled to resort to using Jews who had become unfit for work. The order was given that if the Jews could be made fit and employable within six weeks, they were to be given special care and food. Until then all Jews who had become unable to work were gassed with the next transport or killed by injection if they happened to be in the infirmary. As far as Auschwitz-Birkenau was concerned, this order was sheer idiocy. We lacked everything. There were practically no medical supplies. The housing was such that there was scarcely even room for the most seriously ill. The food was completely insufficient, and every month the Ministry of Food cut the amount of supplies still further. But all protests were useless, and every effort had to be made to carry out the order. The results of the overcrowding of the healthy prisoners could no longer be avoided. The general standard of health was lowered, and diseases spread like a forest fire. As a result of this order the death rate shot up and general living conditions deteriorated tremendously. I do not believe that a single sick Jew was ever made fit again to work in the arms factories.

Jews who were taken to the camp by order of Eichmann's office-RSHA IV B4-were designated as "Transport-Juden." The reports that announced the arrival had the following notice: "This transport is to be included in the given orders and is subject to special treatment [Sonderbehandlung-SB]." The Jews previous to this, i.e., before the orders for extermination were issued, were labeled "Schutzhaft" [protective custody], or Jews who belonged to one of the other categories of prisoners.

During my earlier interrogations I gave the number of 2.5 million Jews who arrived at Auschwitz to be exterminated. This figure was given to me by Eichmann, who had given this figure to my superior, SS General

Glucks, when Eichmann was ordered to make a report to Himmler shortly before Berlin was surrounded. Eichmann and his deputy, Gunther, were the only ones who had the necessary information to calculate the total number of Jews annihilated. According to the orders given by Himmler, all information concerning the number of victims involved was to be burned after each action at Auschwitz.

As head of Department D I, I personally destroyed every bit of evidence which could be found in my office. The other department heads did the same.

According to Eichmann, Himmler and Gestapo Headquarters had also destroyed all their papers.

Only his personal notes contained this information. It is possible that because of the negligence of some departments a few isolated documents, teleprinter messages, or wireless messages remain undestroyed, but they could not give enough information to make a calculation.

I myself never knew the total number, and I have nothing to help me arrive at an estimate.

I can only remember the figures involved in the larger actions, which were repeated to me by Eichmann or his deputies.

From Upper Silesia and the General Government 250,000
Germany and Theresienstadt.....................................100,000
Holland 95,000
Belgium 20,000
France 110,000
Greece 65,000
Hungary 400,000
Slovakia 90,000
Total 1,130,000

I can no longer remember the figures for the smaller actions, but they were insignificant by comparison with the numbers given above.

I regard a total of 2.5 million as far too high. Even Auschwitz had limits to its destructive capabilities.

Figures given by former prisoners are figments of their imagination and have no foundation in fact.

Action Reinhardt was the code name given to the collecting, sorting,

31

and use of all articles acquired as the result of the transports of the Jews and their extermination.

Any member of the SS who laid his hands on this Jewish property was punished with death on Himmler's order. Personal property valued in the millions was seized.

An immense amount of property was stolen by members of the 88, the police, also by the prisoners, civilian workers, and by railway personnel. A great deal of this still lies hidden and buried in the Auschwitz-Birkenau camp area.

When the Jewish transports arrived and were unloaded, their luggage was left on the platform until the Jews had been taken to the extermination buildings or into the camp. During the early days all luggage would then be brought by a transport Kommando to the sorting office called Canada where it would be sorted and disinfected. The clothing of those who had been gassed in Bunkers I and II, or in Crematories II to V, was also brought to the sorting office.

By 1942 Canada I could no longer keep up with the sorting even though new huts and sheds were constantly being added and the prisoners were sorting day and night. Although the number of prisoners employed was constantly increased and several trucks [often as many as twenty] were loaded daily with the sorted items, the piles of unsorted luggage kept on growing. So in 1942 the construction of the Canada II warehouse was begun at the west end of Sector II in Birkenau [B IIg]. Construction was also begun on the extermination buildings and a bathhouse for new arrivals. Thirty newly built barracks were crammed to capacity right after their completion, while mountains of unsorted items piled up outside between the buildings. In spite of the enlarged sorting Kommandos, it was impossible to complete the job during the course of the individual actions, which always lasted from four to six weeks. It was only during the longer intervals that some semblance of order was achieved.

Clothing and footwear were examined for hidden valuables, although hastily in view of the quantities involved. They were then stored or handed over to the camp to supplement the inmates' clothing. Later on they were also sent to other camps. A considerable part of the clothing was passed to welfare organizations for re-settlers and then later to victims of air raids. Large, important arms factories received considerable quantities of these stored items for their foreign workers.

Blankets and mattresses, etc., were also sent to the welfare organizations. When the camp itself required these articles they were kept to complete the inventory, but other camps also received large shipments.

Valuables were taken over by a special section of the camp command and sorted by experts. A similar procedure was followed with the money that was found.

The jewelry was usually of great value, especially when its Jewish owners came from the West. Among these items could be found precious stones worth thousands of dollars; priceless gold and platinum watches set with diamonds; rings, earrings, and necklaces which were quite rare. Money from all countries amounted in the thousands of dollars. Often tens of thousands of dollars, mostly in thousand-dollar bills, were found on individuals. They used every possible hiding place: their clothing, their luggage, and even their bodies.

When the sorting process that followed each major operation had been completed, the valuables and money were packed into trucks and taken to the Economic Administration Headquarters office in Berlin and then finally to the Reichsbank, where a special department dealt exclusively with items taken during the actions against the Jews. On one occasion Eichmann told me that the jewelry and currency were sold in Switzerland, and that the entire Swiss jewelry market was dominated by these sales.

Ordinary watches by the thousands were sent to Sachsenhausen. A large watchmaker's shop had been set up there which employed hundreds of prisoners and was directly administered by Department D II [Colonel Maurer]. The watches were sorted and repaired in the workshop. The majority of these watches were later sent for use by SS and regular army troops at the front lines.

The gold taken from the teeth was melted into bars by the dentists in the SS hospital and sent monthly to the Sanitary Office Headquarters.

Precious stones of great value were also found hidden in the teeth that had fillings.

The hair cut from the women prisoners was sent to a firm in Bavaria to be used for the war effort.

Unusable clothing was sent for salvage; likewise shoes and boots were taken apart and reused as much as possible. What was left over was made into leather dust.

The treasures brought in by the Jews gave rise to unavoidable difficulties in the camp itself. The newly arriving treasure was demoralizing for the SS, who were not always strong enough to resist the temptation of these valuables which lay within such easy reach. Not even the death penalty or a severe prison sentence was enough to stop them.

The arrival of these Jews with their wealth offered undreamed-of opportunities to the other prisoners." Most of the escapes that occurred were probably connected with these circumstances. With the help of this easily acquired money, watches, rings, etc., anything could be arranged with the SS guard troops or civilian workers. Alcohol, tobacco, food, false papers, guns, and ammunition were all in a day's work. In Birkenau the male prisoners obtained access to the women's camp during the night by bribing some of the female guards. This kind of thing naturally affected the discipline of the entire camp. Those who had valuables could get better jobs for themselves and were able to buy the good will of the Kapos and block elders, and even arrange for a lengthy stay in the hospital, where they would be given the best food. Not even the strictest supervision could change this state of affairs. Jewish gold was a catastrophe for the camp.

As far as I know, in addition to Auschwitz, the other extermination centers for Jews were as follows:

Chelmno near Litzmannstadt	Engine exhaust gas
Treblinka on the Bug	Engine exhaust gas
Sobibor near Lublin	Engine exhaust gas
Belzec near Lemberg	Engine exhaust gas
Lublin [Majdanek]	Zyclon B

I personally have seen only Chelmno and Treblinka. Chelmno was no longer being used, but I saw the entire operation at Treblinka.

Treblinka was built directly near the railroad tracks and had several chambers capable of holding hundreds of people. The Jews went straight into the gas chambers without undressing by way of a platform which was level with the railroad cars. An engine room equipped with various types of engines taken from large trucks and tanks had been built next to the gas chambers. These were started up and the exhaust gases were fed by

34

pipes into the gas chambers, thereby killing the people inside. The process was continued for more than a half an hour until everything was silent inside the rooms. In an hour's time, the gas chambers were opened and the bodies were taken out, undressed, and burned on a frame made from metal railroad tracks.

The fires were fed with wood, and the bodies were sprayed every once in a while with used oil. During my visit everyone who was gassed was dead. But I was told that the performance of the engines was not always consistent, so that the exhaust gases were often not strong enough to kill everyone in the chambers. Many of them were only unconscious and had to be finished off by shooting them. I had heard the same story in Chelmno, and I was also told by Eichmann that these problems had occurred in other places.

Another problem which arose in Chelmno was that the Jews sometimes broke through the sides of the trucks and attempted to escape.

Experience had shown that the prussic acid called Zyclon B caused death with far greater speed and certainty, especially if the rooms were kept dry and airtight with the people packed closely together, and provided they were fitted with as large a number of intake vents as possible. So far as Auschwitz is concerned, I have never known or heard of a single person being found alive when the gas chambers were opened half an hour after the gas had been poured in.

The extermination process in Auschwitz took place as follows: Jews selected for gassing were taken as quietly as possible to the crematories. The men were already separated from the women. In the undressing chamber, prisoners of the Sonderkommandos, who were specially chosen for this purpose, would tell them in their own language that they were going to be bathed and deloused, and that they must leave their clothing neatly together, and, above all, remember where they put them, so that they would be able to find them again quickly after the delousing. The Sonderkommando had the greatest interest in seeing that the operation proceeded smoothly and quickly. After undressing, the Jews went into the gas chamber, which was furnished with showers and water pipes and gave a realistic impression of a bathhouse.

The women went in first with their children, followed by the men, who were always fewer in number. This part of the operation nearly always

35

went smoothly since the Sonderkommando would always calm those who showed any anxiety or perhaps even had some clue as to their fate. As an additional precaution, the Sonderkommando and an SS soldier always stayed in the chamber until the very last moment.

The door would be screwed shut and the waiting disinfection squads would immediately pour the gas [crystals] into the vents in the ceiling of the gas chamber down an air shaft which went to the floor. This ensured the rapid distribution of the gas. The process could be observed through the peep hole in the door. Those who were standing next to the air shaft were killed immediately. I can state that about one-third died immediately. The remainder staggered about and began to scream and struggle for air. The screaming, however, soon changed to gasping and in a few moments everyone lay still. After twenty minutes at the most no movement could be detected. The time required for the gas to take effect varied according to weather conditions and depended on whether it was damp or dry, cold or warm. It also depended on the quality of the gas, which was never exactly the same, and on the composition of the transports, which might contain a high proportion of healthy Jews, or the old and sick, or children. The victims became unconscious after a few minutes, according to the distance from the air shaft. Those who screamed and those who were old, sick, or weak, or the small children died quicker than those who were healthy or young.

The door was opened a half an hour after the gas was thrown in and the ventilation system was turned on. Work was immediately started to remove the corpses. There was no noticeable change in the bodies and no sign of convulsions or discoloration. Only after the bodies had been left lying for some time-several hours-did the usual death stains appear where they were laid. Seldom did it occur that they were soiled with feces. There were no signs of wounds of any kind. The faces were not contorted.

The Sonderkommando now set about removing the gold teeth and cutting the hair from the women. After this, the bodies were taken up by an elevator and laid in front of the ovens, which had meanwhile been fired up. Depending on the size of the bodies, up to three corpses could be put in through one oven door at the same time. The time required for cremation also depended on the number of bodies in each retort, but on average it took twenty minutes. As previously stated, Crematories II and III could cremate two thousand bodies in twenty-four hours, but a higher number was not possible without causing damage to the installations. Crematories IV and V should have been able to cremate 1,500 bodies in twenty-four hours, but as far as I know this figure was never reached

During the period when the fires were kept continuously burning without a break, the ashes fell through the grates and were constantly removed and crushed to powder. The ashes were taken by trucks to the Vistula [River], where they immediately dissolved and drifted away. The ashes taken from the burning pits near Bunker II and from Crematory V were handled in the same way.

The process of destruction in Bunkers I and II was exactly the same as in the crematories, except that the effects of the weather on the operation were more noticeable.

The entire operation of the extermination process was performed by the Jewish Sonderkommando.

They carried out their gruesome task with a dumb indifference. Their one goal was to finish the work as quickly as possible so that they could have a longer period of time to search the clothing of the gassed victims for something to eat or smoke. Although they were well-fed and given many additional allowances, they could often be seen shifting corpses with one hand while they chewed on something they were holding in the other. Even when they were doing the most revolting work of digging out and burning the corpses buried in the mass graves, they never stopped eating.

Even the cremation of their close relatives failed to shake them. When I went to Budapest in the summer of 1943 and called on Eichmann, he told me about the future actions which had been planned for the Jews.

During that period there were a little more than 200,000 Jews from the Carpathian Ukraine who were detained there and housed in some brickworks while awaiting transport to Auschwitz.

According to the estimate from the Hungarian police who had carried out the arrests, Eichmann expected to receive about three million Jews from Hungary.

The arrests and transportation should have been completed by 1943, but because of the Hungarian government's political difficulties, the date was always being postponed.

In particular, the Hungarian army, or rather the senior officers, were opposed to the extradition of these people and gave most of the Jewish men a refuge in the labor companies of the front line divisions, thus keeping them out of the grasp of the police.

When in the fall of 1944 an action was started in Budapest itself, only old and sick Jewish men remained.

Altogether there were probably not more than half a million Jews transported out of Hungary.

The next country on the list was Rumania. According to the reports from his representative in Bucharest, Eichmann expected to get about four million Jews from there.

Negotiations with the Rumanian authorities, however, were likely to be difficult. The anti-Semitic elements wanted the extermination of the Jews to be carried out in their own country. There had already been serious anti-Jewish rioting, and Jews who were caught had been thrown into the deep and isolated ravines of the Carpathian Mountains and killed. A section of the government, however, was in favor of transporting unwanted Jews to Germany.

In the meantime, Bulgaria was to follow with an estimated 2.5 million Jews. The authorities were agreeable to transporting the Jews, but they wanted to wait for the results of the negotiations with Rumania.

In addition, Mussolini was supposed to have promised the extradition of the Italian Jews and those from the Italian-occupied part of Greece, although not even an estimate had been made of their numbers. However, the Vatican, the royal family, and consequently all those opposed to Mussolini wanted to prevent these Jews from being surrendered no matter what the cost.

Eichmann did not count on getting these Jews.

Finally, there was Spain. Influential circles were approached by German representatives concerning the question of getting rid of the Jews. But Franco and his followers were against it. Eichmann had little faith in being able to arrange for their extradition.

The course taken by the war destroyed these plans and saved the lives of millions of Jews.

Krakow, November 1946
[signed] Rudolf Höss

II

Early Years

In the following narrative I will try to write about my deepest personal thoughts and feelings. I will attempt to recall, to the best of my memory, all the important events, all the highs and lows of my psychological life, and the experiences which affected me. For the reader to completely understand the entire picture I will sketch, I must return to my earliest childhood memories.

My family lived in an average home outside of Baden-Baden until I was six. Inthe surrounding area there were only isolated farmhouses. I had no playmates at all, because all the children in the neighborhood were older, so my social life depended on adults. This wasn't much fun, and I always tried, whenever possible, to escape their supervision and go off exploring by myself. I was often lured into the nearby Black Forest by the tall pine trees. I never went in very far and always kept sight of our valley from the mountain slopes. Actually, I was not allowed to go into the forest alone because when I was much younger some passing Gypsies had found me playing by myself and had taken me with them. Fortunately, a neighboring farmer happened to pass by, recognized me, snatched me from the Gypsies and brought me home.

I was especially attracted to the large city water tower. For hours on end I would listen in secret to the rushing water behind its thick walls. I never could understand what this was, even though my parents tried to explain it to me. Most of the time, however, I went to the stables to see the horses. If someone wanted to find me, all he had to do was to go to the stables. I was absolutely fascinated by horses. There simply wasn't enough time for stroking, talking to, and feeding them sweets. If the grooming brushes were handy, I would immediately begin brushing and combing the horses. The farmer was always afraid that I would get hurt as I would creep between the horses' legs as I brushed them. Never did any animal ever hit, bite, or harm me in any way. Even the wildest bull the farmer had was my best friend. I was never afraid of dogs, and they never harmed me either.

My favorite trick was to sneak off to the barns when I was supposed to be taking a nap. My mother tried everything to break me of this obsessive love of animals, but it was completely useless because I didn't pay any attention to her. She thought it was too dangerous. I enjoyed playing by myself or finding things to do alone. I didn't like it when others tried to join in and I didn't like being watched by anybody. I was and would always be a loner.

I had an irresistible passion for water. I had to constantly wash and bathe. I would take any opportunity to wash or bathe in a tub or stream that flowed through our garden. I ruined a lot of toys and clothes by doing this. Even today I have this passion for water.

When I was six years old, we moved to the Mannheim area, which was outside the city, but to my deepest regret there were no stables and no livestock. My mother often reminisced how for weeks on end I was heartsick for my animals and my forest. My parents did all they could then to help me get over my great love of animals. They didn't succeed because I always found books with pictures of animals, and I would sneak off and dream about my cows and horses.

On my seventh birthday, I was given Hans, a coal-black pony with flashing eyes and a long mane. I was exploding with joy. I had finally found my friend. Hans was so faithful that he followed me everywhere, just like a dog. When my parents were away, I would even take him up to my room. I got along well with the servants, and they looked the other way as far as my childish behavior was concerned, and they never told on me. In the area where we now lived there were playmates my age. With the few friends I had, I played the same childish games and all the pranks as children have throughout the ages all over the world. But best of all, I enjoyed going with Hans into the Haardt Forest, where we were all alone, riding for hours on end without a living soul around.

Life became more serious once school started. During the first years of elementary school, nothing worth mentioning happened. I studied hard, did my homework as quickly as possible, so that I could have time to play around with Hans. My parents gave me the freedom to do as I wanted because my father had made a vow that I would lead a religious life and become a priest. The way I was raised was entirely affected by this. I was raised in a strong military fashion because of my father. Because of his faith, there was a heavy religious atmosphere in our family. My father was a fanatic Catholic. During our time in Baden-Baden, I seldom saw him because he traveled for months at a time or was busy with other matters. This all changed in Mannheim. My father now took the time every day to give me some attention, whether it was to look over my schoolwork or talk about my future vocation as a priest. I especially liked his stories about his service in East Africa: his descriptions of the battles with the rebellious natives, their culture and work, and their mysterious religious worship. I listened in radiant rapture as he spoke of the blessed and civilizing activities of the missionary society. I resolved that I would become a missionary no matter what, and that I would go into darkest Africa, even venture into the center of the primeval forest. It was especially exciting when one of the old, bearded African fathers who knew my father in East Africa came to visit. I did not budge from the spot so that I would not miss a single word of the conversation. Yes, I even forgot all about my Hans.

My parents constantly had guests at our house so they seldom went to parties. Our house was the meeting place for the religious from all areas. My father became even more devout as the years passed. As time allowed, he would take me on pilgrimages to the holy places of our country, yes, even to the hermitages in Switzerland and Our Lady of Lourdes in France. He fervently prayed for heaven's blessing so I would become an inspired priest. I myself believed deeply, as much as one can as a child, and I took my religious duties seriously. I prayed with the proper childish reverence and was zealous as an altar boy. I was taught to obey all adults, especially older people, and treat them with respect no matter what the circumstances. Most of all, it was essential to be helpful, and this was my highest duty. It was emphatically pointed out again and again that I carry out the requests and orders of parents, teachers, priests, and all adults, even the servants, and that this principle be respectfully obeyed. I was not permitted to leave anything unfinished. Whatever they said was always right. This type of training is in my flesh and blood.

I can still recall how my father was a determined opponent of the Kaiser's government because he was such a fanatic Catholic. But in spite of his political views, he constantly reminded his friends that the laws of the government were to be obeyed unquestioningly. Even from childhood on up, I was trained in a complete awareness of duty. Attention to duty was greatly respected in my parent's home, so that all orders would be

41

performed exactly and conscientiously. Each person always had certain responsibilities. My father paid special attention to see that I obeyed all his orders and instructions, which were to be carried out painfully. I can still remember a time when he got me out of bed because I left the saddle blanket hanging in the garden instead of in the bam where he told me to hang it to dry out. I had simply forgotten about it. He repeated over and over that from little things which seemed unimportant carelessness generally develops into great tragedy. I did not understand what he meant at the time; only later would I learn through bitter experience to follow these principles.

A warm relationship existed between my parents, full of love, full of respect and mutual understanding. And yet, I never saw them being affectionate to one another. But at the same time, it was very seldom that they exchanged an angry or bad word between them. My two younger sisters were four and six years old. They were around my mother a great deal and loved to cuddle with her, but I refused any open show of affection, even from my early years on, much to the constant regret of my mother and all of my aunts and relatives. A handshake and a few brief words of thanks were the most that one could expect from me. Although both of my parents cared for me very much, I could never find a way to confide in them. I would never share any problems, either big or small, which occasionally depress young people. Inwardly I struggled with all these things by myself. The only one I confided in was my Hans. He understood me, as far as I was concerned. My two sisters were very attached to me and tried repeatedly to form a good, loving relationship with me. But I never wanted to bother with them. I played with them only when I had to and then annoyed them until they ran crying to mother. I played many pranks on them. In spite of that, they cared deeply for me, and I regret to this day that I could never display a warm feeling for them. They always remained strangers to me.

I respected and admired my parents very much, my father as well as my mother. However, love, the kind of love which I came to know later as a parent, I could not pretend to show for them. Why was this? I cannot explain, and even today I can find no reason. I was never what you would call a good boy, or even an ideal child. I played all the pranks which a young mind in those years could invent. I ran with other boys through the wildest games and fights or whatever came along. There were always times when I had to be alone.

I always was able to get my way.

If someone did something wrong to me, I did not rest until I felt I had gotten even. I was relentless and I was feared by my classmates. Oddly enough, I sat at the same desk during my whole time in high school with a Swedish girl who wanted to become a doctor. During all the years of struggle in school, we understood each other like good buddies, and we never fought. It was customary in our high school for students to spend all of the school years with the same classmate at the same desk.

Zyclon B (Giftgas= Poison Gas)

III
Early Traumatic Experience

You should know that I took my religion very seriously. The first serious crack in my religious belief happened when I was thirteen years old. On a Saturday morning, during the usual pushing and shoving to be the first one into the gym, I accidentally pushed a classmate down the stairs. Throughout the years, hundreds of students must have sailed down these stairs without any serious injuries. This time he was unlucky; he broke his ankle. I was punished with two hours of detention. I went to confession in the afternoon as I did every week, confessed what I did like a good boy, but I didn't say anything about this incident at home because I didn't want to spoil Sunday for my parents. They would learn about it soon enough during the coming week.

That evening my confessor, who was a good friend of my father, was visiting at our house. The next morning my father scolded me about the pushing incident, and I was punished because I did not report it to him right away. I was devastated, not because of the punishment, but because of this unheard-of breach of confidence by my confessor. Wasn't it always taught that the secrecy of the confessional could not be broken? Even the most serious crimes that a person tells a priest in the holy confessional cannot be reported to the police. And now this priest, whom I trusted so deeply, who was my steady confessor and knew my whole little world of sins by heart, had broken the secrecy of the confessional for such a minor incident. Only he could have told my father.

Neither my father, mother, nor anyone else from our house had been in town that day. Our telephone was out of order, and none of my classmates lived in our neighborhood. No one had visited us except my confessor. For a long, long time, I checked all the details about this over and over because this was such a horrible thing to me. Then and even now I am firmly convinced that this priest had violated the secrecy of the confessional. My faith in the holy profession of the priesthood was smashed and doubts began to stir within me. I never went back to him for confession because I could no longer trust him. I told the priest that I was going to our religious instruction teacher in the church near my school because my father lectured me when he discovered I was no longer going to this priest. My father believed it, but I am convinced that the priest knew the real reason. He tried everything to win me back, but I just couldn't go back to him. **In** fact, I went even further. I didn't go to confession at all anymore if I could get away with it. After this incident I could no longer trust any priest.

In religious instruction we were told that if a person went to communion without confession, he would be severely punished by God. We were told that someone had done that and had dropped dead at the communion rail. With childish simplicity I begged God to be lenient because I could no longer confess faithfully and to forgive my sins, which I now recited directly to him. So I believed I was free of my sins. Full of doubt, I went trembling to the communion rail in a strange church. And nothing happened! So I, poor little earthworm, believed that God would hear my prayers and agree with what I was doing. The deep, true, childlike faith which so calmly and surely guided my soul until this time was smashed.

The following year my father died suddenly. I cannot remember if this loss affected me in any special way. I was still too young [fourteen years old] to understand the whole significance of this. Yet, the death of my father was to send my life in a totally different direction than he had wished.

IV

World War I

World War I began and the Mannheim Garrison went to the front. Replacement units were being formed. The first trains from the front arrived carrying the wounded. I was hardly at home anymore because there was so much to see, and I didn't want to miss anything. I constantly nagged my mother to let me volunteer to help at the Red Cross. Finally, she gave me permission. There were so many impressions at the time that I really cannot remember how the first sight of the wounded affected me. I can still see the blood-soaked head and arm bandages, the uniforms smeared with blood and dirt, our grey prewar uniforms, and the blue French-uniforms with the red trousers. I can still hear the suppressed moaning during the loading of the wounded into the hastily requisitioned streetcars, as I ran among them passing out refreshments, cigarettes, and tobacco. After school I was always in the military hospital, the barracks, or the railroad station watching the passing troop transports or hospital trains and passing out food or gift packages. In the hospitals I saw the seriously wounded as they quietly moaned to themselves. I always crept timidly past those beds. I saw the dying and the dead. A strange feeling shuddered through me, but I can't describe this accurately anymore.

These sad pictures were quickly erased by the humor of the lightly wounded or those who had no pain. I never tired of listening to their stories of a soldier's life. The soldier within me blossomed. Throughout many generations my ancestors on my father's side had been officers. In 1870 my grandfather died as a colonel leading his regiment. My father was a soldier, body and soul, even though his religious fanaticism concealed this passion after he left the army. I wanted to be a soldier and I didn't want to miss this war. My mother, my guardian, and all my relatives wanted me to finish school first. They said that then there would be time to discuss it. Besides, I was supposed to become a priest. I let them talk while I tried everything to get to the front lines. I often hid inside the troop transports and rode with them until I was caught. In spite of my most passionate pleading, the military police brought me back because I was too young. All my thoughts and efforts were directed to becoming a soldier. School, my future, and my home came second.

My mother tried with great kindness to talk me out of joining the army. Her limitless patience with me was touching, but I stubbornly tried everything to become a soldier. My mother was powerless against my efforts. My relatives wanted to send me to a seminary, but my mother refused. Even though I neglected my religion, I still went conscientiously to church and did what was necessary. But now the strong hand of my father was missing.

In 1916, with the help of a captain in the cavalry whom I had met in the hospital, I succeeded in quietly sneaking into the regiment in which my father and grandfather had served. I arrived at the front line after a brief period of training. All this happened without my dear mother knowing. I never saw her again because she died in 1917. I wasn't quite sixteen yet when I arrived in Turkey on the way to the Iraqi front. The fear of being discovered and sent back home, the secret training, and the long trip to Turkey made a tremendous impression on me. I had many new experiences during our layover in Istanbul, which was still rich in Oriental tradition, and on the horseback ride to the distant Iraqi front line. I've forgotten most of these impressions because they weren't important. But I do remember my first firefight with the enemy.

Right after we arrived at the front line we were assigned to a Turkish division. Our cavalry unit was divided into three regiments in order to give the Turks some backbone. As we were being assigned, the English [New Zealanders and Indians] attacked. When the shooting got heavy, the Turks ran away.

Our small German unit lay alone between the rocks and ancient ruins defending our skins in the vast expanse of desert. We didn't have much ammunition because the main supply stayed back with the horses. Very quickly I noticed that our situation was getting damned serious, especially since the explosions of the grenades were becoming more accurate. Comrade after comrade fell wounded, and the one lying next to me didn't answer my calls. When I turned to look at him, I saw he was bleeding from a large head wound and was already dead. Never again in my entire life did I experience the horror that seized me then, and the tremendous fear that the same would happen to me. If I had been alone, I would have run as the Turks did. Something kept forcing me to look at my dead comrade.

But then in desperation I looked at our captain, lying among us behind a large rock. I watched as he returned the fire, shot after shot, with iron discipline. He handled the carbine of my dead comrade as if he were in a shooting gallery. Then, suddenly, a strange, rigid calm came over me that I had never known before. It became clear to me that I was also supposed to fire. Until then, I had not fired a single shot as I fearfully watched the slowly advancing Indians. I can still picture to this day a tall, broad Indian with a distinct black beard, jumping from a pile of rocks. For a moment I hesitated, the body next to me filling my whole mind, then I pulled myself together even though I was very much shaken. I fired and watched the Indian slump forward during his jump. He didn't move. I really can't say if I aimed correctly. He was my first kill! The spell was broken. Still unsure of myself, I began firing and firing, just as they had taught me in training. I didn't think about the danger anymore because my captain who was nearby kept shouting encouragement.

The attack bogged down as the Indians noticed that there was resistance. In the meantime, the Turks had been driven forward again and now a counterattack began. That day we recovered a large part of the ground we had lost. During the advance I hesitated and reluctantly looked at my kill. It made me feel a little squeamish. It was so exciting for me that I can't say whether I wounded or killed any more Indians during this first firefight. After the first shot I aimed and shot carefully at those who emerged from cover. My captain mentioned his amazement at how cool I was during this, my first firefight, my baptism of fire. If he had only known what was really going on inside me!

Later I told him how scared I had been. He laughed about it and said that every soldier had more or less gone through the same experience. It was strange for me to have such a great trust in my captain, my soldier father. I worshiped him a great deal.

It was a much more intimate relationship than I had with my own father. The captain always kept me in his sight. Even though he never let me get away with anything, he always liked me and worried about me as if I were his son. He did not like me to go on long-range reconnaissance patrols, but he always gave in to my constant nagging. He was especially proud when I was decorated or promoted, but he himself never recommended me. When he died in the spring of 1918 during the second Battle of the Jordan, I mourned for him with great pain. His death really hit me hard.

In early 1917 our outfit was transferred to the Palestine front in the Holy Land. All the familiar names from religion, from history, and from the legends about the saints came back to me again. And how different it was from the way we had pictured it in our youthful fantasies from descriptions and pictures. At first they used us at the Hejaz railway station, then later at the front lines near Jerusalem.

One morning, as we returned from a long reconnaissance ride on the far side of the Jordan River, we.met a line of farmers' carts loaded with moss in the Jordan Valley. We had to check all vehicles and pack animals for guns because the English tried in every way imaginable to deliver guns and ammunition to the Arabs and to other nationalities who wanted to overthrow Turkish rule. We asked the farmers to unload their carts and started to talk to them through an interpreter, who was a young Jewish boy. They explained to us that they were bringing the moss to the monasteries for the pilgrims. This didn't make any sense to us at all.

A short time later I was wounded and taken to a field hospital in a German settlement in Wilhelma, between Jerusalem and Jaffa. The settlers there had emigrated a generation before for religious reasons, from the state of Württemberg in Germany. In the hospital, I learned from these people that there was a very profitable trade in the great quantities of moss brought to Jerusalem. The moss is an Icelandic variety, grey-white netting with red dots. The pilgrims were told that the moss came from Golgotha, and that the red dots were the blood of Jesus. It was sold for a great deal of money. The settlers openly told us about the profitable business there was from the pilgrims in peacetime when thousands flocked to the holy places. The pilgrims, they said, would buy anything connected with the holy places or with the saints. The large pilgrim monasteries were the best at it. They tried everything to get as much money from the pilgrims as possible. After I got out of the hospital I looked into this in Jerusalem. Because of the war there weren't many pilgrims, but there were many German and Austrian soldiers. Later I saw the same thing going on in Nazareth. I talked about it with my comrades because this trivial traffic in so-called holy objects by the Church disgusted me. Most of my comrades didn't care and said that if the people were so dumb to fall for such a fraud, they would just have to pay for their stupidity. Others just thought of it as a tourist industry which happens at special places. Only a few, as deeply Catholic as I was, condemned these activities of the Church. They too were disgusted by the sick manipulation of the sincere religious feelings of the pilgrims who often sold everything they owned just to see the holy places once in their lives.

For a long time after my discharge from the army I tried to come to terms with what I experienced, and this was probably the reason I later left the Church. I would like to state that the comrades of my outfit were all staunch Catholics from the Black Forest. During that time, I never heard any words spoken against the Church.

In the hospital at Wilhelma, a young German nurse took care of me.

It was at this time that I had my first sexual experience. I had been shot through the knee and also suffered a terrible relapse of malaria which lasted quite long. I needed special care and had to be watched closely, since I caused a great deal of damage during my delirious ravings due to fever. This nurse took care of me so well that my mother couldn't have done better. As time passed I noticed that it wasn't motherly love which caused her to nurse me in such a loving way. I had never been in love with a woman until then. I had heard about sex in discussions with my comrades, and the way soldiers talk is quite explicit, but I didn't have these desires, perhaps because of the lack of opportunity. Also, the hardships and strain of the campaign didn't exactly bring out feelings of love. Her tender caresses, the way she propped me up and held me, confused me at first, because I had always avoided showing affection, but now I was under the magic spell of love and saw her with different eyes. This love for me was a miraculous experience. She led me through all the steps of love making, including intercourse. I would not have had the courage to do this. This first experience of love, with all its tenderness and affection, became the guideline for the rest of my life. I never again could joke about sex. Sexual intercourse without affection became unthinkable for me. So I was spared from having affairs and from the brothels.

World War I ended. I had matured far beyond my age, both inside and out. The experience of war had put an indelible mark on me. I had torn myself from the security of my parents' home and my horizons had widened. In two and a half years I had seen and experienced a great deal. I met people from all walks of life and had seen their needs and weaknesses.

The schoolboy who had run away from home and trembled with fear during his first battle had become a rough, tough soldier. At the age of seventeen I was decorated with the Iron Cross and I was the youngest sergeant in the army.' After my promotion to sergeant I was sent on deep reconnaissance missions most of the time. It was then that I learned that leadership does not depend on rank, but on better knowledge. The ice-cold, unshakeable calm of the leader is decisive in difficult situations. I also learned how hard it was always to be an example and to keep a straight face, even though inside there were fears and doubts.

At the time of the armistice, we were in Damascus, Syria. I had definitely made up my mind not to be put in a POW camp under any circumstances. I had decided to fight my way back to the Fatherland by my own power. The Army Corps advised against it. After asking around, all the men of my platoon volunteered to fight. their way back with me. Since the spring of 1918 I was leading my own cavalry platoon. All the men were in their thirties; I was only eighteen.

Our adventure took us through Anatolia [Turkey]. We sailed on a miserable derelict ship across the Black Sea to Varna and rode on through Bulgaria and Rumania. We traveled the deepest snows through the Transylvanian Alps, on through Transylvania, Hungary, Austria, and finally we reached the Homeland. After three months of helplessly wandering about with no maps; using only the geography we learned in school, requisitioning food for men and horses, fighting our way through Rumania, which had become our enemy again, we reported to our reserve unit. No one at home expected us to make it back. As far as I know, no complete unit ever returned home from that theater of war.

Even during the war, I had doubts about my vocation to be a priest.

The incident with my confessor and the trade in holy relics that I had seen in the Holy Land had destroyed my faith in priests. I also had many doubts about the Church. Little by little I began to reject the profession my father had always praised, but I didn't consider any other profession. I never spoke to anyone about this. Before my mother died she wrote in her last letter that I should never forget what my father wanted me to be. I struggled with my feelings of rejection toward the priesthood and with my desire to respect my parents' expectations. I still had not decided when I arrived in the Fatherland. After my return, my guardian and all my relatives pestered me to enter a seminary for the priesthood so that I could find the right climate to prepare me for my prescribed profession. Our house and all our belongings were gone and my sisters were placed in convent schools. Now, for the first time, I truly felt the loss of my mother. I no longer had a home! There I was, abandoned, completely dependent on myself. The "dear relatives" had divided among themselves all our precious possessions which made our home so dear. They assumed that I would become a missionary priest and that my sisters would remain in the convent, so we would not need all these worldly goods anymore. There was enough money, however, to pay my way into a seminary, and for my sisters in the convent. I was heartbroken about my lost home and angry at my two-faced, conniving relatives. That day I went to my uncle who was my guardian and told him straight out that I would not become a priest. He wanted to force me to do as my parents had chosen by saying that he would not give me any money to train for any other profession. Without any hesitation, I gave up my inheritance to my sisters. The following day I went to the notary public to put it in writing. I refused to allow my relatives to get involved in my life any longer. I was sure that I could make my own way in the world. Burning with anger, I left my family's home without saying goodbye. The next day I went to East Prussia to sign up with a volunteer outfit destined for the Baltic States.

V
Battles of the Free Corps

So the problem of my profession was solved; I became a soldier again. I found a home again and a feeling of being sheltered in the comradery of my fellow soldiers. And it was strange that I, the loner, who had to struggle with all the inner problems and doubts which occur in one's mind, had to solve it by myself. I always felt myself drawn to the fellowship in which one could always depend upon the other without question in times of need or danger.

The battles in the Baltic States were more brutal and vicious than anything I had experienced before, during World War I, or afterwards in- all of the battles of the Free Corps. There was hardly a front line; the enemy was everywhere. Wherever the opposing forces collided, there was a slaughter until no one was left. The Latvians were the best at this. For the first time I saw the horrors committed against civilians. The Latvians took horrible revenge against their own countrymen who quartered and supplied German or White Russian soldiers. They set fire to their houses and let the people living in them bum alive. Countless times I saw the horrible pictures of the burned-out cottages, the scorched and partially burned bodies of women and children. When I saw this, I could not believe that the mad desire of humans to destroy could be intensified, even though later I repeatedly was to see more horrible pictures. I can still picture these horrors today: the half-burned cottages there on the edge of the forest of the Duna River, whole families murdered. At that time, I could still pray, and I did.

The Free Corps [private armies] in the years 1918-21 were a strange historical phenomenon. Whatever government was in power needed them when there was trouble on the border or inside the country. They were used if the police forces, or later the army, were not enough, or they were used if the government could not openly be involved because of political reasons. When the danger was over, or when France made pointed inquiries, the government disavowed their connection. They were disbanded and the government then persecuted those organizations which formed from the left-over veterans who were waiting for a new mission. The members of these Free Corps were officers and soldiers who had come back from World War I and couldn't fit into civilian life anymore: adventurers who wanted to try their luck in this lifestyle, the unemployed who wanted to escape idleness and public welfare, and young, enthusiastic volunteers who rushed to the soldier's life out of patriotism. Without exception all pledged their allegiance to the particular leader of their Free Corps. With him the unit stood or fell. In this way a feeling of togetherness, an esprit de corps, developed which could not be broken by anything. The more intensely we were hunted by the current government, the stronger we stuck together. Woe to him who broke the ties of this brotherhood or betrayed it.

Since the government had to deny the existence of the Free Corps, it could not prosecute or investigate crimes such as theft of arms, espionage or treason committed by the members of these organizations. A kind of self-justice system based on historical German patterns came into existence within the Free Corps and their offspring organizations. These were the so-called Valmik courts.' Any kind of betrayal was punished by death. And so many traitors were executed. However, only a few cases became known, and only in a few individual cases were the guilty caught and sentenced by a special federal court called the Protection of the Republic, which was created specifically for this purpose.

VI

On Trial for Murder

In the ParchimerVehme murder trial I was sentenced to ten years in prison. This is how my trial came about. A group of us had beaten to death a man named Parchimer, who betrayed a friend named Schlageter to the French. I was accused of being the ringleader and main participant. A man who had taken part in the killing gave the story to the leading Social Democratic newspaper, *Vorwärts*[Forward], because he said his conscience bothered him; in reality however, as it later became known, it was to make money for himself. They could not clear up how it really happened because the informant was not sober enough during the killing to remember the details exactly. Those of us who knew kept silent.

Yes, I was with them, but I was not the ringleader, nor was I a main participant. When I realized during the interrogation that the comrade who actually did the killing could only be incriminated by me, I took the blame upon myself and he was freed while the investigation was still underway. I don't have to emphasize that I agreed with the killing of the traitor for the reasons I explained before; in addition to that, Schlageter was an old comrade of mine from way back. We had fought through many hard battles in the Baltic and Ruhr areas, had worked behind enemy lines in Upper Silesia, and together had traveled many dark paths in order to get weapons.

Then and even now, I am still firmly convinced that this traitor deserved to die. Since in all probability no German court would have sentenced him, we passed judgment on him by an unwritten law which we had instituted ourselves because of the need of the times. Very probably only those who have lived through that time themselves, or who can put themselves into that troubled period, can understand. During my nine months of detention awaiting trial and also during the trial, I never really understood the seriousness of my situation. I firmly believed that it probably would not come to trial and certainly not lead to a prison term.

The political conditions in Germany during 1923 had become so serious that without fail it had to come to a putsch [overthrow of the government], from the political right or the political left. I firmly counted on the fact that at the right time we would be rescued and released by our comrades.

The unsuccessful Hitler Putsch of November 1923 should have taught me a better lesson. In spite of that, I continued to hope for the best. Both of my defense attorneys clearly showed me the seriousness of my situation; that, in fact, I had to count on a death sentence because of the new political composition of the federal court and the more intense prosecution and outlawing of all patriotic organizations. They said that I would at least be sentenced to a long term of imprisonment. During my pretrial detention we had all kinds of privileges, since there were many more left-wingers, mostly Communists, than right-wingers [National Socialists].

Even the minister of justice of Saxony, Dr. Zeigner, sat in his own jail accused of graft and perversions of justice. We were allowed to write frequently, and also to receive mail and packages. We were allowed to subscribe to newspapers, so we were constantly informed of what was happening on the outside. The isolation in the jail itself, however, was very strict. In fact, whenever we were led from our cell, we were blind-folded. We could only communicate by brief shouts to our comrades through the windows every now and then. During the trial, the conversations and the fellowship among us during the breaks and shuttle trips were much more important and interesting than the trial itself. When the sentence was pronounced, it made no impression on me or my comrades. Loudly and cheerfully, singing our old battle songs of defiance, we rode to our prison.

I wonder now if it wasn't gallows humor. I personally doubt it. I simply did not want to believe that I would serve my prison term.

VII
Prison

The bitter awakening came soon, shortly after my transfer to the penitentiary. A new, unknown world opened up for me. Doing time in a Prussian prison was no vacation in those days. Our lives were strictly regulated down to the smallest detail. The discipline was military and it was rigid. The greatest emphasis was placed on the strict and neat performance of the daily work quota, which was calculated for each person. Anyone breaking the rules was severely punished, and the effect of the "in-house punishment" was further increased by having a pending parole denied. Parole was determined by a conference of officials whenever "in-house punishments" were on a man's record. The only concession given to political prisoners [Höss's designation] at the time was that they were given a single cell to themselves.

At first I was not happy about this. I had had enough of being alone for the nine months in Leipzig. But later on I was thankful, despite the many small conveniences which life in a large community hall offered. I was alone in my cell after I finished my duties, and I could divide my day as I wanted. I didn't have to be considerate of a fellow cellmate and I was removed from the terror of the criminal community in those halls.

Even though I only witnessed this terror from the far-away fringes, I came to know it as it went mercilessly against those who did not belong to the guild of criminals, or those who did not hold the same views. Even the closely supervised Prussian prison could not break this terror. Until then I believed that I had seen it all as far as people were concerned, especially since I had become acquainted with all kinds of people from all social levels in many different countries. In my young life I had experienced a great deal of people's customs and even more of their vices. The criminals in the penitentiary taught me differently. Even though I sat alone in my cell, I still came into daily contact with other prisoners, whether it was during exercises in the courtyard or by orders to report to the various departments of the prison administration. I met them in the showers; I met them as prisoner trustees or barbers; I met them when we picked up supplies for work and on many other occasions. Most importantly, I overheard their discussions at the windows during the evening. And those conversations gave me insight about the thinking and psychology of this class of criminals. An abyss opens up to me about human aberration-vices and passions.

At the start of my time in prison, one evening I overheard one prisoner in a nearby cell tell another how he robbed a forester's house after making sure that the forester was safely seated in a tavern. During the robbery he killed the maid with an axe, then murdered the wife, who was in her final month of pregnancy. After that he took the four little children, one by one, and smashed each head against the wall until they stopped screaming, because they were crying. He told about this foul deed with such vile and brazen expressions that I would have loved to get at his throat. I could not get to sleep that night. Later on I heard about many more depraved things, but they did not upset me as much as what I had first heard on that day.

On several occasions the above-mentioned man was sentenced to death as a robber and murderer, but his sentence had been commuted time and again. While I was still in prison, he broke away one evening while returning to the dormitories. Using a piece of iron, he killed a guard who was in his way and escaped over the wall. He struck down an innocent pedestrian and, while robbing the man of his clothes, he was cornered by the pursuing police. He attacked them so furiously that they had to shoot him.

There in the Brandenburg Penitentiary, the cream of Berlin's criminals were assembled, from the international pickpocket to the criminal elite: the famous safe crackers, pimps, crooked gamblers, the great embezzlers, and the brutal sex offenders. There was regular schooling for criminals. The older criminals carefully initiated the younger ones, the novices, into the secrets of their particular criminal craft, but even then they did not share their own personal special trade secrets. For this tutoring, the older gangsters asked for stiff payments of the standard prison money, which was tobacco. Even though smoking was strictly forbidden, every smoker illegally provided himself with tobacco by going fifty-fifty with the younger auxiliary guards. Agreeing to cooperate sexually and firmly agreeing to participate in planned jobs after release was a common form of payment. Many elaborately planned crimes originated while time was being served for previously committed crimes.

Homosexuality was very widespread. The younger, good-looking prisoners were very much desired, and there were often fights and intrigues over these "beauties." The cunning ones set a high price for their desirability. In my opinion, based on my experiences and observations gathered over many years, the homosexuality which occurs in these institutions is pathological or inborn in only a few cases. In humans with strong sex drives, the need for sexual release leads to it. But for most, it was the addiction to excitement and the need to get something out of life in surroundings where there were no moral restraints.

In this mass of criminals driven by urges and desires, there was also a large number of people who became thieves and swindlers during the time of inflation in the poor economic years after the war. There were also people who were not strong enough to resist the temptation of easy gain, or who through unfortunate circumstances were drawn into the whirlpool of crime. Many of them struggled honestly and bravely to extricate themselves from the criminal influence so that they could start an orderly life again after serving their sentences. But many were too weak to withstand the asocial pressures and the criminal terror, year after year, and fell into crime for the rest of their lives.

The cell block in this respect was a real confessional. I heard many a window discussion in Leipzig during my pretrial custody-discussions in which husbands and wives poured out their inner troubles and comforted each other-discussions in which accomplices bitterly accused one another of betrayal, and those which the prosecutor would have been greatly interested in and by which many a dark crime could have been cleared up. At that time I was amazed that through the windows the prisoners so freely and fearlessly told one another often deeply hidden things which were to be kept secret. Was this compulsion to tell one another born of the privation of solitary confinement, or did it stem from the general human desire to tell things to each other? During the pretrial custody, these window discussions were very limited and dangerous because of the constant checking of the cells by the guards. And yet in prison, no guard gave a damn about it except when the conversation became too loud.

In the Brandenburg cell block there sat in solitary three kinds of prisoners: politically motivated criminals, young, first-time offenders with preferential treatment; violent and troublemaking criminals who could not be kept in the larger community halls; and prisoners who had become un-

59

popular because they didn't want to submit to the terror of the criminals. This third group included those who betrayed their friends and now feared revenge. All of these were in a kind of protective custody.

Crematoria II & IV at Birkenau-Auschwitz

VIII
Insights into the Criminal Mind

Night after night I was able to listen to their conversations. And these discussions gave me a deep insight into the mentality of the criminal. While working in the last year of my imprisonment as first clerk in the supply room, I had the opportunity to get to know them even better. The knowledge I gained daily confirmed my insights many times over. The true professional criminal, either because of his nature or his desire, has renounced society. He fights society by committing crimes. He does not wish to be part of society; he loves his crime-his "profession." He knows the feeling of belonging only out of necessity, and also because he submits to it-just like the relationship of a prostitute to her pimp, no matter how badly he treats her. Moral values such as loyalty and trust are laughable to him, and so is the idea of personal property. His sentence and his imprisonment are just a streak of bad luck in his trade; a business mishap, a blunder-nothing else. He tries to make his term of imprisonment as short as possible. Because he knows many of the penal institutions, their idiosyncrasies, their familiar, influential officials, he tries to get transferred to the one most suited to him. I do not think that he is able to conjure up any tender feelings in his heart. Any attempt to educate him, any attempt to lead him back to the right path through kindness is rejected, even though now and then he pretends to be a remorseful sinner in order to get paroled. Generally, he is coarse and mean, and it gives him pleasure when he can trample down the things that others hold sacred.

Let me state one incident as an example. In 1926-27, a humane policy of serving sentences was instituted in the penitentiaries. One of the changes was that on Sunday mornings musical performances were offered in the prison church, where some of the best artists of Berlin's stages performed. One morning there was a performance of Gounod's *Ave Maria* by a famous Berlin female singer with such perfection and tenderness as I have seldom heard. Most of the prisoners were moved by it. Even the most hardened were probably affected-but not all. The last notes had scarcely sounded when an old, depraved fellow behind me said to his neighbor, "Hey, Ed, I'm really dying to get my hands on those diamonds." That was the impression

61

made by this truly heartrending performance on this type of criminal- asocials in the truest sense of the word.

Among this mass of typical professional criminals, there were now a large number of prisoners who did not quite belong to this category. These were the borderline cases who were already on the down slide to the tempting, adventurous world of crime, and others who with all their power fought being enmeshed in the tempting mirages. And finally, there were the first-time offenders, weak-willed creatures who were torn between the outside influences of imprisonment and their own inner feelings. The mentality of this group was multifaceted and ran the entire gamut of human emotions. Often it swayed from one extreme to another. Punishment made no impression at all on the irresponsible and frivolous. Their souls weren't burdened at all, and they went their merry way. They had no care whatsoever about the future. They would just glide on through life as before until they got caught again.

How differently the more serious-natured conducted themselves. They were tremendously depressed by the punishment, and they never came to grips with it. They also tried to escape the bad atmosphere of the community halls; but most of them could not stand life in solitary. They were afraid to be alone and afraid of the constant brooding, and they would ask to be put back again into the swamp of the large halls. Even though there was the possibility to be with only three men in a cell, you could hardly find three prisoners who got along in this confined association for any extended period of time. These small groups had to be constantly dissolved. I didn't see any which lasted a long time. Long-term imprisonment converts even the most good-natured person into someone oversensitive, quarrelsome, and inconsiderate. And consideration for others has to be present if a person wants to live in such a confined environment. But it's not just the imprisonment by itself: the monotonous uniformity of all the daily chores, the constant coercion and pressure by the countless regulations, the continuous yelling and scolding of the corrections officers over trivial things, which depressed the more serious-minded prisoners, but more than that the thoughts about the future and their lives after serving the sentence. Most of the discussions revolved around that.

They worried about whether they could lead a normal life again, whether they would be the outcasts of society. If they were also married, then the nagging worry about the family was added. Furthermore, would the wife remain faithful during the long separation? All of these worries plunged these men into a deep depression from which even the daily work load, or reading serious books during recreation time, could not free them. Frequently they ended up as mental cases, or committed suicide without there being an immediate reason. By immediate reason I mean such bad news from the outside as divorce, death of a family member, refusal of parole, and other setbacks. Those who were unsure of themselves did not bear imprisonment easily. Their inner emotions were too easily influenced by life in prison. A few tempting words from an old con or a small pouch of tobacco could easily cause all their best resolutions to be forgotten. On the other hand, a good book or a serious hour of meditation compelled these characters to explore their inner selves and their consciences quietly. In my opinion, many of the inmates could have been brought back on the right path if the prison officials would have been more humane than just doing their jobs, particularly the priests of both denominations, who just by censoring the letters, alone were aware of the frame of mind and condition of their flock. But all these officials had become gray and dulled by the constant monotony of the work. They didn't recognize the inner needs of the person who was seriously wrestling to become better. If an inmate really got up his courage to ask his spiritual counselor for advice about his inner conflict, it was at once assumed that he wanted to play the penitent sinner in order to get paroled. There is no doubt that the officials had experiences in which they were fooled by those not worthy of compassion and understanding. If there was the slightest expectation, even the most cynical criminals suddenly became very pious when the time for a parole hearing approached. Countless times, however, I overheard prisoners grumbling among themselves how much they needed help from the administration with their inner problems. Such privation had a much more severe psychological effect on the serious prisoners who really wanted to better themselves than the physical hardships and experiences of being locked up could ever have had. In contrast to the easygoing persons, they were doubly punished.

After the consolidation of the political and the economic conditions in Germany after the inflation, a broader, democratic viewpoint came to be accepted. Aside from the many other measures the government took in those years, there was also instituted the humane, progressive management of prison sentences. It was believed that those persons who had broken the laws of the land could be won back for society through kindness and education. From this thesis they concluded that every man was the product of his environment. After the lawbreaker paid his penalty, the government tried to create a job for him in order to give him the incentive to climb up socially and protect him from making further mistakes. Specialized social care was to help him forget his asocial disposition and prevent him from being drawn into the circle of crime again. The intellectual level of the penal institutions was to be raised through general educational measures, like musical leisure time to loosen up the spirit, pertinent lectures about the basic moral laws of human society and the principles of ethics, as well as other themes. The higher officials of the penal institution were supposed to concentrate more on the individual prisoner and see to his concerns but his psychological needs. The prisoner himself was to move through a three-step system with many radically new privileges which were not known to the prisoners beforehand. Little by little the prisoner struggled to the third step through good conduct, diligent work, and evidence of a change of heart-thereby reaching an early release with conditions of parole. The best that could happen would be remission of one half his sentence.

I was the first of the approximately eight hundred prisoners of my penal institution to reach the third step. Until my release there weren't more than a dozen who, in the opinion of the Board of Officials, deserved to wear the three stripes on their sleeve. In my case all prerequisites existed from the beginning: I had no in-house punishment, nor warnings; I always worked above my quota; I was a first offender; I didn't have a bad reputation; and I was considered a political law breaker. But since I was sentenced by a federal court as a political criminal, I could only be released ahead of time by a reprieve from the president, or by an amnesty.

In the first days of my imprisonment my situation *finally* became clear to me. I came to my senses. Without a doubt I had to count on spending the full ten years in the penitentiary. A letter from my defense council about this finally made me realize it, and I prepared myself for the full ten years. I took a hard, critical look at my life. Until then I just lived from day to day, took life as it came without any serious thoughts about my future. Now I had enough time on my hands to think about my life, to see my mistakes, my weaknesses, and to prepare for a life after prison, a life richer in content.

Between the Free Corps campaigns I had learned a profession which I really liked and knew that I could do well in. I had a passion for farming and had accomplished good things, as indicated by my grade reports [Höss was studying farming as an apprentice]. However, the true meaning of life, that which really makes life worth living, was missing, but I didn't realize it at the time. As contradictory as this may seem, I began to do research behind the walls of prison, and found it later!

From childhood on I was taught to be absolutely obedient to the point of the most painstaking neatness and cleanliness, so it was not difficult to fit into the hard life of prison, as far as the prison officials were concerned. I conscientiously performed my duties and did the work I was asked to do-most of the time more-much to the satisfaction of the foreman. Because my cell was always an example of cleanliness and order, even the most critical inspection could not reveal anything to complain about. I even got used to the constant monotony of the daily routine, which hardly ever was broken by special events, although it was against my restless nature. My former life really had been quite hectic and lively.

A special event happened in the first two years, when the permitted quarterly letter arrived from the outside. Even before I got it, I thought about all the possible things which that letter could contain. The letter came from "my fiancée." She was my fiancée as far as the prison administration was concerned. I had never seen or even heard of this girl, who was the sister of a fellow soldier. Since I could only write to relatives or receive mail from them, my fellow soldiers back in Leipzig got me a "fiancée." This girl had faithfully and kindly written to me through all the years and had fulfilled all my wishes and reported about all that went on in my circle of friends and passed on my messages.

I *never* got used to the petty aggravations of the common guards, particularly when they were contrived and hateful. They upset me very much. I was always treated correctly by the higher officials, even up to the prison warden, and also by the majority of the common guards with whom I came in contact during these years. But there were three Social Democrats among them who for political reasons aggravated me whenever they could with little needle jabs. This nevertheless hurt me deeply. Each one of these abuses hurt me more than if I was beaten. Every prisoner with a sensitive nature suffers much more from unjust, malicious, and intended psychological abuse than from physical abuse. He perceives it to be much more humiliating and depressing than any physical abuse. I have often tried to desensitize myself against it, but I never succeeded. I became used to the rough tone of the common guards. The more primitive they were, the more they indulged in their random lust for power. I had also become used to carrying out orders without inner rebellion, even with a silent chuckle at some of the most insane orders which were given by those mentally limited. I became accustomed to the brutal, vulgar manner of speech which was used by most of the prisoners there. Even though it happened daily, I could never get used to the way the prisoners dragged everything that was decent and good in life through the muck and treated things which were sacred to many people in a vulgar, frivolous, and hateful manner. It was particularly upsetting to me to see them doing it all the more when they noticed they could hurt a fellow prisoner. Listening to this has always upset me.

A good book has always been a good friend to me. The only problem was that up to now because of the unrest of the kind of life I led, I had neither time nor leisure for this. In the solitude of my cell it became everything, particularly in the first two years of my imprisonment. It was my recuperation, and with this I could forget my whole situation.

IX

Prison Psychosis

After two years had gone by without anything special happening, suddenly a strange condition came over me. I became very irritable, nervous, and excited. I couldn't stand doing any work. I was a tailor at the time, and I had enjoyed it. However, I was unable to eat. Every bite I forced down my throat came back up again. I couldn't read anything anymore and I couldn't concentrate at all. Like a wild animal I paced rapidly back and forth in my cell. I couldn't sleep anymore. Up until then, I always slept deeply and almost dreamlessly through the whole night. But now I had to. get up and pace back and forth without finding any rest. When I finally did drop on my bed, because I was exhausted, and fell asleep, I would awake after a short time out of a confused nightmare bathed in sweat. In these nightmares, I was constantly persecuted, beaten, or shot to death, or I was plunging into a deep abyss. Those nights became torture to me. Hour after hour, I heard the tower clock strike. The closer the morning approached, the more I dreaded the coming day and the people I would have to see again, and I wished I wouldn't see anyone anymore. With all my power I tried to pull myself together, but I just couldn't fight it. I wanted to pray, but all I could manage was a sad, fearful mumbling. I had forgotten how to pray; I could no longer find the way to God.

In that state of mind, I believed that God didn't want to help me anymore because I had left him. My officially leaving the Church in 1922 tortured me. And yet, this was only the result of a condition which existed since the end of the war. Even though it happened gradually, I had already cut the ties to the Church during the last years of the war. I reproached myself bitterly for not having followed the will of my parents, for not becoming a priest. It was strange how all of that tortured me. My mental agitation grew from day to day, in fact hour to hour. I was close to going raving mad. Physically, I was deteriorating more and more. My foreman noticed my absentmindedness, which I had never shown; I did even the simplest things wrong. And although I worked like a dog, I just couldn't complete my quota. For several days now I had fasted because I assumed I would be able to eat again after that. I was caught dumping my lunch into the garbage by a guard. Even the guard who normally did his job in a tired and indifferent manner and hardly ever cared about the prisoners noticed my behavior and appearance. He himself told me later that he had watched me closely.

I was taken immediately to the doctor. This doctor, an old gentleman who had been practicing in the institution for decades, listened patiently to me, leafed through my files, and said with the greatest calm, "Prison psychosis. That'll take care of itself. It's not so bad!" I was put into an observation cell in the prison hospital, received an injection, and was wrapped in cold towels, after which I immediately sank into a deep sleep. During the following days they put some tranquilizers into my hospital food. My general state of excitement ebbed and I recovered. By my own wish I was returned to my cell. They had intended to put me in a multiple cell, but I had asked to remain alone. During those days the warden advised me that because of my good conduct and work record I was put into the second step and I would receive various privileges.

I was now allowed to write monthly, I could receive as much mail as was sent to me, and I was allowed to keep flowers on my window sill. I was allowed to have a light on until 10 p.m., and could, if I wanted, get together for hours with other prisoners on Sundays and holidays. This ray of hope, the anticipation of all the privileges, helped me to get over my state of depression more than all the tranquilizers. However, the deepest impressions of this condition stayed with me for a long time.

There are things between heaven and earth which one does not experience in the course of the day, about which one entertains serious thoughts when completely alone. Is it possible to communicate with the dead?

In my hours of greatest agitation, before my thoughts became confused, I often saw my parents standing before me in the flesh and I spoke with them as if I were still under their care. To this day I cannot find clarity about the connection between these things. And in all my years I have never spoken about these occurrences to anyone.

In the later years of my imprisonment I was able to observe prison psychosis. Many cases wound up in the padded cell; several of them completely lost their minds. The prisoners I knew who went through this stir-craziness and survived were, however, shy and depressed and pessimistic for a long time afterwards. Some of them never lost their depression. Most of the prisoner suicides that I observed there I attribute to prison psychosis. In this condition all rational thoughts and inhibitions which in normal life prevent suicide fall away. The tremendous agitation which rages through a human drives him to the outer limits of suicide in order to end the torture and find peace! Based on my experiences, the attempt to fake mental breakdown and insanity in order to escape imprisonment is very rare in penal institutions because from the moment of transfer to a mental institution, the term of sentence is suspended until the patient is again able to serve his term. He has to return or remain in that mental institution the rest of his life.

And strangely enough, most prisoners have an almost superstitious fear of becoming insane! After this low, this breakdown, my life in prison passed without particular incident. I became more and more calm and clear-thinking. In my free time I eagerly studied English. I even had textbooks sent to me. Later I had them regularly send me books and magazines in English, so that in about one year I learned this language without anyone helping me. This was a terrific discipline for my mind. I continually received good books on all subjects from fellow soldiers and acquaintances. I was particularly interested in history, ethnology,' and genetics. I enjoyed reading these the most. On Sundays I played chess with those prisoners with whom I got along well. This game is a rather serious mental duel and is particularly suited to exercise the mind and to freshen it up, since the mind is constantly threatened by the monotony of life behind bars. My contact with the outside world increased and was more varied by the letters, newspapers, and magazines that I now constantly received, which was a welcome new mental stimulus. If every once in a while a blue mood came over me, then just the memory of my near mental breakdown acted like a whip and caused the cloud that had appeared to vanish quickly. The fear of a repetition was too strong.

X

Model Prisoner

In the fourth year of my imprisonment I was promoted to the third step, which eased prison life for me because of the new privileges: every two weeks I could write letters with no limit to the number of pages on ordinary paper.

I no longer was required to do any compulsory work. I was allowed to pick out a job of my choice and I received higher pay for it. Up to now the so-called "pay" was eight Pfennigs [about two American cents] for the daily work quota. And from that I was allowed to use four Pfennigs to purchase additional food. Under the most favorable circumstances at the second step I could get one pound of lard in one month. In the third step the daily work quota paid fifty Pfennigs, and one could use all of the earnings for oneself. In addition to that, one could also use up to twenty marks [a mark has one hundred Pfennigs] of his own money monthly.

Listening to the radio was now allowed in the third step and smoking was permitted during designated hours. At that point the clerk's job in the supply room became open, so I requested it.

I now had a daily job which wasn't boring. I saw and heard a great deal from the prisoners of all departments who came every day for a change of clothing, underwear, or to get tools. I also learned about everything that happened in daily prison life from the guards who were on duty or accompanying the prisoners. The supply room was the gathering place for all the prison news and rumors. I also found out how rumors of all kinds got started, and how with the speed of lightning they were spread, and what the effects were. The news and the rumors, both of which are secretly whispered and passed on, are the elixir of prison life. The more isolated the person is, the more effective the rumor. The more naive he is, the more he will believe.

One of my coworkers, who was a prisoner like me working in the supply room-although he really belonged to the inventory since he had been there for more than ten years-took a devilish pleasure in inventing rumors completely out of thin air. He enjoyed whispering them to others and observing their effects. Since he did this so shrewdly, he could never be held to account for some of the serious effects caused by the rumors he started. I myself was once the victim of such a rumor. One day a rumor surfaced that through friends among the senior officials I was able to have women visitors in my cell during the night. A prisoner smuggled this complaint to the officials of the Prison Inspection Bureau via a guard. Suddenly one night the chief of the Prison Inspection Bureau appeared in my cell with several other higher officials, including the warden, who they had gotten out of bed, in order to see for themselves if the complaint was true! In spite of an extensive investigation, neither the person who wrote the complaint nor the one who spread the rumor could be found. When I was released, my coworker told me that he had invented the rumor and that my cell neighbor had written the complaint and then had smuggled out the letter. He did all this just to get back at the warden because he had refused him his parole. Cause and effect! Malicious people can cause a great deal of harm this way.

Especially interesting to me in my job were the new arrivals. The professional criminal was insolent, self-confident, and brash. Even the most severe prison sentence could not subdue him. He was an optimist who somehow believed that a favorable situation would develop. In many cases he had only been on the outside for a few weeks, as if on leave. The penitentiary had become his "home."

The first offenders were depressed, shy, sad, reluctant, and even fearful to talk to anyone. The same was true of those who had bad luck and were caught for a second or third time. Emptiness, misfortune, misery, and desperation could be read on their faces. There was plenty of material there for the psychologist or the sociologist! After a day of seeing and hearing all this, I was always glad when I could withdraw to the solitude of my cell in the evening and with thoughtful calmness draw my conclusions. I buried myself in my books and magazines or read the letters sent to me by kind and dear people. I read about their plans and intentions for me after my release and chuckled about their good intentions to cheer me up and console me. I didn't need this anymore, for it was now the fifth year, and I had gradually become immune to being locked up. Five more years lay ahead of me with not even the smallest reduction of time. Several pleas for mercy by influential persons, even personal supplications by someone very close to Reichspresident von Hindenburg, were absolutely refused by him for political reasons. I did not count on getting out before the ten years were up. With confidence, I hoped to endure the rest of my punishment physically and mentally healthy. I even made plans to keep myself more occupied by learning foreign languages and learning more about my new profession. I thought about everything possible, except an early release.

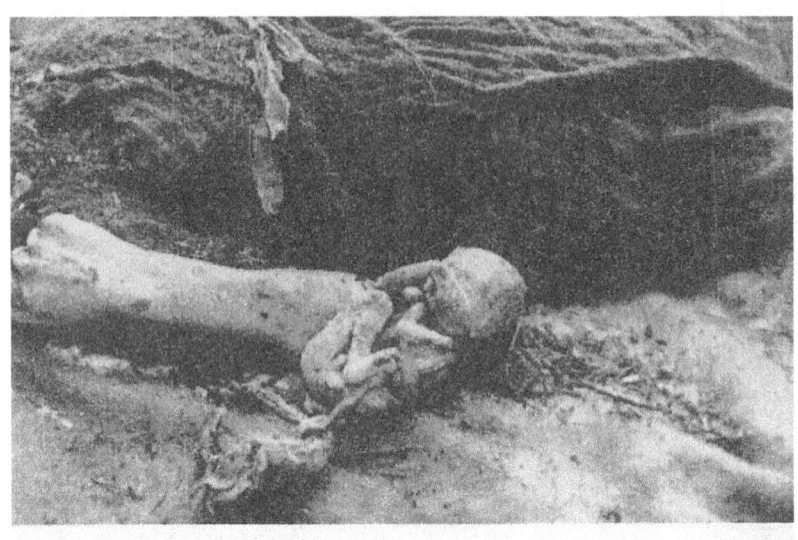

Found by the Red Army

XI

Freedom

It came overnight! In the Reichstag [German Congress] suddenly an unexpected majority had been found among the extreme right and left who had great interest in getting their political prisoners freed. Almost out of nowhere a political amnesty was granted, and along with many others I was freed [on July 14, 1928]. After six years I was free again. The gift of life was given back to me! Even today I can picture myself standing on the large stairway on the Potsdam railroad station in Berlin and looking with great interest at the milling crowd of people on the Potsdam Square. I must have stood there for a long time until a gentleman spoke to me and asked me where I wanted to go. I must have looked at him and answered him quite stupidly because he quickly ran away. All the hustle and bustle did not seem real to me. I thought I was in a movie theater watching a film. My release had been unexpected and too sudden. Everything seemed so incredible, so strange to me.

I had been invited by telegram to stay with a family in Berlin who were friends of mine. Even though I knew Berlin well, and it was easy to get to their apartment, it nevertheless took me a long time to get there. In the first days of my freedom someone always went with me when I dared to walk on the streets, because I didn't pay attention to the traffic signs, nor the frenzied, hurrying city traffic. I wandered around as in a dream. It took several days until I accustomed myself to the harsh reality. They really wanted to be good to me. They dragged me to movies, theaters, and to all the places of entertainment, to parties, in short to everything that a city person considers important in his life. All this rained down on me. There was just too much of a good thing. I became totally confused by it all and yearned for peace and quiet. I wanted to escape the noise, the pace, and bustle of the city as quickly as possible and go out to the country. After ten days I left Berlin to start a position as an agricultural civil servant. To be sure, I still had many invitations for visits, but I wanted to work. I had rested long enough.

The families and soldiers who were my friends suggested many different plans and tried to make me happy. All of them wanted to help me make a living and to make my transition to normal life easier. I was supposed to go to East Africa, Mexico, Brazil, Paraguay, or the United States. Everything was done with the good intention to get me away from Germany so that I would not get involved in the political battles of the extreme right again.

But others, most of all my old comrades, absolutely wanted to see me in the front ranks of the fighting organizations of the NSDAP [National Socialist German Workers Party]. I rejected both ideas. Even though I had been a member of the Party since 1922 and agreed with and was convinced about the aims of the Party, I emphatically rejected the mass propaganda, the pandering for the favor of the masses, the appeal to the lowest mass instincts. Yes, even to the way they expressed themselves. I had become acquainted with "the masses" from 1918 to 1923! Although I was inclined to remain a Party member, I didn't want any office, nor did I want to join the branch organizations. I had other plans. By the same token, I didn't want to go abroad. I wanted to stay in Germany and achieve the farsighted goals of the reconstruction no matter how long it took. I wanted to be a pioneer on the land.

In the long years of seclusion in my cell I became conscious of this: for me, there was only one goal to work and fight for, a farm which I created myself with a large family. This was to be the content of my life, my life's goal.

XII

The Artamans

After my release from prison, I got in touch with the Artamans. I had become acquainted with this organization and its goal during my imprisonment through their writings, and I had occupied myself very intensely with t. This was a community of young patriotic people, young men and women who had come out of the youth movement from all national alignments. They wanted to escape the unhealthy, decaying, and superficial life of the cities, especially the large metropolitan areas. They sought the natural way of life in the country. They abhorred alcohol and nicotine, in fact everything that was not good for the healthy development of mind and body; moreover, through this principle of living they hoped to return to the soil from which their ancestors had come forth, to the fountain of life of the German people, to the healthy farming community. This was also my way, my long-sought goal.

I resigned my position as an agricultural civil servant and joined the community of those who thought as I did. I broke all connections with my former friends and families because they could not understand my decision based on their traditional viewpoints, and because I wanted to start my new life without any interference.

In the first days there I became acquainted with my future wife, who, along with her brother, was inspired by the same ideals and had found her way to the Artamans. We knew from the very first moment that we belonged together. We found within ourselves a harmony of trust and understanding as if we had lived together from childhood on. All our views of life were the same. We completed each other in every respect. I had found the woman I had dreamed of during the long years of my solitude. Through all the years of our life together and even to this day, this inner . harmony remains unchanged even by the misfortunes of life in spite of the outside forces.

But there is one thing that remains a steady sorrow to her. I could never share the things that deeply disturbed me; I had to settle everything alone, within myself. I could not confide even in her about them. We got married as soon as it was possible [in 1929], in order to start our hard life together, a life freely chosen out of deepest inner conviction. Clearly we both saw the long, difficult, and trouble-filled road to our goal, but nothing was going to prevent us from reaching it. Our life truly was not easy in the following five years. But even the biggest hardships could not discourage us. We were happy and content when we were able to win over new believers to our idea by our example and our teaching. During that time three of our children were born for the new tomorrow, for the new future. Our own land was soon to be allotted to us. But it did not happen that way!

Main Gate

XIII

Again a Soldier

Himmler asked me to join the SS in June 1934. This now was to pull me away from our planned path. For a long, long time I struggled trying to make a decision. This was not my usual habit. The temptation to be a soldier again was really strong, much stronger than my wife's doubts about whether this profession would fulfill and satisfy the inner me. She agreed, however, when she saw how very much I felt attracted to becoming a soldier again, even though I would have to deviate from our agreed course. I was confident that we would be able to hold on to our dream, since I was promised quick promotion, and with all the financial advantages connected with it. This goal, the farm as a home, a home for us and our children, remained with us even in the later years. We never deviated from that. After the war I planned to leave active duty and return to the farm. After considering the facts for a long time, still full of doubts, I decided to join the General SS.

Today I deeply regret leaving the course that I had originally chosen.

My life and that of my family would have run a different course, even though we still would now be equally without home or without a farm. But at least we would have shared several years of satisfying work together. But who can foresee the course of people whose fates are intertwined?

What is right? What is wrong?

When Himmler made the call to join the SS, to enter the guard troop of a concentration camp, I had no thought at all about the concentration camps which were mentioned in the postscript. During the isolation of our farm life in Pomerania, we had hardly heard about concentration camps. The only thing I could see was the active military life of being a soldier again.

I arrived at Dachau and became a recruit again, with all its joys and sorrows, and then I became a drill instructor.' The soldier's life captivated me. During instruction and lectures, I learned about the use of arms and about the dangerous nature of the ENEMIES OF THE STATE, as Inspector of the Concentration Camps Eicke called the prisoners behind the barbed wire. I saw prisoners at work marching in and out, and I heard about them from fellow soldiers who had been in service there in the camp since 1933.

I remember precisely the first flogging I ever witnessed. According to Eicke's orders, at least one company of troops had to be present at the administration of this punishment.

Two prisoners had stolen cigarettes from the canteen and were sentenced to twenty-five blows of the cane. The soldiers lined up in aU-shaped formation with their weapons. The punishment bench stood in the middle. The two prisoners were presented by the block leaders. The Kommandant put in his appearance. The camp commander and the senior company commanders reported to him. The duty officer read the sentence and the first prisoner, a small, hardened, lazy man, had to lie down across the bench. Two soldiers from the troop held his head and hands firmly while two block leaders carried out the sentence, alternating after each blow. The prisoner didn't utter a sound.

It was different with the second one, a strong, broad-shouldered, political prisoner. After the first blow, he screamed wildly and wanted to tear himself loose. He continued screaming to the last blow, even though the Kommandant told him repeatedly to be quiet.

I stood in the front rank and I was, therefore, forced to watch the entire procedure in detail. I say forced because if I would have stood further back, I would not have looked. Hot and cold chills ran through me when the screaming started. In fact, the whole procedure, even the first beating, made me shiver. Later, during the first execution at the beginning of the war, I was not as upset as during this corporal punishment. For this I can find no explanation.

Until the 1918 Revolution corporal punishment was a normal procedure, until it was later abolished in the penitentiary. The official who always administered this punishment was still employed in the prison and was called the "bone breaker. " This coarse and depraved man always smelled of alcohol and to him all prisoners were only numbers. One could very well imagine him as a person who liked to beat people. In the solitary confinement area in the basement I once saw the punishment bench and the canes that were used. My skin crawled as I imagined the "bone-breaker" using them. During all the corporal punishments for which I had to be present, and for the whole time I was with the company, I always dis- appeared to the back rank. Later, when I was the block leader, I always avoided being present if possible, at least during the beatings. This was easy because some of the block leaders and camp commanders were always eager to be there. But when I became duty officer and later camp commander, I had to be present. I did not like to do this when I was Kommandant and when I had to order corporal punishment, I was hardly ever present. Certainly I did not thoughtlessly order these punishments.

Why did I shy away from this punishment so much? Even though I try, I cannot explain this. There was another block leader at the time who felt the same way and also avoided being there. It was Schwarzhuber, who was later camp commander in Birkenau and Ravensbrück. The block leaders who were so eager to watch them and whom I really got to know later were almost always two-faced, vulgar, very violent, and vile creatures who behaved in the same way toward their fellow soldiers and their families. To them prisoners were not human beings.

Several years later three of them hanged themselves after they were arrested for brutally mistreating prisoners in other camps and they were held accountable for it. Among the SS troops there were those who looked upon the flogging of prisoners as a welcome spectacle, a kind of entertainment. I certainly was not one of them.

When I was still a recruit in Dachau the following incident happened:

Some SS sergeants together with some prisoners were carrying out an extensive operation of stealing meat from the slaughterhouse and selling it on the black market. Four members of the SS were sentenced to severe prison terms by a Munich civil court because there were no SS courts at the time. The four of them were led in front of the entire guard regiment and stripped of their rank by Eicke and dishonorably discharged from the SS. He personally tore off all the insignia of rank and regiment, had them paraded past all the companies, and then handed them over to the police to serve their sentences. Afterwards he used this incident to give a long lecture and a warning. He said he really would have liked to put the four of them into concentration camp uniforms, and after flogging them, put them behind bars with their partners in crime, but Himmler did not give him permission. A similar fate awaited anyone who got involved with the prisoners behind the barbed wire, regardless of whether it was with criminal intent or out of compassion.

Eicke thought that he would show the ENEMIES OF THE STATE

a weakness which they would immediately take advantage of. Any compassion at all toward the ENEMIES OF THE STATE would be unworthy of an SS soldier. There was no place for weaklings in his ranks, and they would be well-advised to disappear into a monastery as quickly as possible. He said he could use only hard and determined men who would obey every order, no matter what the cost to themselves. They were not wearing the skull insignia and carrying a weapon for nothing. Eicke said that the SS were the only soldiers in peacetime facing the enemy day and night: the enemy behind the barbed wire.

The stripping of rank and the expulsion from the SS were a disturbing experience which affected every soldier who viewed this for the first time.

But at the time I didn't understand what Eicke meant by ENEMIES OF THE STATE, the enemy behind the barbed wire, for I did not get to know them well enough yet. I would find out soon enough.

After I was in service with the outfit for six months, suddenly there came an order from Eicke that all older officers and noncommissioned officers were to be separated from the regular outfit and were to be used in the departments in the camp. I was one of these. I was transferred as a block leader to the concentration camp. I didn't like this at all. Eicke arrived shortly thereafter, and when I reported to him I made a request that he should make an exception in my case, and transfer me back to the General SS. I told him that I was body and soul a soldier, and only the opportunity to become a soldier again had actually brought me into the General SS. He knew my life story completely, and knew, therefore, that I was especially suited for the concentration camp based on my personal experience in associating with and handling prisoners. Noone else, he said, would be more suited for the concentration camp than I. His orders were concrete and would not be changed for anything.

I had to obey, because, after all, wasn't I a soldier? And didn't I choose this course? At that moment I wanted to go back to the difficult but free path that I had followed before. Now there was no turning back for me. With mixed feelings, I entered into my new area of responsibility, into a new world to which I would be chained for the next ten years. Yes, I had been a prisoner myself for six long years, and I knew about the life of a prisoner. I knew his habits, his good and bad sides, all his impulses and his needs, but the concentration camp was new to me. I was to learn the tremendous difference between life in a jail or prison and life in a concentration camp. And I learned it from the ground up, often more thoroughly than I really liked.

Electric Fence

XIV

The Early Concentration Camps

I was turned loose on the prisoners without much instruction by the camp commander, or the executive officer, together with two other beginners, Schwarzhuber and Remmele. Remmele later became the executive officer of one of the industrial factories near Auschwitz.

Somewhat nervous, I stood that evening during Appelle [roll call] in front of the forced labor prisoners who were entrusted to me, as they curiously eyed their new company commander. That's what the block leaders were called then. It was only later on that I understood the question that showed on their faces. My sergeant really had the company running smoothly. The word company was later called a block and the company sergeant was called a block senior. He and his five platoon leaders were political prisoners. They were later called room seniors. They were old, fanatic, dyed-in-the-wool Communists who were former soldiers and who loved to talk about their experiences as soldiers in the army.

At the moment of their induction into the camp most of the forced labor prisoners were very sloppy and degenerate persons; however, the room seniors trained them very quickly to be orderly and clean without my ever having to say a single word. The forced labor prisoners took great care not to attract attention to themselves because after six months their release depended on their conduct and on their work performance. If it was not satisfactory, another three or six months would be added for their reeducation.

In a short time, I knew all of the approximately 270 men of my company very well, and this helped me to form judgments about their readiness for release. There were only a few I found incorrigible during my time as block leader and these were to be transferred to a prison as asocials.

This type stole anything that wasn't nailed down. They tried to get out of work and were sloppy in every respect. Most of them left completely rehabilitated after serving their time in the camp. Very seldom did anyone return. Unless they were criminals or asocials, they were depressed by imprisonment; they felt ashamed, especially the older ones, who had never been in trouble with the law. Now suddenly they were serving time because they hadn't reported to work, either because they didn't feel like going, or because of their Bavarian stubbornness, or because the beer tasted too good, or there were other reasons which caused their loafing which prompted the Bureau of Labor to send them to the concentration camps for reeducation. They all easily survived the hard part of camp life because they had a reasonable assurance that they would be free again after their time was up.

But it was different with the remaining 90 percent of the camp, which consisted of one company made up of Jews, homosexuals, Jehovah's Witnesses, and those who tried to leave Germany; another company of asocials; and seven companies of political prisoners, most of them Communists.

There was no set prison term for political prisoners. It depended on factors which were unpredictable. The prisoners knew this and that's why they suffered so much. And because of this uncertainty, life in the camp became torture for them. I spoke to many intelligent and perceptive political prisoners about this uncertainty. They all said that they could suffer all the indignities of camp life, such as the impulsiveness of the SS guards or the prison seniors in charge, the harsh discipline, living together in close quarters, the monotony of all the daily routines; all of that could be endured, all of that could be overcome, but not the uncertainty of not knowing how long they would remain in the camp. This was the most crushing blow, which paralyzed even the strongest will. From my observation, the unknown length of the sentence and its depending on the whim of low-ranking officials, exerted the strongest and the most negative influence on the mental health of the prisoners.

At least the professional criminal who was sentenced to fifteen years in the penitentiary knew when, at the very latest, he would be free again, and maybe even sooner. The political prisoner, however, was often arrested because of a vague accusation by someone who hated him and was ordered into a concentration camp for an unspecified sentence. This could be for one year or this could last ten years. The quarterly review of sentences which was the law for German prisoners was strictly a matter of form. The final decision rested with the bureau that had ordered him into the camp, and they did not want to admit that they had made any mistakes. The prisoner was the real victim, who, for better or worse, was at the mercy of the bureau that sent him. For him there was no legal defense, nor any legal complaint. Now and then there were extenuating circumstances which allowed exceptional cases to be reviewed which ended with a surprising release. But they were all exceptions. As a rule, the time spent in concentration camp depended on a quirk of fate.

The General Staff: Mengele, 2d from left; Hoss, 2d from right.

XV
The Types of Guards

There were three types of guard personnel everywhere, whether you were in a holding cell awaiting trial, a prison, or a concentration camp. They can make life hell for a prisoner and they can also ease imprisonment, which by itself is difficult, and make it more tolerable.

The first category of guard is the malicious, nasty, basically evil, vulgar, vile, low-natured type. They see the prisoner as an object upon whom they can unleash their perverted urges, their bad moods, and their inferiority complexes without restraint or fear of resistance. They know neither compassion nor any warm feelings for others. They take advantage of every opportunity to terrorize their assigned prisoners, especially those they can't stand, or those they have a grudge against. This begins with the smallest dirty tricks, running the whole scale of disgusting intrigues involving their dark urges up to the most severe abuse, depending on the personality of the guard. They are especially satisfied by the mental anguish of their victims. Not even the strictest order forbidding this prevents them from practicing their inhuman activities. Only the pressure of close supervision prevents them from this kind of torture. They spend their time thinking up new methods of mental and physical torture. Woe to those persons assigned to them when these ugly creatures have supervisors who not only tolerate their wicked urges but, because of the same personality traits, encourage them.

The second category of guard is the majority. These are the apathetic and indifferent ones who ploddingly perform their duties in a careless or deficient manner and do only what is absolutely necessary. The prisoners are objects which they have to supervise and guard. They hardly waste a thought on the prisoners, or the lives they lead. They stick to the orders given or go by the book out of convenience. To think about what they are doing would be too much of an exertion for them. For the most part, their intelligence is somewhat limited. By and large they do not wish to harm the prisoners, but by their indifference, laziness, or limited intelligence, they unintentionally harm, torture, and hurt many prisoners. Above all, they are the ones who make it possible for prisoners to rule over other prisoners, often leading to a disastrous end.

The third category consists of those who by nature are kind, have a good heart, have compassion and empathy for human suffering. However, even here there are vast differences. First there are those who strictly and conscientiously go by the book and do not overlook any breaking of the camp rules by the prisoners, but whose heart and good will interpret the book in favor of the prisoner, who try as much as possible to ease the life of the prisoner, or at least not make it unnecessarily more difficult. There are also those who are too good-hearted, whose naiveté sometimes borders on the miraculous. These guards overlook everything as far as the prisoners are concerned and try to fulfill their every wish; to help them where they can because of their good-heartedness and unlimited compassion. They cannot believe that there are evil men among the prisoners.

The strictness of prison life, paired with kindness and understanding, generally has a calming effect on the prisoners, so they are constantly searching for human understanding. The worse the conditions, the more it is needed. A kind look, a friendly nod of the head, and a pleasant word often work miracles, especially with sensitive prisoners. And if they actually find consideration for their situation and condition, then it has unimaginable impact. Even the most desperate, those who have given up on themselves, find the courage to face life again when they see or feel the slightest sign of human cooperation.

Every prisoner tries to make prison life better for himself and to make his situation easier. He will take advantage of any kindness shown to him. Ruthless prisoners use all their energy and cunning to crack the guards to make life better in prison. Since the prisoner generally is more intelligent than the lower rank of supervisors and guards, he quickly finds a weak spot in their good but limited natures. This is the other side of the coin: too much kindness and gullibility toward prisoners. So it happens that showing human understanding even once to strong-willed prisoners can cause a chain of prison rule-breaking which ends with the harshest punishment. This can start with the harmless smuggling of letters and climax in the worst thing a guard can do, help a prisoner to escape or aid a general breakout.

The following examples will show the different behaviors of the above three categories of guards. In the holding center a prisoner asks the guard to turn up the heat in the cell because he has a bad cold and is freezing.

The malicious guard turns off the heat completely and then constantly watches the prisoner as he runs back and forth and exercises in his cell in order to keep warm. During the night shift when an apathetic guard is on duty, the prisoner again asks for the heat to be turned up. The apathetic guard turns the heat up full blast and doesn't bother to check the cell for the rest of the night. After an hour the cell is so overheated that the prisoner has to keep the window open the whole night, which aggravates his cold even more.

Showers take place at different times of the day in prison. The prisoners are led to the showers by a sadistic guard. In the middle of winter, he orders the men in the locker room to open the windows all the way because there is too much steam in the room. Screaming at the men, he chases them quickly into the showers, turns on the steaming hot water, so hot that no one can stand it; then switches to ice cold and everyone is forced to stand under it for a long time. Later, with a sneering smile, he stands and watches how the prisoners are barely able to dress themselves because they are so cold.

When the apathetic guard is in charge of the shower detail in the winter, the prisoners undress while he sits down and reads the newspaper. After some time has passed, he troubles himself to interrupt his education and turns on the water all the way to hot and returns to his newspaper. No one can get under the water because it is almost boiling. Shouts to get his attention do not disturb him. Only after he has finished his newspaper does he get up and turn the water off. Unwashed, they all get dressed again. He looks at his watch and sees by the elapsed time that he has done his duty.

The following example takes place in a gravel pit in a concentration camp. The good-natured guard takes care to see that the gravel push cars are not overloaded, that a double detachment of men is used to push the cars up the incline, that the rails are not loose, and that the switches are well-lubricated. The day passes without any yelling, yet the ordered quota is achieved. The malicious guard commander has the gravel cars overloaded, a single detachment of men pushes the cars up the incline, and the car has to be pushed the whole way in double time. He also does not assign a prisoner to check the tracks and do the lubricating, so the cars continuously jump the track. The Kapouses this as an excuse to beat the prisoners, so that by noon a large number of prisoners are unable to return to their work detail because their feet are injured. All day long there is terrible yelling and screaming by all the members of the guard detail. The result is that by evening barely half the ordered quota is reached.

The apathetic guard commander cares nothing about his workers. He lets the Kapos work and do as they please or as the mood strikes them. Those prisoners who are the Kapo's favorites have a very easy day, while the others have to work all the harder. The guards don't pay any attention because the commander of the guard is not around most of the time.

I have taken these three examples from a multitude of similar incidents which I personally witnessed; I could fill several books with them. My intention was to show graphically how a prisoner's whole life depends upon the behavior and prejudice of the various guards and supervisors in spite of all the rules and regulations.

It is not just the physical hardships which make a prisoner's life difficult, but also the mental torture caused by the rash, malicious, and vile actions of the apathetic and spiteful guard and supervisors. As difficult as it is, a prisoner can cope with the rigid and lawful strictness of imprisonment, but obvious unjust and spiteful treatment strikes him to the core, like being beaten with clubs. Since he is powerless against this, he must suffer in silence. To put it crudely, one has to look at guards and prisoners as enemies who face each other from two opposing worlds. For the most part the prisoner is assaulted, first by prison life itself and then by the behavior of the guards. If he wants to survive this "war," he has to fight tooth and nail. Since he cannot use the same weapons as the guards, he has to find other ways to defend himself. Depending on his nature, his thick skin becomes an armor against which he lets his enemy rage. He carries on, more or less, indifferently, or he becomes treacherous, underhanded, and deceitful. He outwits his enemy, and in this way achieves relief and favors, or joins the enemy and becomes a spy, a Kapo, or a block leader. He thereby creates for himself a tolerable existence at the expense of his fellow prisoners. Sometimes he bets everything on one card, breaks out and escapes, or he loses his will to live; he gives up on himself, is ruined mentally, and ends up committing suicide. This all sounds very hard and seems unbelievable, yet it is true.

Based on my observations and experiences over the years, I believe

I am able to judge this accurately. Work occupies a large part of a prisoner's life. It can serve to make his life more tolerable but it can also lead to his downfall. Work is a necessity and satisfies an inner need for every healthy prisoner in normal circumstances. But for blatantly lazy people, loafers, and other asocial parasites, it isn't. They can continue to vegetate very well without work without the slightest mental anguish.

Work allows the prisoner to overcome the emptiness of imprisonment. It pushes the unpleasantness of everyday prison life into the background. It can bring him satisfaction if he develops an inner readiness and voluntarily does the work. If, in addition, he finds a job in his trade or suitable work which fits his abilities, he can achieve a state of mind which cannot be shaken, even by very unpleasant circumstances.

Make no mistake, work in prison and a concentration camp is an obligation which is mandatory. Generally, every prisoner voluntarily achieves a considerable amount, provided he is used in the right place. His inner satisfaction about his work situation has an effect on his entire disposition. On the other hand, dissatisfaction in his work causes his whole life to become a burden. How much sorrow, how much hatred, and in fact, how much pain could have been avoided over the years if the work inspectors and the foremen had considered these facts and had walked through the shops and the work areas with their eyes open? All my life I liked to work and I did it willingly. I often did the heaviest physical work under the hardest circumstances in the coal mines, in the oil refinery tanks, and in the brick factory. I chopped down trees, made railroad ties, and harvested peat. There is no important job in agriculture that I did not do. But I didn't just work at those places. I also carefully observed the people who worked with me. I watched their behavior, their habits, and their living conditions. I can speak with authority; I know what it means to work, and I can judge very well how much a man can do. Only when I had done a job well was I satisfied with myself. I never asked a subordinate to do more than I myself was able to do.

Even while waiting for trial in the holding center in Leipzig I missed work. I had lots to occupy my mind, such as the investigation itself, plenty of mail, newspapers, and visitors. I finally asked for work and it was approved. I pasted bags together. Even though it was a truly monotonous job, it was still an occupation which filled out a large part of the day and which forced me into a certain routine. I voluntarily set myself a definite quota; that was the important part of it. During my imprisonment I always tried to choose jobs which forced me to be alert and were not purely mechanical. This work occupied my mind for many hours of the day and saved me from useless, demoralizing brooding. Then in the evening I felt satisfied, not only because I had put another day behind me, but also because I had accomplished a good day's work. The most severe punishment for me would have been to take away my work. What I miss the most now is work. How thankful I am for the present assignment of writing this book, which brings me great satisfaction. I have discussed work with many prisoners in the penitentiary and in the concentration camp, especially in Dachau. All of them were convicted to life behind bars or behind the barbed wire without work would be the worst punishment in the long run. For those locked up, work is an effective, positive disciplinary measure, insofar as it helps maintain self-control, thereby enabling a prisoner to better resist the demoralizing influences of imprisonment. It is also a means of education for those prisoners who are basically unstable; for those who need to get used to regularity and endurance; and for those who, through the beneficial influence of work, can be saved from a life of crime. What I just stated is valid only under normal circumstances. That's how the motto "AR-BEIT MACHT FREI" ["Work sets you free"] is to be understood.! It was Eicke's firm intention that those prisoners, no matter from what category, who stood out from the mass because of their continued diligent work performance, were to be released, no matter what the Gestapo and the civil authorities said. A few prisoners were released in this manner. However, because of the war, these good intentions did not materialize on a larger scale. I have written about work in detail because I myself have experienced the mental value of work to the fullest and because I wish to show how important work is to the mental state of the prisoner. I want my views on this clearly stated.

Later on I will explain what happens regarding the concept of work and the work details of the prisoners.

When I was block leader in Dachau, I had personal contacts with the individual prisoners, even with those not in my block. One of the duties of the block leader then was to censor the outgoing mail. Whoever reads the letters of a prisoner over a long period of time and has enough knowledge of human nature will get a true picture of the inmate's state of mind. Every prisoner tries to describe his needs and worries in his letters to his wife or his mother. He is, more or less, open about it. In the long run, no prisoner can hide his real thinking or disguise himself in prison. He cannot fool the trained eye of the experienced observer, not even in letters.

Eicke had drummed into his SS the concept of dangerous ENEMIES OF THE STATE so intensely, so convincingly, and he kept preaching about it throughout the following years so that everyone who didn't know any better was completely filled with it. I also believed in and now began looking for the dangerous ENEMIES OF THE STATE, and I asked myself: What made them so dangerous?

I found a small handful of hard-core Communists and Social Democrats who, if they could get free, could have caused unrest among the people and would try anything to carry out their illegal activities effectively. They even openly admitted it. The largest number of prisoners had been Communists or Social Democratic officials who had fought and worked personally for their ideas of national policy. They really hurt the Nazi Party and did some damage. But if you looked closer at them in daily life, they showed themselves to be harmless and peaceful persons who, after having realized that their work was in pieces, had only the will left to make a living and be able to return to their families. In my opinion, three out of four political prisoners could have been released in 1935-36, and there wouldn't have been the least bit of harm done to the Third Reich. The other one-fourth was fanatically convinced that their world would rise again. These had to be kept under tight security. These people were the dangerous ENEMIES OF THE STATE. They could easily be identified, even though they did not come out into the open; on the contrary, they tried cleverly to camouflage themselves. As far as the state and the nation were concerned, the professional criminals, the asocials with more than twenty-five or thirty previous arrests, were much more dangerous.

It was Eicke's intention to conduct regular lectures for his SS men, in order to set the tone about the basic criminal danger of these prisoners and issue corresponding orders to prime the SS against the prisoners so that they would suppress any feelings of pity right from the start. Because of his constant hammering he created a hatred, an animosity against the prisoners which is incomprehensible and which outsiders cannot understand. This attitude spread into all the concentration camps, to all the SS men and officers who served in the concentration camps, and continued for many years, even after Eicke's departure as inspector of concentration camps.

This indoctrination of hate explains all the torture and mistreatment of the prisoners in the concentration camps. This basic attitude against the prisoner was intensified by the influence of the senior Kommandants like Loritz and Koch, to whom the prisoners were not human but "Russians," or "Neanderthals." This artificially created hatred against all prisoners did not remain a secret to them. The hard-core fanatics were indeed strengthened in their attitude, while the good-natured were hurt and repulsed.

The hatred could be clearly felt in the camp after Eicke's lectures.

The morale of the prisoners dropped immediately; every move of the SS guards was watched with anxiety. The rumors and camp gossip about the intended measures followed in rapid succession. A general unrest spread. But it wasn't because the treatment became worse. No, it was because a more hostile attitude of the guards and supervisors became evident.

I have to emphasize again: It isn't the physical influence and impression of camp life as a whole which depresses and tortures the prisoner, especially a prisoner of a concentration camp, but the mental aspects which drive him to despair. Most of the prisoners are not indifferent to whether the guards are hostile, neutral, or nice to them. Even though a guard does not have physical contact with a prisoner, his hostility, his hate-filled attitude, and his dirty looks alone scare, depress, and torture the prisoner.

Over and over I had to hear from the prisoners in Dachau, "Why does the SS hate us so? We are human beings too." This alone should suffice to clarify the general relationship between the SS and prisoners.

I do not believe that Eicke personally hated and despised these dangerous ENEMIES OF THE STATE, as he continuously tried to make the troops believe. I am more convinced that his constant priming only served to force the SS men to their utmost alertness and constant readiness. What he caused by this, and what effect his hounding had on everyone, he never realized. And so, raised and trained in the spirit of Eicke, I had to perform my duty in the concentration camp, as a block leader, a duty officer, and as supply administrator. I must now admit, I conscientiously and attentively performed my duty to everyone's satisfaction. I didn't let the prisoners get away with anything. I was firm and often hard. But I had been a prisoner for too long for me not to notice their needs. It was not without inner sympathy that I faced all of the occurrences in the camp. Outwardly I was cold, even stone-faced, but inwardly I was moved to the deepest. I saw many crimes, suicides, or those shot while trying to escape. I was close enough to determine if they were real situations or set up by the guards. I viewed the work accidents, those who died by running into the electrified wire. I was present at the legal identification of bodies in the autopsy room, during disciplinary beatings, and during the punishments Loritz ordered done and often observed himself. These were Loritz's punishment assignments and his way of fulfilling a sentence. By looking at the stone mask on my face he was firmly convinced that he didn't have to "toughen me up," as he loved to do with the SS men who seemed to him to be too weak.

This is when my guilt really begins.

It had become clear to me that I was not suited for this kind of service because in my heart I did not agree with the conditions and the practices of the concentration camp as demanded by Eicke.

My heart was tied to the prisoners because I had suffered their kind of life much too long and had also experienced their needs. Right then I should have gone to Eicke or Himmler and explained that I was not suited for service in the concentration camp because I had too much compassion for the prisoners.

I did not have the courage to do this.

I did not want to reveal myself because I didn't want to admit my sensitivity. I was too stubborn to admit that I had made the wrong decision when I gave up my plans to farm.

I had volunteered to join the active SS. The black uniform had become too precious to me and I didn't want to take it off in this way. If I admitted that I was too soft for the SS, I would have been expelled, or at least been dismissed without ceremony. I did not have the heart for that.

So I fought between my inner conviction and my sense of duty. And I struggled with my loyalty oath of the SS and my allegiance to Hitler. Should I become a deserter? Even today my wife knows nothing of this inner conflict. I have kept it to myself until now.

As an old-time member of the Nazi Party, I believed in the need for the concentration camps. The real ENEMIES OF THE STATE had to be put away safely; the asocials and the professional criminals who could not be locked up under the prevailing laws had to lose their freedom in order to protect the people from their destructive behavior.

I was also firmly convinced that only the SS, the guardians of the new state, could perform this job. But I did not agree with Eicke's views about inmates and his method of enraging the basest feelings of hate among the guard troops. I did not agree with his personnel policy of leaving the prisoners with incompetent people; I did not agree with his practice of unsuitable people in their positions. I was *not* in agreement with the length of sentencing depending on someone's whim.

But by staying in the concentration camp, I adopted the views, orders, and decrees which were in force there. I accepted my fate, which I had voluntarily chosen, even though deep inside I quietly hoped to find another kind of duty in the service in the future. At that time, however, this was unthinkable because Eicke said I was very much suited for prison duty.

Even though I became accustomed to all of the occurrences of the concentration camp, I never became insensitive to human suffering. I always saw it and felt it. But I always had to walk away from it because I was not allowed to be soft. I wanted to have the reputation of being hard. I did not want to be thought of as a weak person.

The Children's Barracks

XVI
Experiences in Sachsenhausen

I went to Sachsenhausen as adjutant [on August 1, 1938]. There I got to learn about the concentration camps, their inner workings and practices. I got to know Eicke better and his influence on the camps and the guards. I came in contact with the Gestapa [Geheimnis Staatspolizeiamt-the administration of the Gestapo secret police (Prussia), not to be confused with the Gestapo]. From all the correspondence, I could see how unified all of the upper departments of the SS were. From my new position I got a broader view.

Through a friend in the highest echelons close to Hitler, I heard about what went on around Hitler. Another old friend had a leading position in the Reich youth leadership; another was on Rosenberg's staff as a public relations officer; another was in the Reich Office of Medicine. I often got together in Berlin with these old friends from the Free Corps days. Through them I became acquainted with the ideology of the Nazi Party. Because I was trusted, I came to know their intentions now more than I ever had before.

During these years Germany experienced a tremendous upsurge. Industry and commerce blossomed as never before. The foreign policy successes of Adolf Hitler were evident enough to silence the doubters or the enemies. The Nazi Party ruled the state. These successes could not be denied. The path and the goal of the Party were correct. I firmly believed this without the slightest doubt.

In spite of the fact that I felt unsuitable for concentration camp service, my inner distress sank into the background because I did not come into direct contact with the prisoners as often as I had in Dachau. Even though Eicke's headquarters was in Sachsenhausen, the atmosphere of hate didn't exist there as it had in Dachau. The guard troops were different. There were many young recruits and young officers from the Junkers School [officer candidate school]. Former guards with the Dachau mentality were seldom assigned there. The Kommandant [Colonel Baranowski] was a different sort of person. Even though he was strict and hard, he nevertheless had a keen sense of justice and a fanatical sense of duty. He became my model of an old National Socialist and SS officer. I always pictured him as the type of officer I wanted to be. He also had moments in which his kindness and his soft heart clearly came out in the open, and yet he was hard and mercilessly strict in all matters concerning the service. And so he constantly showed me how the demanded hardness of the word "MUST" had to silence all the soft feelings in the SS soldier.

The war came and with it a significant turning point in my life in the concentration camp. But at that time who could imagine the horrible tasks that would be assigned to the concentration camps during the course of the war? On the first day of the war Eicke gave a speech to the reserve formations who had replaced the General SS in the camps. In that speech he emphasized that now the harsh laws of war had to be obeyed. Every SS soldier had to give his all fully and completely without consideration for his life. Every order had to be considered sacred and even the hardest and most difficult had to be carried out without any hesitation. Himmler demanded of each SS officer an exemplary sense of duty and performance for the German people and the nation, even to the point of sacrificing his own life.

The main duty of the SS now was to protect Adolf Hitler's nation from all internal dangers during this war. A revolution like the one in 1918, or a strike of the ammunition workers as in 1917 could not be allowed to happen again. Every enemy of the state who surfaced and everyone who sabotaged the war effort was to be annihilated. Hitler demanded that the SS protect the Fatherland against all enemy activities. Eicke therefore demanded that the men of the reserve units servicing the camps now be educated to become inflexibly severe toward the prisoners. They were to carry out the most difficult duty and the harshest orders. This was now our purpose for being in the SS. The SS had to demonstrate that their stern education was indeed the correct way. Only the SS could protect the National Socialist state from all dangers. All the other organizations lacked the necessary toughness for this.

On that very same day the first execution of the war took place in Sachsenhausen. It was a Communist who refused to perform his air raid duties in the Junker aircraft factory in the city of Dessau. Plant security reported him and he was arrested by the State Police and brought to the Gestapo in Berlin for questioning. The report was presented to Himmler, who then ordered his immediate execution by firing squad.

According to a secret mobilization order, all executions ordered by Himmler or the Gestapo were to be carried out in the nearest concentration camp.

At 10:00 p.m., [Major General] Müller of the Gestapo telephoned and reported that a courier was on the way with an order. This order was to be carried out immediately. Shortly afterwards a car arrived with two State Police officials and a handcuffed civilian. The Kommandant broke open the secret order, which stated very briefly, "By order of the Reichs Leader of the SS [Himmler], John Doe is to be shot. He is to be told this during his arrest and the sentence is to be carried out one hour later."

The Kommandant then told the condemned man about the order he had received. The prisoner was very calm about it, even though, as he later stated, he hadn't expected to be executed. He was allowed to write to his family and was given some cigarettes which he had requested.

Eicke was notified by the Kommandant and arrived during that time.

Since I was the adjutant, I was in charge of the headquarters staff. Therefore I had to carry out the execution according to the secret mobilization order. On the same morning that war was declared, neither of us thought that the executions would actually have to be carried out on the very day that the Kommandant opened the secret mobilization orders.

I quickly rounded up three older, mature NCOs of the staff, advised them about what had to be done, and lectured them about how they had to conduct themselves. A pole was quickly set into the sand pit of the factory courtyard. The cars arrived immediately. The Kommandant told the condemned man to stand at the pole. I led him to it. He calmly prepared himself. I stepped back and gave the order to fire. He collapsed, and I gave him the *coup de grace* to the head. The doctor examined the body and discovered that three bullets had pierced the heart. Besides Eicke, there were also a few officers of the reserves present at the execution.

None of us had thought, after Eicke's lecture in the morning, that the announcement would become a cold reality so quickly. After the execution Eicke told us that he too was surprised that it came so soon. I had been so busy during the preparations for the execution that it was only afterwards that I fully realized what had taken place.

All of the officers present at the execution sat for a while afterwards in the officer's mess. Strangely, no real conversation took place. Everyone was immersed in his own thoughts. Everyone recalled Eicke's lecture and was visualizing the hardships of the corning war. Except for myself, all were older gentlemen who had been in World War I as officers. They all were older SS officers who had proven their toughness in the beer hall fights in the early struggles of the Nazi Party. Yet all of us were deeply moved by what we had just experienced. We were to experience much more of the same thing in the corning days. Almost daily I had to report with my execution squad. Most of the cases dealt with saboteurs or those who refused to serve in the army. The reason for the execution was not stated in the execution order, but could only be learned from the Gestapo officer who accompanied the orders.

One case in particular deeply affected me. An SS officer who was also a State Police official with whom I had often worked when he transported important prisoners or delivered important secret documents to the Kommandant, was suddenly brought in one night for immediate execution. Just the day before we had sat in the mess hall and talked about the executions. Now the same thing was going to happen to him, and I had to carry out the order. Even my Kommandant felt that this was going too far. After the execution we both walked around the grounds for a long time without saying a word, trying to calm ourselves.

We heard from the accompanying official that this SS officer was given the job of arresting a former official of the Communist Party. He was told to bring him to the camp. He knew the man he was told to arrest very well, since he had to keep watch on him. The man had always conducted himself very honorably. Out of the goodness of his heart, the SS officer allowed him to go back to his apartment once more and say goodbye to his wife. While the SS officer and his guard were talking to his wife in the living room, the man escaped through another room. By the time the two of them had discovered the escape, it was already too late. The SS officer was immediately arrested at headquarters when he reported the escape. Himmler ordered an immediate court martial hearing. One hour later he was sentenced to death. The guard with him was sentenced to a long prison term. Even Heydrich's and Müller's pleas for mercy were refused by Himmler.

The first serious duty violation of the war by an SS officer was to be punished severely as a deterrent to others. The condemned man was a decent person in his middle thirties, married with three children, who had been conscientious and loyal in his duties prior to this incident. Now he had to pay the penalty for his good heartedness and his gullibility. He went to his death calm and collected.

To this day I still cannot understand how I could have calmly given the order to fire. It was a good thing that the three men who did the shooting did not know who he was, for they surely would have trembled. I was so upset I could barely hold the pistol steady when I had to give him the *coup de grace.*

I did manage to pull myself together in such a way that those who were present did not notice anything conspicuous. I confirmed this when I talked with one of the NCOs of the execution squad about this incident a few days later. Whenever the situation demanded self-restraint and inflexible sternness, this execution came to mind.'

So I believed at the time that this kind of harshness was too much for any person to bear.

Yet Eicke continuously preached about becoming even harder. An SS soldier had to be able to destroy even his own relatives if they went against the state or the ideas of Adolf Hitler. "There is only one thing that is valid: Orders!" This was Eicke's motto, which appeared at the head of all his letters.

What this means and what Eicke meant by it, I began to understand during those first weeks of the war, and not just I, but all of the old-time officers. Some of them who had a higher rank in the General SS with a very low SS number dared to express their opinion. [A low number indicated that the person had joined the SS in the early years.] In the mess hall they said that the hangman's work dirtied the black uniforms of the SS. Eicke heard about this. He reprimanded them, then he scheduled an officers meeting of his Oranienburg District in which he stated, "The comments about the hangman's work of the SS prove that those concerned, in spite of their long membership in the SS, have not yet understood their duty. The most important task of the SS is to protect the new state with any means at hand. Every enemy, depending on how dangerous he is, must be securely locked up or destroyed. Both of these measures can only be carried out by the SS. Only in this way can the safety of the state be guaranteed until new laws can be created which will give true protection to the people and the state. The annihilation of the enemy within the state is just as much a duty as the annihilation of the enemy out in the front lines and, therefore, could never be called dishonorable. The comments about the hangman prove that those who spoke them were contaminated with out-of-date political ideas of the common, middle-class world which have long become obsolete because of the revolution of Adolf Hitler. These statements are proof of weakness and sentimentality which are unworthy of an SS officer; in fact, they could be dangerous." Eicke further stated that he was therefore forced to report those concerned to Himmler for punishment. In his district he forbade once and for all such weak-kneed sentiments. In his ranks he could use only absolutely tough men who understood the meaning of the death's head insignia, which they wore as a symbol of honor.

Himmler did not punish those concerned directly. He personally warned them and gave them a lecture. However, they were never promoted and spent the entire war with the ranks of lieutenant and captain. They also had to remain under the command of the inspector of the concentration camps until the end of the war. They suffered greatly because of this, but they learned to keep their mouths shut and faithfully perform their duty.

At the beginning of the war prisoners in the concentration camps who were fit for military service were drafted by the draft boards of the various army districts according to their status. Those who were fit reported to the Gestapo or the State Police office and either were released to enter the military or were kept in the camps.

There were many Jehovah's Witnesses in Sachsenhausen. A large number of them refused to serve in the military and were, therefore, sentenced to death by Himmler as draft dodgers. They were shot to death in the camp in front of the entire assembly of prisoners. The other Jehovah's Witnesses had to stand in the front rank and watch.

Years earlier I had become acquainted with many religious fanatics at the shrines, in the monasteries in Palestine, at the Hejas railway station, in Iraq and in Armenia. They were Roman and Greek Orthodox Catholics, and Muslims, both Shiite and Sunni, but the Jehovah's Witnesses in Sachsenhausen, especially two of them, surpassed everything I had experienced.

These two fanatics refused to do anything that was connected to the military in any way. They would not stand at attention, or click their heels together, or lay their hands down at the seam of their trousers, and they refused to remove their caps. They claimed that these displays of respect and honor were for God alone, not men. For them there were no human masters. They would only recognize Jehovah as their lord and master. These two had to be removed from the block of the Jehovah's Witnesses and had to be kept in cells because they constantly challenged the others to behave the same way.

Eicke had sentenced them several times to floggings because of their behavior for not obeying the discipline of the camp rules. They withstood the beatings with such an inner passion that they seemed perverted. They begged the Kommandant for further punishment in order to be better witnesses for their ideas and their God. They refused their army physicals-it was not expected that they would submit-but they even refused to sign any military forms. They were sentenced to death by Himmler.

When they were put into cells and told of the death sentence, they went completely insane with joy and happiness. They couldn't stand the wait until the execution. They wrung their hands over and over, looked up joyously and called out repeatedly, "Soon we will be with Jehovah. What good luck we have that we have been chosen for this." A few days earlier they had attended an execution of one of their fellow believers and could hardly be controlled even then. They continuously asked to be shot. This frenzy became a burden to watch. When they were first arrested, they had to be taken by force, but now when their time came, they practically ran double time to their own execution. They did not want to be tied up, so that they would be able to raise their hands to Jehovah. They stood in front of the wooden execution wall with a radiance and ecstasy which was no longer human. This is the way I had always pictured the first Christian martyrs as they waited in the arena to be tom apart by wild beasts.

With their faces completely transfigured, eyes directed to heaven, hands folded in prayer and exalted, they went to their death. All who saw them die were deeply moved. Even the execution squad was numbed.

The Jehovah's Witnesses became even more possessed in the faith because of the martyrs' deaths suffered by their fellow believers. In order to gain their freedom several had already signed the declaration which stated they would not recruit for Jehovah anymore, but now had changed their minds as they gladly wanted to suffer further for Jehovah.

Generally, in their everyday life, the men and women of the Jehovah's Witnesses led a quiet, hard-working life and were sociable people who were always ready to help. Most of them were tradesmen and many were fanners in Prussia. As long as they confined their activities to prayer services and get-togethers, they were harmless to the state in peacetime. However, from 1937 on, when they increased the recruiting, this sect made some impact. The investigations were increased. Workers for the church were caught who furnished proof that the enemy was deliberately and zealously helping to spread the idea of the Jehovah's Witnesses, and thus using religion to undermine the will of the people for military preparedness. So it was evident at the outbreak of the war the kind of danger which could arise if the most active workers and the most fanatic Jehovah's Witnesses were not taken into custody. The recruiting for the Jehovah's Witnesses came to a halt after 1937.

In the camp itself the Jehovah's Witnesses were hard-working and dependable; they could have been sent out on work details without guards since they wanted to suffer imprisonment for Jehovah. The only problem was that they stubbornly refused to have anything to do with the military or with the war. For example, the female Jehovah's Witnesses in Ravensbriick refused to roll up first-aid bandages for military field dressings. Female fanatics refused to line up for the morning roll call and had to be counted in a disorderly mob. Even though the imprisoned Jehovah's Witnesses were members of the International Bible Students Association, they really didn't know anything about how their association was organized. All they knew were the workers who handed them the leaflets, led the meetings, and held the Bible instruction. They had no idea to what political purposes their fanatic belief was used. When this was explained to them, they laughed about it and could not understand. Their duty was only to follow the call of Jehovah and to be faithful to him. Jehovah spoke to them in visions through inspiration, through the Bible, if you read it correctly, and through the preachings and the writings of their association. This was the whole truth and could not be argued. To suffer for Jehovah and his teachings, in fact to die for him, was their goal. They believed that only in this way would they rise to become the chosen witnesses of Jehovah. This is also the way they looked at their imprisonment in the concentration camp. They willingly accepted all abuses. It was touching the way they cared and helped one another in brotherly Christian love whenever it was possible.

However, there were countless cases of Jehovah's Witnesses voluntarily reporting to the "swearing off." That's how the process was labeled by the Jehovah's Witnesses. They signed a "reverse" in which they renounced their membership in the International Bible Students Association, and in which they pledged to recognize and fulfill the laws and regulations of the state. They also declared that they would not recruit new witnesses for Jehovah. It so happened that based on these renunciations many Jehovah's Witnesses were released immediately in later years. Himmler originally wanted to assure himself by keeping them imprisoned after they had signed that the renunciation was true, and full of conviction. The turncoats were put upon quite nastily by their brothers and sisters because of their turning away from Jehovah. Many, especially the women, had retracted their signature because their consciences bothered them. The continuous moral pressure was too strong. It was totally impossible to shake the Jehovah's Witnesses in their belief. Even the turncoats wanted to remain faithful to Jehovah under any circumstances, even though they had divorced themselves from their congregation. Even when contradictions were pointed out in the Bible itself to the Jehovah's Witnesses, they simply declared that one could only see with human eyes, but in Jehovah there were no contradictions; he and his teachings were infallible.

On many occasions Himmler, as well as Eicke, referred repeatedly to the fanatical faith of the Jehovah's Witnesses as an example to the SS. Just as fanatically and unshakably as the Jehovah's Witnesses believed in Jehovah, that's exactly how an SS man must believe in the idea of National Socialism and Adolf Hitler. Only when all SS men would become such believing fanatics would the state of Adolf Hitler be secure far into the future. Only by fanatics who were willing to give themselves completely for the idea could a philosophy be carried and maintained far into the future.

I have to return again to the executions at the beginning of the war in Sachsenhausen.

How different each person's approach to death was. The Jehovah's Witnesses were in a way strangely satisfied. One could say they had an almost transfigured mood and had a rock-hard awareness that they were to be allowed to go into Jehovah's kingdom. The draft dodgers and the saboteurs calmly composed and reconciled themselves to the inevitability of their fate. The professional criminal and the truly asocial appeared to be quite different, either cynical, insolent, or apparently vigorous. Trembling inside with the fear of the great unknown, they raged and fought all the way or whined for a priest to help them.

I will give you two striking examples. The Sass brothers had been arrested in Denmark during a raid and, according to international treaty, were extradited to Germany. Both were internationally notorious burglars, escape artists, and specialists in safe cracking. They had been convicted many times before but never finished serving a complete sentence because they always succeeded in escaping from jail. All precautionary measures were useless against them. They always found a way to escape. Their last brilliant "piece of work" was to break into the most modem, secure vault in the basement of a large Berlin bank. Starting from a grave situated in a cemetery opposite the bank, they dug a tunnel underneath the street. After carefully removing all the alarms they worked in total security until they reached the vault of the bank. The theft was of great value, consisting of gold, foreign currency, and jewelry. They safely buried their loot in several graves and made withdrawals from their "bank" when they needed it, until they were caught.

These two super criminals had been sentenced to prison, one for twelve years, the other for ten, by a Berlin court after their extradition, which, according to German law, was the maximum sentence they could receive. Two days after the sentencing Himmler, by authority of his special powers, had both of them taken from the holding center and brought to Sachsenhausen for execution by firing squad. They both were to be shot without delay.

They were taken by car directly to the sand pit of the industrial courtyard.

The officials who brought them said that while they were on their way they had behaved in a defiant and arrogant manner, demanding to know where they were being taken. At the site of the execution, I read the death sentence to them. Immediately they began to yell, "This is impossible. How can you do this? We want to see a priest immediately," and several other things. They absolutely refused to stand at the pole, so I had to have them tied to it. They fought with all their strength against this. I was relieved when I finally gave the order to fire.

A sex offender with several previous arrests had lured an eight-year-old girl into a hallway of a Berlin house. As he was raping her, he strangled her to death. He was sentenced to fifteen years in prison by the court. On that very same day he was brought to Sachsenhausen for execution. Even today I can see him getting out of the car at the entrance to the industrial courtyard. Grinning cynically, he was a depraved-looking older man, a typical asocial. When I read him the death sentence, his face turned a pale yellow: He began to cry, scream, and carry on. Then he cried out for mercy-a disgusting display. I had to have him tied to the pole also. Could it be that these amoral people were in fear of the "great beyond"? I cannot explain their behavior in any other way.

Before the [1936] Olympic Games the streets were cleaned of beggars and bums, who incidentally were sent for reeducation to the workhouses or the concentration camps, and also all the prostitutes and homosexuals were removed from the cities and bathhouses. They were to be reeducated in the concentration camps for useful work. Even though there were as many homosexuals in Sachsenhausen as in Dachau, the homosexuals had become a problem in the camp. The Kommandant and the camp commander believed that the best way to handle them was to separate them into all the barracks of the entire camp. I did not agree because I remembered them from my years in prison. And it didn't take long for the reports about homosexual activities to flow back from all the blocks. Punishing them didn't change a thing. The epidemic spread. On my suggestion, all homosexuals were put together and assigned a block senior who knew how to handle them. They were also sent to work isolated from the other prisoners, where they pulled the big iron street roller for a long time.

Some of the prisoners from other categories who were also addicted to this habit were transferred to them. With one stroke the homosexual epidemic ended. Even though now and then this unnatural activity took place, they were only isolated cases. In their barracks they were so carefully watched that it was impossible to engage in these activities.

I still can remember one incredible case.

A Rumanian prince who lived in Munich with his mother had become a public disgrace because of his unnatural behavior. In spite of all the political and social considerations shown him, the publicity which he brought on himself had become intolerable. He was sent to Dachau. The police thought that his excessive sexual wickedness had made him disgusted and bored with women, and that he had turned to homosexuality in order to get a new thrill. Himmler believed that hard work and the strict life in a concentration camp would soon cure him.

The minute he arrived he attracted my attention without my knowing what was wrong with him. The way his eyes roamed everywhere, the way he jumped at the slightest noise, and his feminine, dancer-like movements made me suspect that he was a true homosexual. He started to cry when the Kommandant barked at him in a very harsh tone as he was being presented to the Kommandant, as all new prisoners were. He didn't want to shower because he said he was ashamed to undress. We discovered rather quickly why, when he undressed. His entire body, from his neck to his wrists and ankles, was tattooed with pornographic pictures. These tattoos depicted every kind of sexual perversion that the human mind could possibly invent, even, curiously, normal sexual intercourse with women. He was a living picture book. Researchers of human sexuality would have gotten some new and unusual material for their research. During his questioning, he admitted that he had been tattooed in every seaport in Europe and America.

He became sexually aroused, especially when someone touched him, as when his sexual tattoos were being photographed by the police. All tattoo marks had to be recorded for the state criminal police files. I told his room senior that he was personally responsible for this prisoner and that he was never to let him out of his sight. After a few hours I went to check on this strange character, and I was immediately approached by the room senior, who begged me to relieve him of this responsibility. He said that the newcomer was truly driving him crazy. The prince stood in front of the stove the entire time, just staring off into nowhere. When anyone came near him or just touched him in order to move him out of the way, he became sexually aroused and began to masturbate. I took him to the doctor. As the doctor began to ask him questions about his strange condition, he became aroused again. He explained that since his earliest childhood he had suffered from very strong sexual impulses he could never completely satisfy, no matter what he did. He was constantly looking for new ways to try to satisfy these impulses.

The doctor prepared a report for Himmler which stated that this prisoner should be in a nursing home and not in a concentration camp. The doctor reported that any attempt to cure him by hard work was doomed to fail from the start. He sent the report to Himmler and in the meantime the prince was sent to work as had been ordered. He was given the job of moving sand in a wheelbarrow, but he could barely lift the shovel full of sand. He collapsed just trying to push an empty wheelbarrow. I had him taken back to my office and reported all this to the Kommandant.

The Kommandant wanted to see this the next day with his own eyes, since Himmler had ordered that this man must work. The following day the prince was staggering so much that he could hardly get to the sand pit, which was not very far away. Even Loritz now realized that work was out of the question for this man. So he was taken back to his room and put to bed. This was also a mistake, because he was constantly masturbating. The doctor pleaded with him as if he was a sick little child. It was all useless. They tied down his hands, but even this could not be done for very long. They gave him sedatives and cold packs, but this too was useless, since he was becoming weaker and weaker. In spite of his weakness he still tried to crawl out of bed to reach the other prisoners. He was put under arrest, as it was becoming impossible to allow him in the camp with others, while we awaited Himmler's decision. He died two days later while masturbating. He had been in the camp for a total of five weeks.

Himmler ordered an official court autopsy and a detailed report, which was to be sent to him. Much to my regret, I had to be there at the autopsy. The examination revealed that he was completely run down physically, but there was nothing abnormal. The professor from the Munich Judicial Court of Medicine who performed the autopsy had never seen anything like this case in all his many years of practice.

I was present when the Kommandant showed the prince's body to his mother. The mother said that his death was a blessing for the both of them because his uncontrolled sexual behavior had made life impossible for everyone. She remarked that she had consulted the most famous specialists in Europe without any success. He had run away from every nursing home and had even spent some time in a monastery, and even there he could not be stopped. In her despair she even begged him to commit suicide, but he didn't have the courage to do it. At least now he would be at peace. Even now cold shivers run through me as I recall this case.'

From the beginning the homosexuals in Sachsenhausen were housed in a special block. Some of them were put to work in the clay pit of the Gross-Klinker brick factory, separated from the other prisoners. This was hard work and everyone had to produce a certain quota. They were exposed to all kinds of weather because there were a certain number of clay trains which had to be filled daily. The baking process could not be stopped just because of lack of material. So they had to work outdoors, summer or winter, regardless of the weather. Depending on the kind of person the homosexual was, the heavy work, which was supposed to make him "normal" again, had a varying effect on him. The purpose of this kind of work had visible results with the "Strichjunge." This was the Berlin slang word for the male prostitutes who wanted to earn their living in an easy way and absolutely avoid even the lightest work. They were not considered homosexuals, since this was only their trade. The strict camp life and the hard work quickly reeducated this type. Most of them worked very hard and took great care not to get into trouble so that they could be released as soon as possible. They also avoided associating with those afflicted with this depravity and wanted to make it known that they had nothing to do with homosexuals. In this way countless rehabilitated young men could be released without having a relapse.

One lesson was effective enough, since it dealt mostly with young boys.

Some men were homosexual because they became weary of women through overindulgence or because they looked for new highs in their parasitic life. These men could also be reeducated and' turned away from their vice.

But those who were inclined and had become addicted to their vice could not be reeducated. They were on the same level with those few who were genuine homosexuals. With those not even the hardest work and not even the strictest supervision were of any help. Whenever they found an opportunity they lay in each other's arms. Even when they were completely physically debilitated, they were slaves to their vice. They were easily recognizable. They exhibited a soft, female prudishness and affectation, expressed themselves in a sweet manner, and conducted themselves toward others of their kind with a charming behavior. Those who had turned away from this vice and who wanted to be free from it were different. Their recovery could be carefully observed step by step. Those who had a firm resolve to renounce this vice were able to withstand the hardest work while the others, depending on their inner strength, died. Since they could not or would not give up their vice, they knew that they would never be free again. This most effective mental pressure accelerated the physical decay in these sensitive characters. If in addition to that they lost a "friend" through sickness or perhaps through death, one could predict the future. Many committed suicide. In this situation the homosexual's friend meant everything. It happened several times that two friends decided to commit suicide together.

In 1944 Himmler carried out "renunciation tests" in Ravensbrück. If there was doubt that they were completely cured, the homosexuals were inconspicuously brought together to work alongside whores and were closely observed. The whores were told to approach the homosexuals quietly and to excite them sexually. Those who were cured immediately took advantage of this opportunity and they hardly had to be seduced. The incurables didn't even notice the women. If the women were too obvious in their approach, the incurables turned away from them shuddering with loathing and disgust.

After this procedure, those who were about to be released were once more given the opportunity to get together with other men. Almost all spumed this opportunity and absolutely refused any advances by the true homosexuals. But there were also borderline cases who took advantage of both opportunities. Whether they could be designated as bisexuals, I have no opinion.

It was in any case very educational to observe the psychological make-up of the homosexual in prison, their lifestyle, and all kinds of activities as far as prison life was concerned.

In Sachsenhausen there were a great number of prominent people and also some special prisoners. Prisoners were considered "prominent" if they formerly played a role in public life. They were treated as political prisoners and they were dispersed among the others of the same category in the camp and received no special privileges. As the war began, their number increased considerably because of the rearrests of former officials of the Communist and Socialist parties. Special prisoners were those who were to be separately housed in the concentration camp. The Federal Police had their own reasons not to allow them to have any contact with other prisoners. Only those directly concerned knew about their place of arrest or that they were in prison. There were only a few of these special prisoners before the war, but as the war progressed the number increased considerably. I will come back to this later.

In 1939 Czech professors, students, and also some Polish professors from Krakow were imprisoned in Sachsenhausen. They were housed in a special block in the camp. As far as I can remember they were not allowed to be used for work and there was also no special treatment planned for them. The professors from Krakow were released again after a few weeks because a great number of German professors had pleaded with Hitler through Goring for their release. As far as I recall there were approximately one hundred university teachers involved. I saw them only at their arrival and heard nothing further about them during their imprisonment.

However, I have to discuss one special prisoner in more detail because his behavior while in custody was strange. I was able to closely observe him and knew all the circumstances concerning him.

I am referring to the Evangelical Pastor Niemoller. who was a famous U-boat commander during World War I. After the war he became a pastor of the German Protestant Evangelical Church, which split into numerous factions. One prominent faction, the Lutheran Confessional Church, was headed by Niemoller, Hitler wanted to see the Protestant church united and had appointed a Protestant Reich's bishop, but many of the Protestant factions refused to recognize him and strongly challenged him. Niemoller was one of them. He had a congregation in Dahlem, a suburb of Berlin. In this congregation there were gathered together all the Protestant reactionaries of the Berlin-Potsdam area and all the old nobility from the Kaiser's time, including those who were dissatisfied with the National Socialist government.

Niemoller preached resistance and that led to his arrest. He was housed in a cell block in Sachsenhausen and generally had all kinds of privileges which eased his life in prison. He was allowed to write to his wife as often as he wanted. Every month his wife was allowed to visit and bring him as many books and as much tobacco and food as he desired. He was allowed to take a walk in the courtyard of the cell block whenever he wanted. His cell was made as comfortable as possible. In short, whatever was possible was done for him. It was the Kommandant's duty to constantly worry about him and to ask him about his wishes.

Hitler had a personal interest in persuading Niemoller to give up his opposition. Prominent personalities appeared in Sachsenhausen to persuade Niemoller, even Admiral Lans, his former navy superior of many years and a member of his church, but it was all in vain. Niemoller persisted in his view that no state had the right to interfere with church laws, or in fact to make them. This was solely a matter of each church congregation. The Confessional Church continued to grow and Niemoller became its martyr. His wife busily continued his work. Since I read all of his mail and listened to all his conversations with visitors, which took place in the Kommandant's office, I knew exactly what was going on.

In 1938 he wrote to the commander-in-chief of the navy, Grand Admiral Raeder, that he would renounce his right to wear the uniform of a naval officer because he did not agree with the state which the navy was serving. When the war broke out, he volunteered for service and asked to be assigned as a U-boat commander. The tables were now turned; Hitler refused him because he did not wish to wear the uniform of the National Socialist state. As time went by, Niemoller started to flirt with the idea of changing to the Catholic Church. He brought up the strangest arguments for it, stating that his Confessional Church agreed in essential matters with the Catholic Church, but his wife very energetically advised him against this. I believe he wanted to secure his release by converting to the Catholic Church. His congregation would never have followed him.

I often had long conversations with Niemoller. He was interested in all questions about life, and he also had an understanding about things which were outside his field. However, as soon as the conversation drifted to a discussion about matters of the church, an iron curtain fell. Stubbornly he returned to his point of view and refused to accept any criticism about his perceptions, no matter how convincing. And in spite of his willingness to convert to the Catholic Church, he would have had to recognize the state, since the Catholic Church had done so by its concordat [agreement between church and state].

Niemoller suffered a personal fiasco because of one of his daughters.

He had seven children who eagerly continued his work along with their mother, as much as their young ages allowed them. But one of his daughters fell out of line when she stubbornly decided to marry a naval officer who was not a Christian, but rather a follower of the modern German cult of pseudo-humanism, a form of non-Christian belief in God. Niemoller tried everything to talk her out of this. During one of the authorized visits of this daughter he tried to persuade her using all his powers of argumentation based on religious and church doctrine. It did not move her. She married him anyway.

In 1941 Himmler issued the order that all clergymen were to be transferred to Dachau, and Niemoller was sent there. I saw him in 1944 in a cell block where he had even more freedom of movement and had the company of Bishop Wurm, the former Protestant state bishop of Posen," He was in good health and had survived all the years of imprisonment well. His well-being was constantly and adequately taken care of and no one ever offended him. He was always treated courteously.

While Dachau was mainly RED because the majority of the prisoners were political prisoners, Sachsenhausen was GREEN [criminals]. The whole atmosphere in the camp was influenced by the criminal element, even though the most important executive positions were filled by political prisoners. In Dachau there was a certain *esprit de corps* among the prisoners which didn't exist at Sachsenhausen.

The two main colors constantly fought against each other, so it was easy for a camp administrator to play one against the other. That's why the escapes were more numerous from there than from Dachau. For the most part they were much more cunning, better planned, and much better carried out than in Dachau.

An escape in Dachau was a special event, but in Sachsenhausen they really made it a big deal because of Eicke's presence. As soon as the siren sounded Eicke was in the camp, if he happened to be nearby in Oranienburg. He immediately wanted to know all the details down to the smallest item about the escape. He searched doggedly for the guilty SS, who, because of inattention or carelessness, made the escape possible. The chain of guards around the camp often stood for three to four days if there was any indication that the prisoner could still possibly be within the circle of guards. Night and day everything was carefully searched again and again, so that no stone was left unturned. Every SS soldier of the garrison was dragged into the search. The officers, most of all the Kommandant, the camp commander and the officer of the day did not have a quiet hour because Eicke was constantly asking about the status of the search. Eicke felt that no

112

escape should be allowed to succeed. Because the chain of guards was kept in place most of the time, the prisoner was usually found, either hiding someplace or buried by someone in a remote area.

But what a strain all of this was for the camp. The men often had to stand continuously for sixteen to twenty hours while the prisoners had to stand at attention until the first chain of guards was relieved. As long as the search was in progress, no one was allowed to move out of the work details and only those functions were carried out which were absolutely necessary to stay alive. If a prisoner succeeded in breaking through the chain of guards, or if he had run away from an outside work detail, a tremendous network was set in motion to recapture him. Every SS soldier and policeman who could be reached was brought into action. Railroads and streets were watched. The motorized branch of the sheriff offices combed the streets and roads guided by radio. The vicinity of Oranienburg had countless waterways and all bridges were posted with guards. The inhabitants of isolated houses were notified and warned. Most of them already knew what happened when the siren sounded. With the help of the local residents, some of the prisoners were caught again. The people living around the camp knew that the prison housed mostly professional criminals. They were scared when there was a breakout. Every sighting was immediately reported to the camp or the search patrols.

When an escapee was found he was paraded past the assembled prisoners of the camp, if possible in front of Eicke, and a big sign was hung around his neck with the words, "I am back again." Not only that, he also had to beat a large drum which also hung around his neck. After this parading, he was punished with twenty-five lashes with a cane and transferred to the punishment company. The SS soldiers who had found him or caught him were praised in the order of the day and received special leave. Outsiders, police or civilians, received cash rewards. If an SS soldier had prevented an escape by being thoughtful and attentive, Eicke rewarded this with special leave and a promotion. Eicke wanted to be absolutely guaranteed that everything was done to prevent an escape, and also, if an escape succeeded, that nothing was left unsearched which might lead to his recapture. SS guards who made an escape possible were severely punished, even if they were only slightly at fault. Prisoners who assisted in an escape were punished even harder. At this point I would like to tell you about some unusual escapes.

Seven professional criminals, all felons, were housed in a barracks near the wire barrier. They succeeded in digging a tunnel underneath the barrier into the nearby forest and escaped during the night. They spread the earth dug from the tunnel under the barracks, which was raised on pilings. The entrance to the tunnel was under the bed. They had worked several nights on this without their fellow prisoners in the barracks knowing. A week later one of the escapees was recognized on a Berlin street by a block senior and was arrested. During the interrogation, he told where the others were staying so that all could be arrested again. A homosexual prisoner was able to escape from the clay pits in spite of the tightest security, a sufficient number of guards, and a wire barrier. There was no clue as to how the escape was possible. As the clay handcarts left, each was personally searched by two SS soldiers and the officer in charge. A tremendous search was undertaken that involved days of searching the adjacent forest area. Not a trace was found. Ten days later a wire arrived from the border crossing at Warnemünde [on the Baltic seacoast] that the escaped prisoner had just been brought in by fishermen. SS were sent to get him, and he had to show the escape route. For weeks he thought about his escape and had considered all the possibilities. He concluded the only way to escape was the train of hand carts that left the compound. He worked very hard and thereby became noticed, so he was chosen to lubricate the carts and inspect the tracks. He then watched carefully day after day how the departing train was searched. Every car was inspected on the top and the bottom. The diesel engine was checked, but no one looked underneath the engine because the metal guards reached almost to the tracks, but he had noticed that the rear guard was only loosely attached. While the train was standing at the control point at the exit, he quickly crawled underneath the engine, wedged himself between the pair of wheels and moved out with the train. At the nearest steep curve, helet himself fall, let the train roll over him, and disappeared into the forest. He knew he had to head north since the escape would be noticed very quickly because the leader of the work detail notified the camp by telephone.

The very first thing done in cases such as this was the guarding of bridges by motorized patrols. As the prisoner reached the great shipping route from Berlin to Stettin, he saw the bridge was already guarded. He hid in a hollow willow tree, so that he could keep the canal and the bridge under observation. I myself have driven past this willow tree several times. During the night he swam across the canal. He then ran straight north, kept away from streets and villages, and obtained civilian clothes from a work shed in a sand pit. He lived off the milk which he got from milking cows in the pastures and vegetables growing in the fields. In this way he passed through Mecklenburg to the Baltic Sea. In a fishing village he succeeded in getting away unnoticed in a sailboat and started sailing in the direction of Denmark. Just before reaching the Danish territorial waters, he met fishermen who recognized the boat. They stopped him, and since they immediately suspected him of being an escaped prisoner, they took him to Warnemünde and handed him over to the authorities.

A professional criminal from Berlin who was a painter worked in some houses in the SS village which was situated within the guard chain. He began an affair with one of the servant girls of a doctor who lived there, and thereby repeatedly visited the house, where he always found something to do. Neither the doctor nor his wife noticed anything about the intimate relationship of their servant girl and the prisoner. The doctor and his wife left for a time, during which the servant girl was also to have a vacation. This was his chance. The girl left the basement window unlocked. After he had watched them leave, he climbed through the unlocked window into the basement. In the upper story he removed a section of the wall, creating a hideout in the space between the slanting roof and the wall; he then drilled a hole through the wooden wall, where he now could observe most of the chain of guards and the village. He had food, drink, and a pistol just in case. When the siren started, he crawled into his hideout, pulled a large piece of furniture against the hole in the wall, and simply waited. During escapes, the houses of the village were thoroughly searched. I myself was in this particular house on the same day because I thought it was suspicious, since at the time no one was there, but I could see nothing wrong. I was also in the room where the criminal sat behind the edge of the roof with the pistol ready, safety off. He later said that if he had been discovered, he would have without a doubt used his pistol. No matter what, he had to be free, because an investigation was underway about a murder committed during a robbery. This crime happened many years before and his accomplice had implicated him because of homosexual jealousy in the camp. The chain of guards was in place for four days.

On the fifth day, he went to Berlin with the first morning train. Very calmly he had picked the best clothes from the doctor's wardrobe and lived very well during those days on the food found in the basement storage and the kitchen. Several empty liquor and wine bottles gave evidence of this. Taking his time in the selection, he packed two heavy suitcases for himself in which he put the family silver, clothing, cameras, and other valuable items. After a few days, he was arrested by chance in an obscure Berlin bar by a detective making the rounds, just as he was in the process of converting the last items from the suitcases into 'cash. Even the girl with whom he had made a date was taken to Ravensbrück. The doctor was quite surprised as he entered his house again. Eicke was going to make him account for the pistol, but he didn't when the doctor threatened to sue for damages done to his property by an escaped prisoner.

These were only three examples which I can remember at this moment, only a small segment of the never-boring life in a concentration camp.

- January '47 Rudolf Höss

If I remember correctly, I became executive officer of Sachsenhausen around Christmas 1939.In January 1940, the surprise visit of Himmler resulted in a change of Kommandants,

Loritz arrived. He let us know that in Himmler's opinion there was no discipline in the camp and that he would bring it up to standards. This Loritz could do. I had gone through the process once before, in 1936, when I was duty officer. It was quite rough on me because Loritz was continually on my back. I had gotten on his bad side by leaving in 1938 to become adjutant to his most hated enemy [SS General Baranowski]. He assumed that I had schemed my transfer behind his back, but this was not true. The Kommandant of Sachsenhausen [Baranowski] had asked for me because he saw that I was put into a dead-end job at Dachau, because I was too loyal to him when he had been the commander in Dachau.

Loritz carried a big grudge and made sure I felt his disfavor many times in unmistakable ways. In his opinion everything was done too softly in Sachsenhausen, not only by the SS guards but by the prisoners as well. Former Kommandant Baranowski had died in the meantime. Eicke, who was busy putting together an SS division, was occupied in other places, therefore he allowed Loritz to do as he pleased. [SS Major General] Glucks had never cared much for Baranowski. He was therefore very pleased about Loritz's being called back to the concentration camp because, as one of the original Kommandants, Loritz made Glucks look good in his new job as inspector of concentration camps.

XVII
Kommandant of Auschwitz

When Auschwitz was chosen as the site for a concentration camp, the powers that be did not have to look very hard to find a Kommandant. Loritz now could get rid of me and find a camp commander who would better suit him. He chose an officer named Suhren who had been Loritz's adjutant in the General SS, and who would later become Kommandant of Ravensbriick. So I became the Kommandant of the new quarantine camp called Auschwitz.

Auschwitz was far off the beaten track in the backwoods of Poland.

There the pain-in-the-neck Höss could indulge his mania for work to his heart's desire-at least, this was Glucks's opinion. Under these conditions I began my new assignment. I had never figured to move up so quickly to a command position in view of the fact that some of the older camp commanders had waited for a long time for a vacant Kommandant's post. This assignment was not easy.

In the shortest possible time I was supposed to create a transition camp for ten thousand prisoners from the existing complex of well-preserved buildings. The buildings were filthy and teemed with lice, fleas, and other bugs, and as far as sanitation was concerned, practically nothing was available. In Oranienburg I was already told that I could not expect much help for the most part, and I would have to help myself. I would find everything that I needed in Poland that was unobtainable in Germany for years. It is much easier to establish a new camp than it is to take an unsuitable group of buildings and barracks without major remodeling and quickly create a useful concentration camp as I was originally ordered.

I had barely arrived at Auschwitz when the inspector of the security police and the secret service from Breslau asked when we could receive the first transports. It was clear from the beginning that the only way Auschwitz could become useful would be through exhausting hard work by everybody, from the Kommandant on down to the very last prisoner. In order to get everyone to cooperate in this task, I had to break with all the customs which had become traditions in a concentration camp. I was going to ask my officers and soldiers to give 100 percent, then I had to set a good example. When the common SS soldier was awakened, I also got up; before he reported for duty, I was already on my way and I didn't get to bed until late at night. There were only a few nights in Auschwitz when I was not disturbed by urgent telephone calls about events which had occurred. If I expected to get good, useful work from the prisoners, then they had to be treated better, even though that was not normally done in a concentration camp.

I assumed that I would be successful in providing better housing for them and feeding them better than in the old camps. I thought the way some things were done in the old camps was wrong. I wanted to do things differently here. Under these conditions I believed I would be able to win the prisoners over to willingly rebuild the camp. I also had to be able to ask the prisoners for their very best performance. These were the factors on which I had firmly counted. However, in the first month, in fact, the first weeks, I became bitterly aware that all of my good aspirations and the best of my intentions were ruined by the human shortcomings and stubbornness of most of the officers and men who were assigned to me. I tried everything I could to convince all of my colleagues to do things as I wanted them done, to persuade them to my way of thinking, and to try to make it clear to them that by working together in this way the assigned task could be accomplished. All my attempts failed. After all the years of working in concentration camps, even the most cooperative of them simply could not break out of the mold, since it was drilled so deeply into their flesh and blood by the training of men like Eicke, Koch, and Loritz. I am referring to the "old guard." The beginners picked this method up very quickly from the "old guard," much to my regret. All my requests to get at least a few good officers and NCOs from the inspector of concentration camps were ignored. Glucks simply would not cooperate. The same thing happened with the Kapos.

[SS Sergeant Gerhard] Palitzsch was supposed to pick out thirty professional criminals, since Himmler would not allow any political prisoners to be selected to begin building Auschwitz. These men were to be chosen from all criminal categories. He brought thirty criminals he thought to be the best and who were available from Sachsenhausen. Not even ten of them were the type that I wanted. Palitzsch selected prisoners who he thought would be the best based on his ideas and opinions as to how a concentration camp should be run, and also according to the way he had been trained. In fact, because of his personality and outlook, he wasn't able to do this in any other way. So the whole internal framework of the camp was ruined from the beginning. Because of this early failure, patterns were developed which later on were to have tremendously disastrous consequences. These errors, however, could have been kept to a minimum, in fact, could have been corrected, if the camp commanders and the duty officers would have done it the way I wanted it. They, however, did not wish to do this and, in fact, couldn't because of their own narrow-mindedness, stubbornness, maliciousness, and, last but not least, for their own convenience. These prisoners suited them just fine, considering their inclinations and viewpoints.

In every concentration camp the true ruler of the camp is the camp commander. There is little doubt that the Kommandant leaves his mark on all of prison life, more or less, depending on his energy and intent. There is also little doubt that the Kommandant sets policy and is the controlling authority and, in the final instance, is responsible for everything, but the real ruler of the prisoner's life, of his total inner state of mind, is the camp commander or the duty officer, if he happens to be more intelligent or stronger willed. It is true that the Kommandant sets the guidelines, makes the regulations, and gives the orders for the whole organization of all prison life as he thinks best. But how all of this is carried out lies completely in the hands of the executive officers in the camp. The Kommandant is totally dependent on the good will and intelligence of his executive staff. However, if he does not trust them, or if he feels they are incompetent, he may take over this function himself. Only then can he have the guarantee that his directions and orders will be carried out according to his intentions.

For example, it is quite difficult for a regimental commander to have his orders carried out, according to his plans, down to the smallest squad, especially when they deal with matters which are beyond the daily routine. How much more difficult is it then for a Kommandant to know that his orders concerning the prisoners are carried out to the last letter, and are understood correctly, orders which are so often of far-reaching importance The Kapos are especially difficult to control when it comes to the administration of prisoners.

For reasons of prestige and discipline, a Kommandant must never question prisoners about SS officers. The greatest exception to this would be to help solve a crime and even then only in extreme cases. In spite of this, a prisoner will invariably know nothing, or he will answer evasively in order not to have to fear reprisals. I really came to understand this in Dachau and Sachsenhausen, when I was a block leader and duty officer. I know very well how camp orders that do not suit certain individuals are twisted and even turned around to the opposite intent without the person who gave the order noticing it. In Auschwitz I learned with certainty that this was the general practice; a radical change would only have been possible by immediately changing the entire camp administration. Never in a million years would the inspector of the camps [Glücks] approve this step.

In order for me to see that my orders were carried out to the smallest detail, I would have had to take over the duties of the camp commander and set aside my main task, which was to create a usable concentration camp as quickly as possible. But this was not possible, especially in the early period, during the creation of the camp. I would have had to be in the camp day and night, considering the mentality of the camp staff. It was precisely during this early period that I was forced to be outside the camp almost continuously because of the incompetence of those in charge of logistics and supplies. Just to get the organization of the whole camp going and to maintain it I had to have conferences with the Ministry of Economics, the governor, and the local officials. Because my executive officer was a total nincompoop, I had to preside over all the meetings which dealt with the clothing and food supplies of the troops and the prisoners. It didn't matter if it was about meat, bread, or potatoes. I even had to drive to the farms to get straw. Since I could not expect any kind of help from the inspector of the concentration camps, I had to take care of everything myself: I had to scrounge up cars, trucks, and the necessary gasoline for them. In fact, I had to drive all the way to Zakopane in Rapka [on the Polish-Czechoslovakian border] just to get a couple of huge cooking kettles for the prisoners' kitchen, and I had to go all the way to the Sudeten-land [western Czechoslovakia] for bedframes and straw sacks. Since my construction foreman was unable to get even the most basic materials, I had to drive around with him to look for them and buy them.

In Berlin they were still arguing about who had jurisdiction over Auschwitz, because according to the contract the whole project still belonged to the army and was on loan to the SS only for the duration of the war. SS headquarters, the chief of security in Krakow, the inspector of the secret police and the secret service in Breslau, all continually made inquiries as to when larger transports of prisoners could be accommodated, while I still didn't even know where I could get a hundred meters of barbed wire. In Gleiwitz there were mountains of barbed wire in the engineers' depot in the harbor. But I could not get any of it without a release from the Engineering Headquarters in Berlin. I could not persuade Glucks to help me in this matter, so I had to steal the urgently needed barbed wire from various places. Wherever I found abandoned field trenches with barbed wire, I gutted them. We even took old bunkers apart just to get the armor plate from them. Whenever I found a warehouse with the materials that I needed urgently, I simply had it carted away without worrying about going through channels. After all, I was supposed to help myself. At the same time the evacuation of the first zone around the camp area was taking place and the evacuation of the second zone was beginning. Because this included a large area of farmland, I had to plan for the use of that also.

By the end of November 1940 I could make the first progress report to Himmler about the expansion of the total camp area as he had ordered. If I thought that the construction and expansion of the actual camp site were more than enough work for me to do, I had another guess coming. After my first report I learned that this only triggered the beginning of a never-ending chain of new assignments and new projects.

Right from the beginning I was completely absorbed by my new assignment and my orders; in fact, I was obsessed. Every new problem that appeared lashed me on to even greater intensity. I didn't want this situation to get the best of me. My ambition would not permit it. I lived only for my work. It is easy to understand that because of the amount of these overall responsibilities, I had little time for the prison camp or the prisoners. I had to leave the prisoners entirely in the hands of those thoroughly distasteful persons like Fritzsch, Meyer, Seidler, and Palitzsch, even though I knew that they were developing the prison camp contrary to my orders and instructions. However, I could devote myself fully and completely to only one task: either I applied myself only to the prisoners, or I pushed ahead with the development and expansion of the camp with all my energy. Either task demanded my complete attention. I could not do both equally well. My job was, and still remained, to finish the building and development of the camp. Many other assignments were added to this in the course of the years, but the main task, which took all of my time and energy, remained the same. All of my striving and thinking went into it; everything else had to take second place. Only from this position could I direct the entire camp. Consequently, I saw everything from this perspective. Glucks often told me that my greatest mistake was in trying to do everything myself instead of delegating the work. The mistakes they made out of incompetence would just have to be endured. He said that this was something we all had to live with. Things could not always turn out the way one wished them to.

Glucks refused to accept my objections that in Auschwitz I had certainly the worst material as far as subordinates were concerned, and that it was not just their inability, but also their deliberate neglect and maliciousness which simply forced me to do the most urgent and important things myself. In Glucks's opinion, a Kommandant should direct and control the whole camp from his office by issuing orders and using the telephone. It would be enough if he would occasionally walk through the camp. What simple-mindedness! He had this attitude only because he had never worked in a concentration camp; therefore, he could never understand my problems. This lack of understanding on the part of my superior nearly drove me to despair. I applied all my knowledge and resolve to my job; in fact, I lived for nothing else. Glucks saw it only as a craze or game on my part. He claimed I was far too immersed in my assignment and that I could not see beyond my assignment.

When Himmler came on March 1, 1941, my last hopes of ever getting better and more dependable coworkers disappeared because this visit now brought new and even greater responsibilities, but no help for our most urgent needs. I had to make do with the "big shots" that were at hand, and I had to continue to endure more of their irritation. Only a few, really good, dependable coworkers were on my side. Much to my sorrow, they were not in the most important and responsible positions. I had to pile the work on them; in fact, I overloaded them, so much so that I often saw too late that this was self-defeating.

I became a different person in Auschwitz because in general I could not rely on my staff. Until then I always saw the good in people, until I was convinced otherwise. My gullibility had often fooled me. However, in Auschwitz, where I saw myself cheated and disappointed at every step of the way by my so called coworkers, I changed. I became suspicious. Everywhere I saw only deceit and day after day I was disappointed. In every new face I looked immediately for malice or the worst in everyone. Because of this I hurt and snubbed many honest and decent men. I was unable to confide in or trust anyone anymore. The feelings of comradeship 'which had been a holy concept to me appeared to be a farce. I felt this way because my old comrades so disappointed and deceived me.

I did not want to have anything to do with them socially. I repeatedly put off going to such social events, and I was glad when I could find a suitable excuse for my absence. This behavior of mine was constantly thrown up to me by my comrades. In fact, Glucks himself pointed out several times that in Auschwitz there were no comradely ties between the Kommandant and the officers. I just couldn't do it anymore. I had been disappointed too much.

More and more I was withdrawing into myself. I buried myself in my work and became unapproachable and visibly hardened. My family suffered because of it, particularly my wife, because I was unbearable to live with.

I saw only my work, my duty. All human feelings were pushed aside by this. My wife tried repeatedly to tear me away from this isolation. She invited friends from outside the camp to visit us, as well as my comrades from the camp, hoping that this would draw me out and help me to relax. She arranged parties away from the camp even though she disliked the social life as much as I did. Now and then this pulled me out of my self-imposed isolation for a while, but new disappointments quickly drove me back behind my wall of glass.

Even people who hardly knew me felt very sorry when they saw how I behaved. But, I didn't want to change. I became unsociable in certain respects because of the tremendous amount of disappointment I experienced. Often, even when I was with friends I had personally invited I would suddenly become non-talkative or even rude. I would have loved to run off and be alone because I suddenly felt that I didn't want to be among other people any longer. That's when I struggled to pull myself together and tried to get rid of the bad mood by drinking. With alcohol I became talkative again and at times funny and even loud.

In general, alcohol put me into a happy mood, and I wished the whole world well. I have never had an argument with anyone when I was drunk. In this mood people were able to coax out of me things which I would have never revealed when I was sober. However, I never drank when I was alone, and I never had a craving for alcohol either. I also never got dead drunk or let myself go too far because I had too much to drink. When I felt I had had enough I quietly disappeared. I was never derelict in my duty because I had too much to drink. No matter how late I came home I arrived for work in the mornings completely refreshed. For disciplinary reasons I also expected my officers to behave the same way at all times because there is nothing more demoralizing for subordinates than when the superior is not there at the start of work because he got drunk the night before. My attitude about this was not very popular.

They only obeyed because they were forced since I was on the job watching them. They complained bitterly about the "old man's spleen." If I wanted to be fair in my duty, I had to be the tireless motor which relentlessly spurred the construction work and drove everyone forward, or dragged them along, whether they were SS soldiers or prisoners. Not only did I have to fight all the difficulties and unfavorable conditions caused by the war during this construction, but also daily, even hourly, I had to contend with the laziness, the carelessness, and the disobedience of my staff.

A person can fight active opposition but is powerless against passive resistance. A person cannot put his hands on it even though he feels it everywhere. And yet, I had to spur them on, even the reluctant ones, even if there was no other way than by direct force.

Before the war, the concentration camps were used to protect Germany from its internal enemies, but because of the war Himmler ordered that their main purpose now was to serve the war effort. Every possible prisoner was to become a defense plant worker; every Kommandant was to have his camp absolutely ready for this purpose. According to Himmler's orders Auschwitz was to become a tremendous prisoner defense center. His announcement during his visit in March 1941 was clear enough in this respect. The following plans for the camp spoke clearly enough: preparation of the camp for 100,000 POWs, the remodeling of the old camp for 30,000 prisoners, and the allocation for the "Buna" [synthetic rubber] factory of 10,000 prisoners. At that time these numbers were unheard of in the history of concentration camps. Before, a camp containing 10,000 prisoners was considered tremendously large.

The emphasis that Himmler put on the ruthless, quickest possible acceleration of the construction, while at the same time ignoring the existing and anticipated difficulties and abuses which I doubted could be eliminated, caught my attention even then, and made me suspicious. The way in which he dismissed the considerable objections of the regional governors and the governor general [Hans Frank] led me to believe that something very unusual was in the works. And let me tell you I was accustomed to quite a bit when it came to the SS and Himmler. But what was new with him was how severe and relentless he became in demanding the quickest execution of his orders. Even Glucks noticed this.

Now all this responsibility fell on my shoulders. From nothing and with nothing, I, together with my "coworkers," had to build an enormous enterprise in the quickest possible manner without any significant help from above because of the conditions at the time. My experiences to this point confirmed this fact.

And what did my work force look like? And what had happened to the concentration camp in the meantime?

The SS staff in the camp had done their very best to maintain Eicke's tradition of handling prisoners. In fact, Fritzsch from Dachau, and Palitzsch from Sachsenhausen, and in addition Meier from Buchenwald all tried to outdo one another with better "methods." They did not accept my continuous objections that Eicke's methods were out of date because of the way concentration camps had changed. It was impossible to drive out Eicke's indoctrination from their limited brains. Eicke's methods better suited their mentality. My orders and decrees which conflicted with their training were simply modified because they, not I, were actually running the camp. They trained the Kapos, from the senior prisoners down to the last block clerk. They trained the block leaders and taught them how to deal with the prisoners, but I have said and written enough about this already.

Against this passive resistance I was powerless. Only someone who had been serving in a concentration camp for years could understand and believe this.

I have already related above how much influence, in general, the Kapos have on their fellow prisoners. In a concentration camp this has significant consequences. Considering the limitless masses of prisoners at Auschwitz-Birkenau, this was a significant and deciding factor. One should have been able to assume that the fate and suffering, which was common to all, would have led to an indestructible, invincible community and a rock-hard loyalty to each other. Quite the contrary, nowhere can one see naked self-interest so pronounced as in prison. The harder the life is in these situations, the more pronounced the selfish behavior becomes. The drive to survive dictates this. Even people who in their normal life outside prison had always been helpful and good-natured will now mercilessly tyrannize their fellow prisoners in a harsh prison environment, if there is even the slightest chance to better their life by doing so.

But how much more brutally do those people act who are already selfish, cold, and criminal? They will walk without mercy over the misery of their fellow prisoners if they can see even the tiniest advantage.'

Besides the physical results of this often cruel, vile treatment by their fellow prisoners, there is this consequence: prisoners who are not yet dulled by the harshness of prison life suffer tremendous psychological damage because of this behavior. Nothing hits them as hard as this severe treatment from their fellow prisoners, not even the mean, impulsive brutality of the guards. It is just this helplessness, this powerlessness of being forced to watch how these trusties torture their fellow prisoners, that acts so destructively on the whole mind of the prisoners. Woe to the prisoner who tries to interfere or tries to stand up for the person being tortured. The terror of these powers inside a concentration camp is much too strong for someone to dare help a prisoner.

And why do the Kapos and the privileged prisoners treat their fellow prisoners who are suffering the same fate in this brutal manner? Because they want to make a good impression on those guards and camp supervisors who think like them; they want to show how well-suited they are so they can obtain favors, making their life in prison more comfortable, but always at the expense of their fellow prisoners. They behave in this manner because the guards and supervisors callously watch this behavior and are too lazy to stop it. Then there are those guards who enjoy this behavior because they themselves have a low and mean disposition and, in fact, encourage the Kapos to incite prisoners against each other because it gives them a satanic pleasure. However, there are also enough Kapos who, because of a mean, raw, vile mentality and criminal attitude, willingly torture their fellow prisoners physically and mentally; they even hound them to death through pure sadism.

Even now, as I sit in prison, I have had and still have enough opportunity from my limited perspective to confirm what I have written, even though it is on a much smaller scale. Nowhere does the real "Adam" appear so clearly as in prison, where he sheds all acquired and adopted manners and all that he was not born with. While he is in prison he is forced to give up all that is usually concealed and faked. He stands naked before the world, for better or for worse, as he really is.

How then did the overall prison life in Auschwitz influence the various categories of prisoners?

For German citizens of all triangle colors there was no problem. Almost without exception they sat in the preferred position and, therefore, had everything they needed to physically survive. What they could not obtain by legal means they "organized." This ability to "organize" was prevalent among all of the senior Kapos in Auschwitz, regardless of their color triangle or nationality. The only limit to their success was their intelligence, daring, or lack of scruples. There was never a lack of opportunity. Once the campaign against the Jews had begun, it was possible to get almost anything. The senior Kapos definitely had the necessary freedom of movement to do this.

Until the beginning of 1942 the main body of prisoners was Polish.

They all knew that they would have to remain in the concentration camp at least for the duration of the war. Most of them believed that Germany would lose the war; after Stalingrad! practically everyone agreed. By listening to the enemy broadcasts they were accurately informed about Germany's "real situation." It was not very difficult to listen to enemy news since there were enough radios in Auschwitz.

We listened to them even in my house. Later on, there were opportunities for extensive letter smuggling with the help of civilian workers from the outside and even SS soldiers themselves. In other words, there were plenty of news sources. The new arrivals also brought the latest information with them. Since according to enemy propaganda the defeat of the Axis powers was only a question of time now, one could say that the Polish prisoners had no reason to despair. There was only one question. Who would be lucky enough to survive the imprisonment? It was the uncertainty and the fear of random bad luck which made life so emotionally difficult for the Polish prisoner. Anyone on any day could be struck down by diseases to which his physical condition had no more resistance; anyone could suddenly be shot or hanged as a hostage or could unexpectedly be caught up in a resistance movement and thereby brought before Summary Court and sentenced to death; or anyone could be executed in a reprisal or be killed accidently at work in a situation which was set up by fellow prisoners who didn't like him; and finally, anyone could die from the mistreatment of the guards. There were many other chance happenings to which he was always exposed.

The anxious question always remained. Would he survive physically, since the food situation was becoming steadily worse, the housing more overcrowded, and the overall sanitary conditions worse and worse? Would he be able to withstand the hard labor which he had to do in all weather conditions? In addition to all this, he constantly worried about his family and his relatives. Were they still living at home? Had they been arrested, or transported away somewhere to work? Most of all, were they still alive? Many of them were tempted to escape from all this misery.

In Auschwitz escape was not difficult. Since there were many possibilities, it was easy to set up a situation to escape. The guards were easily fooled. With a little daring, and a little luck, it could be done. When you bet everything on one card, you also have to take into account that it might end in death. There were additional drawbacks to escaping, such as reprisals against the family members and the shooting of ten or more fellow prisoners. Many who escaped cared little about reprisals and took the chance in spite of them. Once they were outside the ring of guards, the civilian population living in the area helped them. The rest was easy. If they had bad luck, then it was all over. Their motto was: Either way you're dead. Their fellow prisoners, their companions in sorrow, had to march by the corpse of the shot escapee so that they could see how an attempt to escape would end. Viewing the body probably frightened many of them to abandon their ideas of escape. The diehards dared it anyway. They figured that they would be lucky and belong to the 90 percent who succeeded. I often wondered what they were thinking as they paraded past the bodies of their dead comrades. If I am able to read faces, I saw the following in them: hardened feelings because of what happened, compassion for the unlucky one, and a desire for revenge and retribution when the time came. I could see the same things in their faces when they were assembled to watch the hangings. The only difference was that at that occasion the fear of suffering the same fate was more noticeable.

I also have to mention here the Summary Court and the killing of hostages, since this affected only the Polish prisoners.

Most of the hostages had been in the camp for quite some time. Neither they nor the camp administration knew they were hostages. Suddenly a telegram would arrive from the Gestapo or from Himmler stating, "The following prisoners are to be shot or hanged as hostages." Compliance with this order had to be reported within a few hours. Those prisoners concerned were taken away from their work areas or pulled out during roll call and brought to the detention block [Block II]. Those who had been imprisoned for quite some time knew what this meant; at least they had an idea of what was in store for them. In the detention block they were informed of the order to execute them. At first, in 1940 and the early part of 1941, they were shot in the back of the neck. The bedridden patients in the hospital infirmary [Block 10] were killed by injection [phenol injection directly into the heart].

The Summary Court in Katowice generally came to Auschwitz every four to six weeks and met in Block 11. Most of the prisoners who had been imprisoned there, including those who were brought in shortly before, were led before the presiding tribunal and questioned through interpreters about their testimony and confessions. The prisoners whom I had witnessed there freely, openly, and firmly admitted what they had done. Some of the women bravely pleaded their cases. In most cases the death sentence was pronounced and carried out immediately. All of them went to their death proudly. They were as calm as the hostages. They were convinced that they were sacrificing themselves for their country. I often saw in their eyes a fanaticism which reminded me of the Jehovah's Witnesses and the way they died.

But the criminals sentenced by the Summary Court, the men who had committed robberies or gang theft died in a completely different manner. They were either numb or totally hardened even toward the very end, or, on the other hand, they whined, cried, and begged for mercy. We could see here the same picture and behavior as during the executions in Sachsenhausen. Those dying for their ideals were brave, upright, and strong; the asocials were dull or struggling and trying to resist their fate.

Although the general conditions were anything but good, no Polish prisoners liked being transferred to a different concentration camp. As soon as they found out they were being transferred they tried to move heaven and earth to be treated as an exception or tried to get a delay. When the general order arrived in 1943 that all Poles had to be transferred to concentration camps in Germany proper, I was swamped with petitions for deferment from all the factory branches. No one could spare the Poles. We simply had to transfer a number of them by force. I never heard of Polish prisoners volunteering to go to a different concentration camp. I never understood this clinging to Auschwitz.

Among the Polish prisoners there were three large political groups whose members were constantly feuding. The strongest group was the National Chauvinists. These groups fought constantly among themselves to occupy the important jobs in the camp. If one of the group achieved an important position he quickly pulled members of his group with him and fired the other group members within his sphere of power. Many times this did not happen without serious intrigues. In fact, I dare say that many cases of spotted fever or typhus which ended in death resulted from these power struggles. From the doctor I learned that, especially in the infirmary, there was always a serious struggle about who was in charge. The same happened in regard to the assignment to the work details. The infirmary and work details were the most important power positions in all of prison life. Whoever held these positions was able to rule over the rest. Make no mistake about this; they ruled quite generously with their friends. From these positions of power, a man could place his friends wherever he wanted them; he could also get rid of them or even totally eliminate the people he disliked. Everything was possible in Auschwitz. These power struggles occurred not only among the Polish prisoners in Auschwitz but in every concentration camp and among all nationalities. Even among the Spanish Communists in Mauthausen there were two factions which violently fought each other. In fact, even in jail and later in prison, I learned through first-hand experience how those from the right and left plotted

against each other,

In the concentration camp the rivalries were passionately maintained by the camp administration and constantly fanned in order to prevent any strong movement of solidarity among the prisoners. Not only the political prisoners but also the various colored triangle categories played a part in this. Without the help of these rivalries, it would have been impossible to keep thousands of prisoners in harness no matter how strong the camp leadership. The moregroups fighting each other and the more intense the power struggle among them, the easier it was to control the camp. "Divide and conquer" is used not only in high politics, but also in the operation of a concentration camp. It is an important factor that should not be underestimated.

In 45 minutes, they will be ashes....

XVIII

The Russian Prisoners of War

The second-largest group, who were supposed to build a POWcamp at Birkenau, were the Russian prisoners of war. They came from the army POWcamp in Lamsdorf [presently Lambinowice] in Upper Silesia and were in a very run-down physical condition. They arrived in Auschwitz after long weeks of marching with very little food supplied to them on route. During the breaks in their march they were simply led into nearby fields and told to "graze" like cattle on everything that was edible. Camp Lamsdorf reportedly held approximately 200,000 Russian POWs. The camp was simply a square area of land where most of the Russians huddled together in huts made from the earth which they had built themselves. Food distribution to the camp was irregular and totally inadequate. The prisoners cooked for themselves in fire pits in the ground. Most of them gobbled up their food raw as soon as they could get their hands on it. One could not call what they did eating.

The army was not prepared for the masses of prisoners captured in 1941. The entire bureaucracy handling POWs was much too rigid and immovable and could not improvise quickly to meet the situation. By the way, the German POWs did not fare any better during the collapse in May 1945. The Allies also were not prepared for this mass influx. The prisoners were simply herded together on suitable terrain, surrounded by barbed wire, and then left to themselves. The German POWs suffered the same way as the Russians did.

I was supposed to build the POWcamp at Birkenau with these prisoners, who barely had enough energy to stand up. According to Himmler's orders, only the strong and able-bodied Russian POWs were transferred. The officers accompanying the Russians said that these were the best available in Lamsdorf. They were perfectly willing to work but were unable to accomplish anything because of their weakened condition. I remember precisely that we continued to increase their food rations when they were still housed in the original camp, but without any results. Their emaciated bodies could not digest any food. The entire body organism was finished and could no longer function. They died like flies because of their weakened physical condition or from the slightest illness, which their bodies could no longer fight off. I saw countless Russians die as they were swallowing turnips and potatoes. For a period of time I had detailed approximately five thousand Russians almost daily to unload the turnip trains. The entire railway complex was jammed because the turnips lay like a mountain on top of the railroad tracks. It was almost an impossible task because the Russians simply could no longer do any physical labor. They walked around aimlessly in a daze, or they crawled anywhere into a protected area to swallow something edible that they found. They tried to force it down their throats, or they just simply, quietly found a place to die. The situation really became terrible during the muddy period in the winter of 1941- 42. They could bear the cold, but not the dampness and wearing clothes which were always wet. This together with the primitive, half-finished, hastily thrown-together barracks at the start of Camp Birkenau caused the death rate to steadily climb. Even those who in the beginning had shown some physical strength became fewer and fewer as the days passed. Extra rations no longer helped. They gulped down whatever they could get their hands on, but their hunger could not be satisfied.

Once I witnessed a column of several hundred Russian prisoners on the road between Auschwitz and Birkenau suddenly charge into nearby piles of potatoes stored next to the street on the other side of the railroad tracks. All in unison, they completely surprised the guards and ran right over them. The guards didn't know what to do. Luckily I just happened to be driving by and was able to restore order. The Russians threw themselves into the piles of potatoes. It was almost impossible to tear them away. Some of them died while digging into the pile; others died while still chewing, their hands full of potatoes. They no longer exercised the slightest restraint toward each other. The most flagrant desire for self-preservation didn't allow for any human feelings.

Cases of cannibalism happened quite often in Birkenau. Once I found the body of a Russian lying between two piles of bricks. The body had been ripped open with a dull instrument. The liver was missing. They beat each other to death just to get something to eat.

One day while riding on my horse outside the barbed wire fence, I spotted a Russian huddled behind a pile of stones chewing on a piece of bread. Another Russian struck him with a brick so that he could grab the bread away. The victim was already dead behind the pile of stones by the time I got through the entrance to the scene of the action; his head was caved in. I could not find the killer among the swarm of Russians.

During the leveling of the land and the trench-digging in the first section of Birkenau [B 1], the men discovered several corpses of Russians apparently beaten to death and partially eaten. They had been dumped there and hidden in the mud. The puzzling disappearance of many Russians came to be explained with these discoveries. From the window of my house, one day I saw a Russian busily scratching around in his food bucket, then dragging it between the block [probably Block 12] and the Administration Building. Suddenly another Russian came around the comer, then, after a moment of surprise, pounced on the man with the bucket, pushed him into the electrified barbed wire and disappeared with the bucket. The guard in the tower had also witnessed this but was unable to get the running man in his gunsight. I immediately called up the block leader of the day and had him turn off the electricity in that section; I then went into the camp to find the attacker. The Russian who was pushed into the wire was dead; the other could not be found.

They were no longer human. They had become animals who looked for only one thing, food. Of the ten thousand Russian prisoners of war who were supposed to be the main labor force for the construction of the POW camp at Birkenau, only a few hundred were alive by the summer of 1942. This remnant became the elite. They worked with distinction and were employed as mobile work Kommandos wherever something had to be done quickly. But I never lost the impression that these survivors made it through only at the expense of their fellow prisoners because they were more ruthless, more unscrupulous, and were basically tougher.

In the summer of 1942, I believe this remnant achieved a mass break-out. A large number were shot in the attempt, but many managed to escape. Those who were recaptured explained that they ran because of the fear of being gassed, which they expected when the announcement was made that they would be transferred to a newly built section of the camp. They assumed that this transfer was just a trick.' There never was any intention to gas these Russians. It was certain that they knew about the killing of the Russian politruks and commissars, so they feared they would also suffer the same fate. This is how a mass psychosis develops, and these are the results.

XIX

The Gypsies

The next largest contingent in the camp were the Gypsies. Long before the war the Gypsies were rounded up and put into concentration camps during the campaign against the asocials. One branch of the Federal Criminal Police was solely concerned with supervision of the Gypsies. There were continuous investigations in the Gypsy camps to uncover those who were not true Gypsies; those who had merely drifted in with them. These persons were then delivered to the concentration camps as work dodgers or asocials. Furthermore, the Gypsy camps were continuously checked for biological reasons. Himmler wanted to preserve the two main tribes of Gypsies, the names of which I have forgotten, at all costs. Himmler believed they were direct descendants of the Indo-Germanic aborigines and had preserved their customs and culture pure and intact. For research purposes they were all gathered together, accurately registered, and put under state protection as an historical treasure. Later they were to be assembled from all over Europe and granted a limited reservation.

In 1937-38 all wandering Gypsies were brought together in so-called living camps near large cities, so that the police could watch them. In 1942 the order came that all Gypsies, including those with Gypsy blood living in Germany proper, were to be arrested and transported to Auschwitz regardless of sex or age. The only exceptions were those who were officially recognized as pure Gypsies of the two main tribes. These were to be settled in the district of Odenburg on Lake Neusiedler. Those transported to Auschwitz were to be housed in a family camp for the duration of the war.

The guidelines by which the arrests were carried out had not been precise enough. The various police departments interpreted them in different ways and thereby arrested persons who could not possibly have been considered Gypsies. In many cases highly decorated soldiers who had been wounded several times were arrested while on leave from the front because their fathers, mothers, grandparents, or other relatives were either Gypsies or of Gypsy blood. Even a very early member of the Nazi Party whose grandfather had settled in Leipzig was among them. He had a large business in Leipzig and was a World War I veteran who was decorated several times. A female university student who was a group leader of the Berlin League of Nazi Girls was also found to be among them. Many more such cases happened. I reported these matters to the Federal Criminal Police Headquarters. This resulted in continual checking in the Gypsy camp, and many were released. Because of the size of the prison population, it was hardly noticeable.

I can no longer recall how many Gypsies, or those with mixed blood, were in Auschwitz.' I only know they completely filled the section of the camp designed for ten thousand prisoners. However, the general conditions were suited for everything but a family camp. Every condition was lacking, even if the intention was to keep these Gypsies only for the duration of the war. It was almost impossible to feed the children properly, even though for a time I was able to cheat my way through the Nutrition Supply Office by referring to the Himmler order, so that I could get suitable food for the infants. However, soon even this source dried up since the Nutrition Center vetoed any kind of special food for children in the concentration camps.

Then came Himmler's visit in July 1942. I showed him every aspect .of the Gypsy camp. He inspected everything thoroughly. He saw the overcrowded barracks, the inadequate hygienic conditions, the overflowing infirmaries, and the sick in the isolation ward. He also saw the cancer-like illness in children called "Noma," which always gave me a chill because this illness reminded me of the lepers I had seen in Palestine a long time before. The emaciated bodies of children had huge holes in their cheeks, big enough for a person to look through; this slow rotting of the flesh of the living made me shudder.

Himmler learned about the death rate, which, compared to the whole camp, was still relatively low, even though the death rate among the children was exceptionally high. I do not believe that many of the newborns survived the first weeks. Himmler saw everything in detail, as it really was. Then he ordered me to gas them. Those who were still able to work were to be selected, just as was done with the Jews.

I pointed out to him that the types of people being sent did not really correspond with what he had planned for Auschwitz. He then issued the order that the Federal Criminal Police Office was to begin screening the Gypsies as quickly as possible. This took two years. The Gypsies able to work were transferred to other camps. By August 1944 there were only about four thousand gypsies left, and these had to go into the gas chambers. Until that time, they did not know what fate was in store for them. Only as they were marched barrack after barrack to Crematory I did they figure out what was going on. It was not easy to get them into the gas chamber. I personally did not witness this. Schwarzhuber told me that no previous extermination of the Jews had been as difficult as this. It had been especially hard for him because he knew almost every one of them and had a good relationship with them. By nature, the Gypsies were as trusting as children.

In spite of the adverse conditions, the majority of the Gypsies, as far as I could tell, had not suffered psychologically very much because of the confinement; if one overlooks the fact that they could not travel around anymore as they were accustomed to doing. Their previous primitive life-style had accustomed them to close living quarters, poor hygienic conditions, and poor nourishment. Even illness and the high death rate were not taken seriously by them. In fact, for the most part they still behaved like children. They were still spontaneous in their thinking and behavior. They loved to play even during work, which they never took seriously. They were able to see humor even in the most difficult situations. They were optimists.

I have never seen a scowl or a hate-filled expression on a Gypsy's face.

Whenever I arrived in their camp, they immediately ran out of their barracks, played their instruments, let their children dance, and performed their usual tricks. There was a large playground where the children could frolic to their heart's desire with every kind of toy. When I talked to them, they were open and trusting in their answers and made all sorts of requests. It always seemed to me that they really didn't understand that they were imprisoned.

There was fierce feuding among them. Their hot blood and quarrelsome natures made this inevitable because the many different tribes and clans were forced to live in close association. Within their clans, however, they stuck together as if they were glued and they were very devoted to one another. When the selection of the able-bodied workers began, it was necessary to separate and tear apart the clans. There were many emotional scenes, much sorrow and many tears.

We were able to calm and console them somewhat by telling them that they would all soon be together again. For a while we kept the working Gypsies in Auschwitz proper. They did everything possible to see their clans again, even though it was only from a distance. Oftentimes we had to search for the younger ones after roll call because they had sneaked back to their clans by using all kinds of tricks, because they were homesick.

In fact, when I was in Oranienburg with Camp Inspector Glucks, I was often approached by Gypsies who recognized me from Auschwitz. They always asked for news of their clan members, even though they had been gassed long before. It was difficult for me to evade their questions because they were so trusting.

Even though they caused me a great deal of aggravation when I was Kommandant of Auschwitz, they were my favorite prisoners, if one could say something like that.

They simply could not stick to one job for a long period of time. They loved to "Gypsy around" everywhere. The job they wanted the most was the transport Kommando because it allowed them to move around everywhere and satisfy their curiosity and also get a chance to steal. This urge to steal and to roam around is born into them and cannot be stamped out. Also, they have an entirely different moral viewpoint. They do not believe that stealing is absolutely bad. They cannot understand why a man should be punished for it. I am talking about the majority of those in prison, of the true, restless, wandering Gypsies who constantly move about and also those of mixed Gypsy blood who have adapted to this lifestyle. I am not referring to those who settled in the cities. They have already adopted too much from civilization, even though it wasn't always the best part.

It would have been interesting to observe their lifestyle and their activities, if I didn't know all the horror that lay ahead for them, namely the extermination order. In Auschwitz only the doctors and I knew about this order until the middle of 1944. The doctors had the order from Himmler to separate the sick, especially the children, without making it noticeable. It was the children who had the most trust in the doctors. Surely nothing is more difficult than to have to go through all this, to be cold, without mercy, and without compassion.

XX

The Jews

How did imprisonment affect the Jews, who were the majority in Auschwitz from 1942 on? How did they behave?

Even in the beginning there were Jews in the concentration camps.

I knew them very well from my time in Dachau. However, in those days Jews still had the opportunity to leave Germany and go to anywhere in the world that gave them permission to enter. Their stay in the camp was only a question of time or money, and having connections in a foreign country. Many got the necessary visas together within a few weeks and were freed. Only Jews who had violated racial laws, or who were very politically active during the Weimar Republic, had to remain in the camp. Those who had hopes of leaving the country had only one thought: that their life in the concentration camp would pass as smoothly as possible. They worked as hard as they could, even though most of them were totally unaccustomed to hard physical labor. They kept as quiet as possible and fulfilled their duties with quiet willingness.

The Jews in Dachau did not have it easy. They had to work in the gravel pit, which was very hard work for them. The guards had been tremendously incited by Eicke and the newspaper *Der Sturmer)* which was posted everywhere in the SS barracks and in the mess halls. The Jews were harassed and persecuted enough as "corrupters of the German people," even by their fellow prisoners. Since there was a *Der Sturmer* bulletin board within the concentration- camp, the impact was also noticeable even among those prisoners who were otherwise not really anti-Semitic. Of course, the Jews protected themselves in the typically Jewish way, by bribing their fellow prisoners. They all had plenty of money and could therefore buy anything they wanted in the mess hall. Because of this it was easy to find prisoners who had no money and were therefore very willing to do them favors in return for tobacco, candy, sausages, and other items. Through bribery, the Jews were able to influence the Kapos to get them easier work details or spend time in the infirmary by bribing the prisoner nursing staff. One Jew had the nails of both large toes pulled out by a prison nurse for a pack of cigarettes, just to get into the hospital. Mostly they were tormented by people of their own race, whether they were Kapos or block seniors. Their block leader, a man named Eschen, was particularly active in doing this. This person later hanged himself after being involved in a homosexual affair. He was afraid of being punished for it. This block leader not only tormented the Jews with all sorts of dirty tricks, but he also tormented them mentally and emotionally. He constantly applied pressure on them. He lured them into breaking the rules of the camp, and then put them on report. He provoked them to physically fight each other, or with the Kapos, so that he would have the threat of reporting them for breaking the rules. However, he did not report them, but instead just kept up the steady pressure by constantly threatening to report them. He was the personification of the devil. He exhibited a sick eagerness to please the SS, but towards his fellow prisoners and members of his own race he was ready to commit any foul deed. Several times I wanted to demote him, but I ran into a stone wall. Eicke personally insisted that he remain in his position.

Eicke invented a special collective punishment just for the Jews. Each time another hate campaign was started against the concentration camps [by the foreign press], the Jews had to remain anywhere from one to three months in their beds. They were allowed to get up only for meals and to step outside of their barracks during roll call. The barracks were not allowed to be aired out and the windows were screwed shut. This was a cruel kind of punishment which had severe psychological effects. Because they were forced to lie down continuously, the prisoners became very nervous and irritable, so much so that they could not stand to look at each other and could not tolerate each other anymore. Terrible fist fights took place among the prisoners.

Eicke believed that only Jews who had been in Dachau could have caused the hate campaign against the concentration camps and, therefore, the Jews as a whole should be severely punished for this.

I have to say something about this. I have always rejected *Der Stürmer,* [Julius] Streicher's anti-Semitic newspaper, because of the disgusting sensationalism calculated to work on man's basest instincts. Then there was also the constant emphasis on sexual matters, which were extremely pornographic. This newspaper did a lot of damage and has never been of any use to serious scientific anti-Semitism. In fact, it has damaged the cause of anti-Semitism by turning people off. It was no wonder after the collapse of Germany I learned that a Jew edited this newspaper and wrote most of the depraved articles

Since I was a fanatic National Socialist, I was firmly convinced that our idea would take hold in all countries, modified by the various local customs, and would gradually become dominant. This would then break the dominance of international Jewry. Anti-Semitism was nothing new throughout the whole world. It always made its strongest appearance when the Jews had pushed themselves into positions of power and when their evil actions became known to the general public. Such depraved hate campaigns in the manner of *Der Stürmer* did not serve the cause of anti-Semitism. If you wanted to fight the Jews intellectually, you had to use better weapons than this. I believed that because our ideas were better and stronger, we would prevail in the long run. Eicke's collective punishment would have no effect whatsoever against the hate reports about the concentration camps. The hate campaign would have continued even if hundreds or thousands were shot. In those days I thought that it was right that the Jews we held in custody should be punished for the spread of the hate campaign by their fellow Jews.

Then came Kristallnacht, instigated by Goebbels in November 1938; throughout all of Germany Jewish businesses were destroyed, or at least all the windows were smashed in retaliation for the killing of von Rath in Paris by a Jew. Everywhere fires broke out in the synagogues and the firemen were deliberately prohibited from fighting the fires. "In order to protect them from the wrath of the German people," all Jews who still played a role in commerce, industry, and business were arrested and brought to the concentration camps as "Jews in protective custody." This is when I first became acquainted with them as a group. Until then Sachsenhausen was almost free of Jews, but now this tidal wave of Jews came all at once. Before then bribery was an almost unknown concept in Sachsenhausen. Now it started to become widespread and it took all forms.

The Greens welcomed the Jews with great pleasure as objects of exploitation. We had to take their money away from them, otherwise there would have been chaos in the camp.

The Jews did damage to each other whenever they could. Each tried to get an easy job for himself. In fact, with the tacit approval of the Kapos, whom they had bribed, new jobs were constantly being invented to avoid real work. In order to get a nice easy job, they did not shrink from getting rid of their fellow prisoners by making false accusations against them. When they had achieved a certain position, they mercilessly bossed and tormented members of their own race in a beastly manner. They far surpassed the Greens in every way. In order to escape this torment and often out of desperation, many Jews threw themselves into the electrified barbed wire or attempted to escape with the hope of being shot. Some just hanged themselves.

The Kommandant reported these continuous occurrences to Eicke. He replied, "Just let them be. Let the Jews devour each other without our interference."

I want to emphasize here that I personally never hated the Jews. I considered them to be the enemy of our nation. However, that was precisely the reason to treat them the same way as the other prisoners. I never made a distinction concerning this. Besides, the feeling of hatred is not in me, but I know what hate is, and how it manifests itself. I have seen it and I have felt it.

The original order of 1941 to annihilate all the Jews stated, "All Jews without exception are to be destroyed." It was later changed by Himmler so that those able to work were to be used in the arms factories. This made Auschwitz the assembly point for the Jews to a degree never before known.

The Jews who were imprisoned during the 1930s could still count on the fact that someday they might be released again, which made being in prison psychologically much easier. But for the Jews in Auschwitz, there was no such hope. They knew without exception that they were sentenced to death, and that they would stay alive only as long as they worked. The majority also had no hope or expectation that their sad fate would be changed. They were fatalists. Patiently and apathetically they allowed all the misery, deprivation, and torment to happen to them. The hopelessness of escaping the foreseeable end caused them to become totally withdrawn from what was happening in the camp. This mental breakdown accelerated the physical breakdown. They no longer had the will to live. They had become indifferent to everything and even the slightest physical shock caused them to die. Sooner or later death was certain for them.

From what I observed, I firmly maintain that the death rate of most of the Jews was caused not only by the unaccustomed work, or the inadequate food, or the overcrowded living conditions and all the other unpleasantness and poor conditions of the camp, but mainly and most importantly because of their psychological condition.! The death rate of the Jews was not much lower in other places of work in other camps under much more favorable conditions. It is significant that it was always relatively higher than the death rate of other prisoners.

During my inspections of the camps as camp inspector [after November 1943], I had seen and heard this often enough. This was even more noticeable among the Jewish women. They collapsed even quicker than the men, even though, from my observation, women generally are much tougher and have more stamina psychologically and physically than do men. This applies to the majority of the Jewish prisoners. In many ways the more intelligent ones conducted themselves differently. These were mostly the Jews who were psychologically strong, who had the will to live, and who came mostly from the Western countries. These were the exact ones, especially the doctors, who knew precisely what was going to happen. But they hoped and counted on good luck sparing them. They hoped that somehow or sometime their lives would be saved. They also counted on Germany's collapse because the enemy propaganda reached them easily. For them, the goal now became to get a job or a position which would lift them from the mass of prisoners and bring them special privileges. This then would protect them somehow from the chance of getting killed accidently and improved their entire living condition. In order to win such "protection for life," in the truest sense of the word, they applied all their knowledge and tough will. The safer the position, the more desirable it was, and the more it was fought over. There was no consideration for others. This was a fight in which everything was at stake. No means were spared, no matter how depraved, in order to free up such a position or to hold on to it. For the most part the unscrupulous were the winners. Many times I heard about the fights to dislodge others from their positions in the camp. In different camps I had become familiar with the methods and intrigues of these power struggles for higher positions among the different color triangles and the various political groups. Even then I was still able to learn a lot from the Jews in Auschwitz. "Necessity is the mother of invention," and here it actually concerned survival itself.

It repeatedly happened that those who occupied safe positions suddenly began to slowly waste away when they learned about the death of close family members, in spite of the fact that there was no physical reason, such as illness or poor living conditions. The Jews have a tremendously strong sense of family cohesiveness. The death of close relatives affects them so much that life does not seem worth living or fighting for anymore. However, I have also witnessed the opposite during the gassings, but more about that later.

The Railway Entrance- Birkenau-Auschwitz

XXI

The Women's Camp

All of the above also applies to the female prisoners of the various groups. For the women, however, everything was much more difficult and depressing and could be felt more because the general conditions in the women's camp were worse. They were jammed together much more than the men. The sanitary and hygienic conditions were considerably worse. Added to that, it never had been possible to get the women's camp organized properly because of the disastrous overcrowding with all its consequences from the beginning.

Everything was much more crowded than with the men. When the women had reached a point of no return, they let themselves go completely. They stumbled through the area like ghosts, completely without will, and had to be literally pushed everywhere by others until one day they just quietly died. These walking corpses were a terrible sight. The Green triangles among the female prisoners were of a special type. I believe that Ravensbrück had selected the "best" for Auschwitz. They far exceeded their male counterpart in their ability to survive in toughness, vileness, and depravity. Most of them were prostitutes with considerable records. Often they were loathsome females. One can understand that it was unavoidable that these beasts satisfied their evil desires by exploiting the prisoners they were in charge of.

When Himmler visited Auschwitz in 1942, he thought that they would be especially well-suited to act as Kapos for the Jewish women. Not many of them died unless they were victims of an epidemic. They never suffered any mental anguish.

I can still visualize the bloodbath which took place at Budy. I don't believe that men could ever turn into such monsters. The way the Green triangles mutilated and had tom the French Jewish women apart, killed them with axes, and strangled them to death was simply horrible. Fortunately, not all the Greens and Blacks were such depraved creatures. There were also some useful ones among them who still had a heart for their fellow prisoners. But these women were persecuted terribly by their comrades of the same triangle color. Most of the female SS guards showed no understanding of this situation.

A pleasant contrast to this type were the female Jehovah's Witnesses, called "Bible Bees" or "Bible Worms." Unfortunately, there were too few of them. In spite of their more or less fanatical philosophy, they were very much in demand. They worked as servants for the SS who had large families, in the Waffen SS clubhouse, even in the officer's club, but for the most part they worked on the farms. They needed no guards or supervisors. They worked on the chicken farms at Harmense and on different farm estates. They chose to work hard since this was Jehovah's commandment. They were mostly middle-aged German women but there were also a number of Dutch females represented. I had two older women working for more than three years in our household. My wife often said that she personally could not take better care of the household than these two women. They were especially touching in the way they cared for our children.

The children hung on them as if they were members of the family.

At first we feared that they might try to convert the children to Jehovah. But this never happened. They never spoke about religious subjects, which was truly surprising because of their fanatical attitude. There were also peculiar types among them. One of them worked for an SS officer and was able to anticipate his every wish, but absolutely refused to clean or even to touch his uniforms: not the cap, the boots, or, in fact, anything connected with the military. But as a whole, she was satisfied with her lot. By her suffering imprisonment for Jehovah, she hoped to gain entry into his kingdom, which was expected to come soon. Strangely, all of them were convinced that the Jews were justly suffering and had to die because their ancestors had betrayed Jehovah. I have always believed Jehovah's Witnesses to be poor lunatics who were happy in their own way.

The rest of the able female prisoners of Polish, Czech, Ukrainian, or Russian nationalities were used for farm work. Because of this they escaped the mass camp and all its bad effects. They were much better off in the living quarters of the farms and Raisko [a large estate owned by the SS]. I have always found that all of the prisoners who worked on the farm and were living away from the main camp made quite a different impression. They just weren't under the same psychological pressures as those in the mass camps. Otherwise it would not have been possible to get them to do the work willingly and without question. The fact that the regular women's camp was overcrowded from the very beginning meant mental breakdowns for the mass of the female prisoners, which was sooner or later followed by physical breakdown. In the women's camp the worst possible conditions always prevailed. This was true right from the beginning, when it was still part of the original main camp. When the transports of Jews from Slovakia began [March 26, 1942], within a few days the women's camp was crammed full to the rafters. Washing and toilet facilities were barely able to satisfy even the smallest needs for one third of them. To bring order into this scurrying anthill, I would have needed other manpower requirements than the few available female guards sent to me from Ravensbrück. I have to emphasize once again; they did not send me their best.

In Ravensbrück the female guards had been spoiled rotten. Everything had been done to persuade them to stay in the women's concentration camp service and also to attract new female guards by providing a very high standard of living. They were housed extremely well and were paid a salary which they could never have achieved in civilian life. They also were not overworked in their duties. In short, Himmler and especially Pohl wanted us to give them the greatest consideration.

At the time conditions were still normal in Ravensbrück, so there was no question as yet of overcrowding. None of these guards came to Auschwitz voluntarily, and yet, they were supposed to start under the most difficult conditions. From the very beginning most of them wanted to run back to the quiet, comfortable, easygoing life at Ravensbrück. The female officer in charge of the women guards, Mrs. Langefeldt, was in no way able to handle the situation, but she stubbornly refused any advice from the camp commander. I finally had to admit this mess could not continue like this, so on my own authority I simply put the women's camp under the control of the camp commander. Hardly a day passed in which there weren't discrepancies in the roll call count. In this confusing situation the female guards ran around like excited chickens and didn't know what to do. The three or four competent female guards were driven crazy by the others. Since the female officer in charge of the guards felt that she was an independent leader of the camp, she complained about being put into a lower position than her equally ranked male counterpart. I actually had to reissue the order putting her under the camp commander.

When Himmler visited Auschwitz in July 1942, in Mrs. Langefeldt's presence I listed all of the poor conditions and I told him that she was not, nor ever would be, able to lead and build the women's concentration camp at Auschwitz properly. I once again asked him to make her subordinate to the camp commander.

In spite of the most convincing proofs of her incompetence and the incompetence of the other female guards in general, he absolutely refused. He wanted a woman in charge of the women's camp and told me that I was to put one of the SS officers under her command as her assistant. But, which of the officers would subject himself to be placed under the command of a woman? Every officer I ordered to do so out of necessity begged me to be relieved from this duty as soon as possible. When time permitted I was present at the unloading of the larger transports in order to ensure a smooth transition. So right from the beginning of the women's camp, the female prisoners took control. Therefore, the larger the camp became, the more difficult it was for the female guards to control it, and the easier it was for the prisoners to gain self-rule. Since the Greens were predominant, shrewder, and had less scruples, they actually ruled the women's camp, in spite of the fact that the camp seniors and the other top prison trusties were Red. The "instructors," as the female Kapos were called, were mostly Green or Black triangles. This was the reason that in the women's camp, the most miserable conditions always prevailed.

The senior female camp guards were head and shoulders above those who came after them. In spite of the tremendous recruiting throughout the Nazi women's organizations, very few women volunteered to be concentration camp guards. The rising daily demand for women guards had to be met by force. Every armament factory to which female prisoners were detailed had to supply a certain percentage of female employees as women guards. It can be understood that these companies did not send the best material, since there was a general shortage of capable women workers because of the war. These guards were now given a few weeks of half-hearted training in Ravensbrück and then let loose on the prisoners. Since the selection and the allocation took place in Ravensbrück, Auschwitz again was put at the bottom of the barrel. It is only natural that Ravensbrück kept the best workers, since they had to put up a new women's work camp themselves.

That's how the guard situation in Auschwitz looked. Their moral qualities, almost without exception, were very, very low. Many female guards ended up appearing before the SS court during the Reinhardt Action for stealing. However, these were only the few who were caught. In spite of the most severe punishment designed to deter them, the stealing continued, and they continued to use prisoners as middlemen. I will give one very flagrant case as an example.

A female guard sank so low that she became sexually involved with some of the male prisoners, mostly Green Kapos. As payment for her sexual favors, she accepted valuable jewelry, gold, and other items. In order to cover up her shameless conduct, she had an ongoing affair with a staff sergeant. She hid her hard-earned pay in his room by packing it up and locking it away. This fool had no idea what his sweetheart was doing and was very much surprised when all those nice things were found in his quarters. This female guard was put into the concentration camp for life by Himmler and received an additional punishment of two lashings of twenty-five strokes each.

Similar to the homosexuality in the men's camp, the infection of lesbian love was widespread in the women's camp. Even the strongest punishments, in fact, even the transfer to a punishment company, could not stop it. Many times cases of sexual contact between female guards and female prisoners were reported to me. All this shows the low quality of these guards. Obviously, it can be understood that they did not take their duties very seriously and were mostly undependable.

There weren't many possible ways to punish the breaking of service rules. Confinement to quarters was, in fact, considered to be a privilege because it kept them indoors during bad weather. All forms of punishment needed the authorization of the inspector of concentration camps or Pohl. There was to be as little punishing as possible, but, instead, by kind teaching and able leadership, these deviations were supposed to be set straight. The female guards, of course, knew all of this and the majority acted accordingly.

I have always had a great respect for women in general. In Auschwitz, however, I learned that I had to reserve my general opinion, so that I had to look very closely at a woman before I could consider her with the greatest respect. The above applies to the majority of the female guard personnel. However, there were good, dependable, and very decent women among them, even if they were just a few. It does not need to be emphasized that these few suffered very badly in the environment of Auschwitz, but they could not escape their fate, since they were drafted into the service. Several of them poured out their troubles to me, and even more so to my wife. We could only console them by pointing out that at the end of the war their troubles would be over. This truly was poor consolation.

In addition to the guard detachment for the work Kommando outside the camp, the women's camp also had the dog handlers. In order to save guard personnel the female guards were allotted dogs in Ravensbrück. Even though the female guards were armed with pistols, Himmler counted on the use of dogs to have a deterring effect on the prisoners. While the men care less about this, women have a tremendous respect for dogs for the most part. In Auschwitz there were never enough guards to guard the outside work Kommandos, considering the large number of prisoners. Chains of guards remedied this when larger work areas had to be guarded. However, on the farms the work areas constantly changed and moved during the day. Chains of guard posts didn't work in this situation, or in ditch digging, or with other, similar work details. This is why the largest possible number of dog handlers became a necessity, since there were so few female guards available. However, even the approximately 150 dogs were not enough. Himmler estimated that one dog could replace two guards. This was possible in the women's camp because they feared dogs so much.

The dog detail of Auschwitz was perhaps the most splendid soldier material that ever existed. When volunteers were sought for training as dog handlers, half of the SS regiment reported. They thought they would have an easier and more varied duty in this job. Since all of the volunteers could not be accepted, the companies hit upon an extremely clever solution, or so they thought. Instead of sending the volunteers, they sent all of the black sheep of the company and thus got rid of them. Let someone else have the headaches with them. Most of these men had been punished for one offense or another. If the commanders of the guard units would have examined their conduct reports more accurately, they would not have allowed them to be sent for training. This is why, during the training period at the Learning and Research Institute for Dog Training in Oranienburg, some of them were sent back as totally useless. After the rest came back to Auschwitz and the dog squad was formed, one could then see what a magnificent organization had been created.

One should have seen them in use; they either played with their dogs, or they lay hidden somewhere and slept. They weren't worried, since the dog would wake them immediately should an "enemy" approach. If they weren't doing the above, then they were having friendly conversations with the female guards or the female prisoners. A large majority had regular affairs with the Green women Kapos. Since the dog handlers were constantly used in the women's camp, it was not difficult for them to be posted on "their" special work detail. When they were bored or just wanted to have some fun, they would sic the dogs on the prisoners. When they were caught doing this, they explained that the dog had done it on its own by going after prisoners who were not behaving properly, or they had lost hold of the leash, and so on. They always had an excuse.

According to their regulations, they were supposed to continue training their dogs daily in order to save the time and trouble of training new dog handlers. They could only be relieved of their duties if they had committed serious infractions which required sentencing by an SS court, or by abusing or neglecting their dogs. The officer in charge of the kennel, an old police sergeant whose career as a dog handler spanned more than twenty-five years, was often in despair over the behavior of the dog handlers. They knew that nothing much could happen to them, and that it wasn't easy to have them relieved of duty. A stronger commanding officer would have brought this gang to their knees, but those gentlemen had much more important things to do. Countless times I became upset with the dog company. There was a great deal of friction between myself and the camp commander [Hartjenstein]. According to Glucks, however, it was I who had little understanding of what was actually required of soldiers. This was the reason I could never get those officers promptly relieved of their duties when they became impossible in their camp jobs. A lot of problems could have been avoided if Glucks had had a different attitude toward me.

As the war progressed Himmler wanted to save on even more manpower by using mechanical means. The guards were replaced by movable barbed wire fences, electrically charged fixed barbed wire fences at the regular work sites, even minefields, and even by using more dogs. Any Kommandant who could invent a truly practical method to decrease the number of guards was to be promoted at once. Nothing came of this. Himmler continued to picture in his mind that dogs could be trained to constantly circle the prisoners as if they were a herd of sheep, thereby preventing an escape. Using Himmler's method, one guard with several dogs was supposed to be able to guard up to one hundred prisoners safely. The continued experiments had no results. Men are not sheep. Even when the dogs were highly trained to recognize prisoners by their uniforms or by scent, no matter how thoroughly they were trained to maintain the proper distance and react to any approach, they were still just dogs who could not out-think a human being. If they were tricked by the prisoners to go to one spot to divert their attention, they left a large section unguarded, which was then used to escape. Besides that, the dogs were not able to prevent a mass escape. True, they could have badly mutilated a few prisoners, but in the process they would have been beaten to death along with their handlers.

In addition to all this, Himmler wanted to replace the guards in the watchtowers with dogs. The dogs were supposed to run free all around the camp, or at regular work sites between the two rows of barbed wire. In this way the dogs would give notice by their barking if prisoners came near and thus prevent them from breaking through the wire. This also had no results. The dogs either found some place to sleep or they let themselves be tricked. If the wind blew from the opposite direction the dog didn't notice anything at all, or the guard in the listening post didn't hear the barking.

Burying land mines around the area was a double-edged sword because the mines went dead after three months and had to be changed. The mines had to be laid in a precise manner and their placement had to be written down accurately on a map of the minefield. From time to time the mined area had to be entered for various reasons; this enabled the prisoners to remember the mine-free lanes.

Globocnik used this method of mining at the extermination sites where he was in charge. In spite of the carefully laid mine fields at Sobibor, the Jews were able to achieve a mass breakout because they knew where the safe lanes were. Almost all of the guards were brutally beaten to death. Dogs or mechanical gadgets cannot replace human intelligence. Even the double electrified barbed wire fence can be overcome, if a person gives it some thought, has cold-blooded determination, and some help from the dry weather. Many escapes were successful. On several occasions the guards on the outside had gotten too close to the electrified wire and had to pay for this carelessness with their lives.

I have written in other places in these memoirs about my main task and how I believed it should be done. I firmly believed that I had to use all means and materials at my disposal to speed the development of all the 'SS factories in the area of the Auschwitz concentration camp. I used to think that I could see an end to this constant enlarging of the camp. I thought I could look forward to a quieter period when I would be able to manage all of Himmler's directives and building plans, but new plans kept arriving. This meant that I personally could not perform the necessary checking and supervising of the building sites because new duties needed my immediate attention. The increasing pressure I felt from Himmler, from the difficulties caused by the war, from the daily problems which occurred in the camp, and finally from the unending river of prisoners pouring into the camp, caused me to think only of my work and allowed me to see everything only from that view. Pressured by all these circumstances, I, in turn, hounded everybody in my command, whether they were SS, civilian employees, other government agencies, the people in charge of the factories, or the prisoners.

There was only one goal that was important to me: to continue trying to improve the general situation, so I could carry out my orders. Himmler demanded that each SS man perform his duty. But more than that, he demanded that each SS man be willing to sacrifice himself completely in performing it, if necessary. Everyone in Germany had to give 100 percent so that we could win the war. Himmler ordered that the concentration camps be made to manufacture war materials. Everything else came second. All other considerations had to be swept aside. An example of this was Himmler's deliberate disregard of the deteriorating general condition of the camp. The war effort came first. Whatever got in the way was pushed aside.I was not permitted to let anything come in conflict with these orders. I had to be like steel—colder, harder, and even more merciless toward the misery of the prisoners. I saw everything clearly, often too clearly, but I could not allow feelings to overcome me. I could not allow any emotion to stand in the way. Winning the war was the final goal; the rest didn't matter. We had to win the war. Since I was not allowed to go to the front lines, I believed I had to do my best at home to help those at the front. Today I can see that in spite of my pushing and striving, we could not have won. But back then, I truly believed and was convinced of our final victory. I believed I had to work to this goal and that I certainly could not neglect anything.

According to Himmler's orders, Auschwitz became the largest human killing center in all of history. When he gave me the order personally in the summer of 1941 to prepare a place for mass killings and then carry it out, I could never have imagined the scale, or what the consequences would be. Of course, this order was something extraordinary, something monstrous. However, the reasoning behind the order of this mass annihilation seemed correct to me. At the time I wasted no thoughts about it. I had received an order; I had to carry it out. I could not allow myself to form an opinion as to whether this mass extermination of the Jews was necessary or not. At the time it was beyond my frame of mind. Since the Führer himself had ordered "The Final Solution of the Jewish Question," there was no second guessing for an old National Socialist, much less an SS officer. "Führer, you order. We obey" was not just a phrase or a slogan. It was meant to be taken seriously.

Since my arrest I have been told repeatedly that I could have refused to obey this order, and even that I could have shot Himmler dead. I do not believe that among the thousands of SS officers there was even one who would have had even a glimmer of such a thought. Something like that was absolutely impossible. Of course, many SS officers moaned and groaned about the many harsh orders. Even then, they carried out every order. Himmler had offended many SS officers because of his inflexible harshness, but I am convinced that not even one would have dared raise a hand against him, not even in his most secret thoughts. As leader of the SS, Himmler's person was sacred. His fundamental orders in the name of the Führer were holy. There was no reflection, no interpretation, no explanation about these orders. They were carried out ruthlessly, regardless of the final consequences, even if it meant giving your life for them. Quite a few did just that during the war.

It was not in vain that the leadership training of the SS officers held up the Japanese as shining examples of those willing to sacrifice their lives for the state and for the emperor, who was also their god. SS education was not just a series of useless high school lectures. It went far deeper, and Himmler knew very well what he could demand of his SS.

Outsiders cannot possibly understand that there was not a single SS officer who would refuse to obey orders from Himmler, or perhaps even try to kill him because of a severely harsh order. Whatever the Fuhrer or Himmler ordered was always right. Even democratic England has its saying, "My country, right or wrong," and every patriotic Englishman follows it.

Chosen to Work

XXII
The Gassings

Before the mass destruction of the Jews began, all the Russian politruks [Communist Party members] and political commissars were killed in almost every camp during 1941 and 1942. According to the secret order given by Hitler, the Einsatzgruppe [special troops of the SS] searched for and picked up the Russian politruks and commissars from all the POW camps. They transferred all they found to the nearest concentration camp for liquidation. The reason for this action was given as follows: the Russians were murdering any German soldier who was a member of the Nazi Party, especially SS members. Also, the political section of the Red Army had a standing order to cause unrest in every way in any POW camp or places where the POWs worked. If they were caught or imprisoned, they were instructed to perform acts of sabotage. This is why these political officials of the Red Army were sent to Auschwitz for liquidation. The first small transports were shot by firing squads of SS soldiers.

While I was on an official trip, my second in command, Camp Commander Fritzsch, experimented with gas for these killings. He used a gas called Zyclon B, prussic acid, I which was often used as an insecticide in the camp to exterminate lice and vermin. There was always a supply on hand. When I returned Fritzsch reported to me about how he had used the gas. We used it again to kill the next transport.

The gassing was carried out in the basement of Block 11. I viewed the killings wearing a gas mask for protection. Death occurred in the crammed-full cells immediately after the gas was thrown in. Only a brief choking out-cry and it was all over. This first gassing of people did not really sink into my mind. Perhaps I was much too impressed by the whole procedure.

I remember well and was much more impressed by the gassing of nine hundred Russians which occurred soon afterwards in the old crematory because the use of Block 11 caused too many problems. While the unloading took place, several holes were simply punched from above through the earth and concrete ceiling of the mortuary. The Russians had to undress in the antechamber, then everyone calmly walked into the mortuary because they were told they were to be deloused in there. The entire transport fit exactly in the room. The doors were closed and the gas poured in through the openings in the roof. How long the process lasted, I don't know, but for quite some time sounds could be heard. As the gas was thrown in some of them yelled "Gas!" and a tremendous screaming and shoving started toward both doors, but the doors were able to withstand all the force. It was not until several hours later that the doors were opened and the room aired out. There for the first time I saw gassed bodies in mass. Even though I imagined death by gas to be much worse, I still was overcome by a sick feeling, a horror. I always imagined death by gas a terrible choking suffocation, but the bodies showed no signs of convulsions. The doctors explained to me that prussic acid paralyzes the lungs.' The effect is so sudden and so powerful that symptoms of suffocation never appear as in cases of death by coal gas or by lack of oxygen.

At the time I really didn't waste any thoughts about the killing of the Russian paws. It was ordered; I had to carry it out. But I must admit openly that the gassings had a calming effect on me, since in the near future the mass annihilation of the Jews was to begin. Up to this point it was not clear to me, nor to Eichmann, how the killing of the expected masses was to be done. Perhaps by gas? But how, and what kind of gas? Now we had discovered the gas and the procedure. I was always horrified of death by firing squads, especially when I thought of the huge numbers of women and children who would have to be killed. I had had enough of hostage executions, and the mass killings by firing squad ordered by Himmler and Heydrich.

Now I was at ease. We were all saved from these bloodbaths, and the victims would be spared until the last moment. That is what I worried about the most when I thought of Eichmann's accounts of the mowing down of the Jews with machine guns and pistols by the Einsatzgruppe. Horrible scenes were supposed to have occurred: people running away even after being shot, the killing of those who were only wounded, especially the women and children. Another thing on my mind was the many suicides among the ranks of the SS Special Action Squads who could no longer mentally endure wading in the bloodbath. Some of them went mad. Most of the members of the Special Action Squads drank a great deal to help get through this horrible work. According to [Captain] Hoffle's accounts, the men of Globocnik's extermination section drank tremendous quantities of alcohol.

In the spring of 1942 [January] the first transports of Jews arrived from Upper Silesia. All of them were to be exterminated. They were led from the ramp across the meadow, later named section B-II of Birkenau, to the farmhouse called Bunker 1. [Camp Commander] Aumeier, Palitzseh, and a few other block leaders led them and spoke to them as one would in casual conversation, asking them about their occupations and their schooling in order to fool them. After arriving at the farmhouse they were told to undress. At first they went very quietly into the rooms where they were supposed to be disinfected. At that point some of them became suspicious and started talking about suffocation and extermination. Immediately a panic started. Those still standing outside were quickly driven into the chambers, and the doors were bolted shut. In the next transport those who were nervous or upset were identified and watched closely at all times. As soon as unrest was noticed these troublemakers were inconspicuously led behind the farmhouse and killed with a small-caliber pistol, which could not be heard by the others. The presence of the Sonderkommando' and their soothing behavior also helped calm the restless and suspicious. Some of the Sonderkommando even went with them into the rooms and stayed until the last moment to keep them calm while an SS soldier stood in the doorway. The most important thing, of course, was to maintain as much peace and quiet as possible during the process of arriving and undressing. If some did not want to undress, some of those already undressed as well as the Sonderkommando had to help undress them.

With quiet talk and persuasion even those who resisted were soothed and undressed. The Sonderkommando, which was composed of prisoners, took great pains that the process of undressing took place very quickly so that the victims had no time to think about what was happening. Actually the eager assistance of the Sonderkommando during the undressing and the procession into the gas chambers was very peculiar. Never did I see or ever hear even a syllable breathed to those who were going to be gassed as to what their fate was. On the contrary, they tried everything to fool them. Most of all, they tried to calm those who seemed to guess what was ahead. Even though they might not believe the SS soldiers, they would have complete trust in those of their own race. For this reason, the Sonderkommando was always composed of Jews from the same country as those who were being sent to the gas chamber.

The new arrivals asked about life in the camp and most of them asked about their relatives and friends from earlier transports. It was interesting to see how the Sonderkommando lied to them and how they emphasized these lies with convincing words and gestures. Many women hid their babies under piles of clothing. Some of the Sonderkommando watched carefully for this and would talk and talk to the woman until they persuaded her to take her baby along. The women tried to hide the babies because they thought the disinfection process would harm their infants. The little children cried mostly because of the unusual setting in which they were being undressed. But after their mothers or the Sonderkommando encouraged them, they calmed down and continued playing, teasing each other, clutching a toy as they went into the gas chamber.

I also watched how some women who suspected or knew what was happening, even with the fear of death all over their faces, still managed enough strength to play with their children and to talk to them lovingly. Once a woman with four children, all holding each other by the hand to help the smallest ones over the rough ground, passed by me very slowly. She stepped very close to me and whispered, pointing to her four children, "How can you murder these beautiful, darling children? Don't you have any heart?"

Another time an old man hissed while passing me, "Germany will pay a bitter penance for the mass murder of the Jews." His eyes glowed with hatred as he spoke. In spite of this he went bravely into the gas chamber without worrying about the others.

Another young woman stands out in my mind. While constantly running back and forth, she helped to undress the little children and old women with great care. At the point of selection, she had two little children at her side and she caught my attention by her agitated behavior and her appearance. She didn't look Jewish at all. At this point the children were no longer with her. Staying until the end with several other children, she kept speaking softly and calming those who weren't finished undressing. She then went into the bunker with the last group. In the doorway she stopped and said, "I knew from the beginning that we were destined to be gassed at Auschwitz. I got through the selection of those who were chosen to work by taking children in my hands. I wanted to experience the process fully conscious and accurately. I hope it will be quick. Farewell!"

Occasionally some women would suddenly start screaming in a terrible way while undressing. They pulled out their hair and acted as if they had gone crazy. Quickly they were led behind the farmhouse and killed by a bullet in the back of the neck from a small-caliber pistol. Sometimes, as the Sonderkommando were leaving the room, the women realized their fate and began hurling all kinds of curses at us. As the doors were being shut, I saw a woman trying to shove her children out of the chamber, crying out, "Why don't you at least let my precious children live?" There were many heartbreaking scenes like this which affected all who were present.

In the spring of 1942 hundreds of people in the full bloom of life walked beneath the budding fruit trees of the farm into the gas chamber to their death, most of them without a hint of what was going to happen to them. To this day I can still see these pictures of the arrivals, the selections, and the procession to their death.

As the selection process continued at the unloading ramps, there were an increasing number of incidences. Tearing apart families, separating the men from the women and children, caused great unrest and excitement in the entire transport. Separating those who were able to work only increased the seriousness of the situation. No matter what, the families wanted to stay together. So it happened that even those selected to work ran back to the other members of their family, or the mothers with their children tried to get back to their husbands, or to the older children. Often there was such chaos and confusion that the selection process had to be started all over again. The limited amount of standing room did not permit better ways to separate them. There was no way to calm down these overly excited masses. Oftentimes order was restored by sheer force.

As I have said repeatedly, the Jews have a very strong sense of family.

They cling to each other like leeches, but from what I observed, they lack a feeling of solidarity. In their situation you would assume that they would protect each other. But no, it was just the opposite. I heard about, and also experienced, Jews who gave the addresses of fellow Jews who were in hiding. These Jews in particular came from Western Europe.

A woman who was already in the gas chamber shouted out the address of a Jewish family to an SS soldier. One man who, judging by the way he was dressed and the way he behaved, came from the best social class, actually gave me a slip of paper on which was a list of quite a few addresses of Dutch families who were hiding Jews. I cannot explain what motivated them to reveal this information. Was it personal revenge, or were they jealous because they did not want the others to live on?

As strange as that was, so was the general behavior of the Sonderkommando. All of them knew with certainty that when it was over, they themselves would suffer the same fate as thousands of their race had before them, in whose destruction they were very helpful. In spite of this they still did their job with an eagerness and in a caring, helpful way during the undressing, yet they would also use force with those who resisted undressing. This always amazed me. They never spoke to the victims about what was ahead of them. They also led away the troublemakers and then held on to them firmly while they were being shot. They led these victims in such a way that they could not see the NCO who stood ready with his gun. This enabled him to aim at the back of their necks without being noticed. It was the same when they dealt with the sickly and feeble who could not be brought into the gas chambers. All this was done in a matter-of-fact manner, as if they themselves were the exterminators. They dragged the bodies from the gas chambers, removed the gold teeth, cut off the hair, then dragged the bodies to the pits or to the ovens. On top of that, they had to maintain the fires in the pits, pour off the accumulated fat, and poke holes into the burning mountains of bodies, so that more oxygen could enter. All these jobs they performed with an indifferent coolness, just as if this was an everyday affair. While dragging the bodies, they ate or smoked. Even the gruesome job of burning the bodies dug up after being in mass graves for a long time did not prevent them from eating. It often happened that Jews from the Sonderkommando discovered close relatives among the bodies and even among those who went into the gas chambers. Although they were visibly affected there never was any kind of incident.

This incident I witnessed myself: As the bodies were being pulled out of one of the gas chambers, one member of the Sonderkommando suddenly stopped and stood for a moment as if thunderstruck. He then pulled the body along, helping his comrades. I asked the Kapo what was wrong with him. He found out that the startled Jew had discovered his wife among the bodies. I watched him for a while after this without noticing anything different about him. He just kept dragging his share of bodies. After a while I again happened on this work party. He was sitting with the others and eating as if nothing had happened. Was he really able to hide his feelings so completely, or had he become so hardened that something like this really didn't bother him?

Where did the Jews of the Sonderkommando get the strength to perform this horrible job day and night? Did they hope for some special luck that would save them from the jaws of death? Or had they become too hardened by all the horror, or too weak to commit suicide to escape their existence? I really have watched this closely, but could never get to the bottom of their behavior. The way the Jews lived and died was a puzzle I could not solve.

I could relate countless more of these experiences and occurrences of the type I have described so far. These are only excerpts from the total process of the annihilation. They are only glimpses.

The mass annihilation with all the accompanying circumstances did not fail to affect those who had to carry it out. They just did not watch what was happening. With very few exceptions all who performed this monstrous "work" had been ordered to this detail. All of us, including myself, were given enough to think about which left a deep impression. Many of the men often approached me during my inspection trips through the killing areas and poured out their depression and anxieties to me, hoping that I could give them some reassurance. During these conversations the question arose again and again, "Is what we have to do here necessary? Is it necessary that hundreds of thousands of women and children have to be annihilated?" And I, who countless times deep inside myself had asked the same question, had to put them off by reminding them that it was Hitler's order. I had to tell them that it was necessary to destroy all the Jews in order to forever free Germany and the future generations from our toughest enemy.

It goes without saying that the Hitler order was a firm fact for all of us, and also that it was the duty of the SS to carry it out. However, secret doubts tormented all of us. Under no circumstances could I reveal my secret doubts to anyone. I had to convince myself to be like a rock when faced with the necessity of carrying out this horribly severe order, and I had to show this in every way, in order to force all those under me to hang on mentally and emotionally.

Everyone watched me. They all wanted to see what kind of impression this made on me, and how I reacted. Following these scenes, I was observed carefully. Everything I said was thoroughly discussed. I had to make a tremendous effort to pull myself together in order not to show, not even once, in all the excitement after an incident, or to allow my inner doubts and depressions to come out in the open. I had to appear cold and heartless during these events which tear the heart apart in anyone who had any kind of human feelings. I couldn't even turn away when deep human emotion rose within me. Coldly I had to stand and watch as the mothers went into the gas chambers with their laughing or crying children.

On one occasion two little children were involved in a game they were playing and their mother just couldn't tear them away from it. Even the Jews of the Sonderkommando didn't want to pick up the children. I will never forget the pleading look on the face of the mother, who certainly knew what was happening. The people in the gas chamber were becoming restless. Everyone was looking at me. I had to act. I gave the sergeant in charge a wave, and he picked up the screaming, kicking children in his arms and brought them into the gas chamber along with the mother, who was weeping in the most heart-breaking fashion. Believe me, I felt like shrinking into the ground out of pity, but I was not allowed to show the slightest emotion.

Hour upon hour I had to witness all that happened. I had to watch day and night, whether it was the dragging and burning of the bodies, the teeth being ripped out, the cutting of the hair; I had to watch all this horror. For hours I had to stand in the horrible, haunting stench while the mass graves were dug open, and the bodies were dragged out and burned. I also had to watch the process of death itself through.the peephole of the gas chamber because the doctors called my attention to it. I had to do all of this because I was the one to whom everyone looked, and because I had to show everybody that I was not only the one who gave the orders and issued the directives, but that I was also willing to be present at whatever task I ordered my men to perform.

Himmler sent various high-ranking Party officials and SS officers to Auschwitz to see the process of the extermination of the Jews. All of them were deeply impressed by what they saw. Some of them who had lectured before very fanatically about the necessity of this extermination became completely silent while viewing the "Final Solution of the Jewish Question" and remained so. I was asked repeatedly how I and my men could watch these proceedings day after day. How we could stand it? I gave the same answer time and time again, that only iron determination could carry out Hitler's orders and this could only be achieved by stifling all human emotion. Even [SS General of the Gestapo] Mildner and Eichmann, who had a reputation for being truly hard, said they would not want to change places with me. No one envied me my job.

I had many detailed discussions concerning every phase of the "Final Solution of the Jewish Question" with Eichmann without ever letting him know what was going on inside me. I tried everything possible to get Eichmann to open up about what his deepest convictions were about the "Final Solution." But, even when we were alone and the wine and schnapps were flowing so that he was in the most talkative mood, he revealed that he was totally obsessed with the idea of destroying every Jew he could get his hands on. Ice cold and without mercy, we had to carry out this annihilation as quickly as possible. Any compromise, even the smallest, would bitterly avenge itself later on.

Faced with such grim determination I had to bury all my human inhibitions as deeply as possible. In fact, I have to confess openly that after such conversations with Eichmann these human emotions seemed almost like treason against the Führer. There was no escaping this conflict as far as I was concerned. I had to continue to carry out the process of destruction. I had to experience the mass murder and to coldly watch it without any regard for the doubts which uprooted my deepest inner feelings. I had to watch it all with cold indifference. Even minor incidents, which others probably would not have noticed or been affected by, stayed on my mind for a long time.

And yet, I really had no reason to complain about being bored at Auschwitz.

When something upset me very much and it was impossible for me to go home to my family, I would climb onto my horse and ride until I chased the horrible pictures away. I often went into the horse stables during the night, and there found peace among my darlings.

Often at home my mind would suddenly recall some incident at the killing sites. That's when I had to get out because I couldn't stand being in the loving surroundings of my family. When I watched our children happily at play, or saw my wife bubbling with happiness over the baby, this thought often came to me: how long will your happiness continue? My wife never understood my troubled moods and merely blamed them on the problems connected with my work. Many a night as I stood out there on the railroad platforms, at the gas chambers, or at the burnings, I was forced to think of my wife and children without connecting them to what was taking place. The married men who worked the crematory or the open-pit burnings often told me that the same thoughts had occurred to them. When they watched the women enter the gas chambers with their children, their thoughts naturally turned to their own families.

I was no longer happy at Auschwitz once the mass annihilation began.

I became dissatisfied with myself, my main responsibility, the neve-rending work, and the undependability of my coworkers. I was also not happy with my superior's lack of understanding and the fact that he would not even listen to me. Truly, it was not a happy or desirable situation. And yet, everyone in Auschwitz believed the Kommandant really had the good life. Yes, my family had it good in Auschwitz, every wish that my wife or my children had was fulfilled. The children could live free and easy. My wife had her flower paradise. The prisoners tried to give my wife every consideration and tried to do something nice for the children. By the same token no former prisoner can say that he was treated poorly in any way in our house," My wife would have loved to give a present to every prisoner who performed a service for us. The children constantly begged me for cigarettes for the prisoners. The children especially loved the gardeners. In our entire family there was a deep love for farming and especially for animals. Every Sunday I had to drive with them across all the fields, walk them through the stables, and we could never skip visiting the dog kennels. Their greatest love was for our two horses and our colt. The prisoners who worked in the household were always dragging in some animal the children kept in the garden. Turtles, martens, cats, or lizards; there was always something new and interesting in the garden. The children splashed around in the summertime in the small pool in the garden or the Sola River. Their greatest pleasure was when daddy went into the water with them. But he had only a little time to share all the joys of childhood.

Today I deeply regret that I didn't spend more time with my family.

I always believed that I had to be constantly on duty. Through this exaggerated sense of duty I always had made my life more difficult than it actually was. My wife often urged me, "Don't always think of your duty, think of your family too." But what did my wife know about the things that depressed me? She never found out.

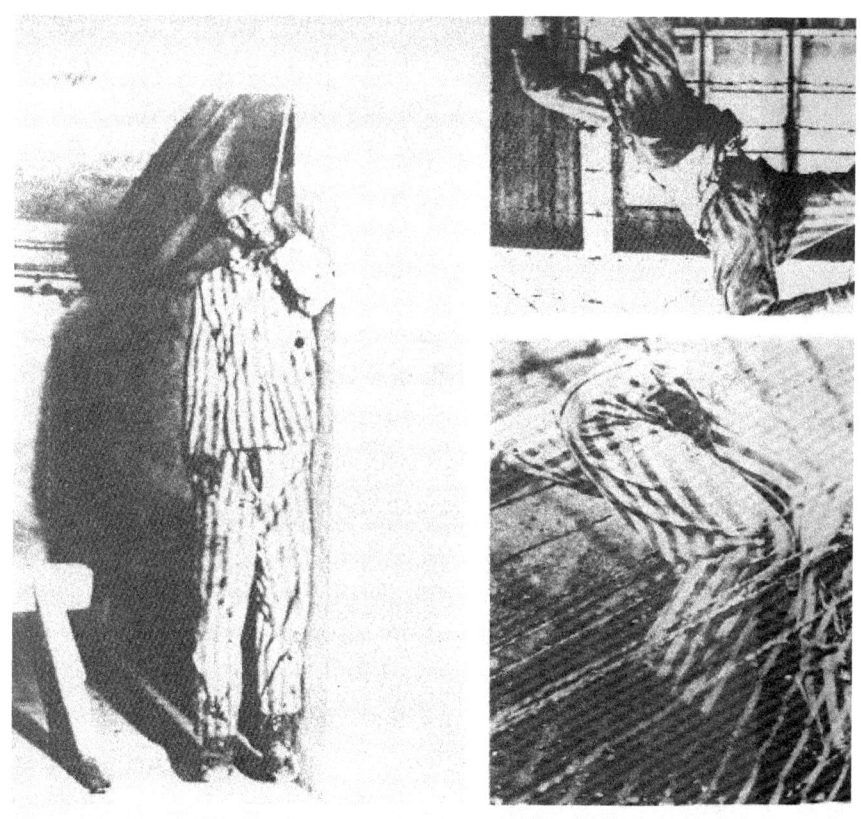

The Only Escape

XXIII

Chief of the Department of Inspectors of Concentration Camps

According to Pohl's suggestion Auschwitz was divided up. He gave me a choice of becoming Kommandant of Sachsenhausen, or becoming chief of concentration camps inspectors. It was very unusual for Pohl to let an officer actually choose his assignment, and even more extraordinary that he gave me twenty-four hours to think it over. This was a gesture of goodwill on his part for what I had accomplished at Auschwitz. At first I was not happy about moving away because Auschwitz had become my life precisely because of the difficulties, the problems, and the many difficult duties. But afterward, I was glad that I was free from all of it. I knew I did not want a concentration camp again-no matter what the situation. I had had enough after nine years' general service in concentration camps and three-and-a-half years at Auschwitz.

I chose to become the chief of concentration camps inspectors. There really was nothing else for me. I was not allowed to go and fight at the front lines because Himmler had refused both my requests. As a matter of fact, I really didn't like office work, but Pohl had told me that I could reorganize the department the way I wanted. When I started my new post on December 1, 1943, Glucks also let me have a free hand, even though he was not pleased with Pohl's choice; me, of all people, around him. However, he accepted the inevitable because Pohl wanted it. *H* I wanted to do more than just sit back and use my job as a nice easy cushion, I would first have to help the Kommandants and make sure that the duties of my department were based on the needs of the camps. This was the exact opposite of the usual procedure by the previous inspector of the camps [Liebehenschel]. Most of all, there had to be steady contact, along with personal inspections of the camps, to be able to correctly understand the problems. This way we would be in a position to be able to alleviate the problems that we could by pushing our solutions through the higher departments. From my new position I was able to get a complete picture. All the files, orders, and correspondence about the development of all the camps dating back to Eicke's time as inspector were stored in my department.

Many of the camps I didn't even know personally. All of the correspondence to the camps by the inspector of the concentration camps was officially filed in my department. The only things we didn't have were the work schedules, medical records, or administrative matters. In other words, from my position I could get an overview of all the camps, but no more than that. What actually happened in the camps, how the camps actually looked, could not be judged by the documents or the files. In order to really understand each camp it was necessary to walk through the camp with eyes wide open. That's what I wanted to do. I made a lot of inspection trips. Most of these were at Pohl's request, because he thought I was a specialist concerning internal camp affairs.

Now I saw what really went on in the camps: the hidden defects and the deplorable conditions. With the assistant director, [Colonel] Maurer, who actually was Glucks's representative, and the actual inspector [Höss was actually a deputy inspector], we were able to correct a lot of the faults. However, in 1944 there wasn't much that could be changed. The camps were becoming more and more overcrowded, causing all the problems that accompany this situation. Tens of thousands of Jews were moved from Auschwitz to be used for the new arms industry, and conditions went from bad to worse. These camps were thrown together in accordance with the official guidelines by those in charge of camp construction under such unbelievably difficult conditions that they were absolutely primitive. In addition, the hard work, to which most of the prisoners were not accustomed, and the constantly decreasing supply of food presented a truly wretched picture. If they had been gassed in Auschwitz, they would have been saved from a great deal of suffering. They died anyway within a short time without having contributed anything substantial to the war effort, in fact, nothing. In my reports I referred again and again to this fact, but the pressure from Himmler for "more prisoners for the arms industry" was stronger. He became intoxicated with the increasing numbers which showed the deployment of prisoners from week to week. He no longer paid any attention to the death rates. Before, he always became enraged when the death rate rose. Now he said nothing.

I always thought that the healthiest and strongest Jews should be selected. Of course, we would have fewer able-bodied workers, but they would have been truly useful and for a longer period of time. The way things stood, they had a lot of large numbers on paper, but in reality a large percentage of them were useless. They only put a strain on the camps, took away space and food from the able-bodied workers, and produced nothing. In fact, their presence caused many of those able to work to become unproductive. The end result was so obvious that you didn't need a calculator. However, I have said enough about this and described this in detail in the notes made about the SS officers.

My new position brought me closer and in direct contact with the Gestapo. I got to know all the departments and officials who were responsible for the concentration camps. I also came to know their views, which differed from person to person, concerning the purpose of the concentration camps. Each person's view depended on the attitude of his department head. I have already written extensively about the head of Department IV [Müller], whose viewpoints I could never clearly find out because he only repeated Himmler's views.

Subsection IV -B, whose concern was protective custody, was still locked into the old prewar guidelines. More effort was put into the paper war than the real war, whose demands were disregarded. Many of the officials in this department should have been fired from their jobs.

I believe that the arrest of the former officials of the opposition parties at the beginning of the war was a mistake. This only created more enemies of the state. Those people who posed a threat to the state could have been arrested much earlier because there still would have been plenty of time in the peaceful prewar years. However, this subsection was governed by the arresting departments. I often fought with the department heads who were responsible.

The department in charge of the western and northern areas, including their special prisoners, was very sensitive because the West and North were under Himmler's direct control. This meant that the utmost caution was necessary. These prisoners were to be given special consideration. They had to be given easy work assignments, plus many other considerations.

The subsection concerned with the eastern regions was much looser.

The main body of prisoners in all the camps was from the East. In addition, the Jews were the main work force used in the arms industry.

Orders to execute prisoners just kept rolling in. Using hindsight, I can now see the situation much more clearly. My requests, which tried to remedy the deplorable conditions in Auschwitz by requesting a halt of any new transports, were simply filed away by the Gestapo, because they could not or would not show any consideration to the Poles. Their main concern was that the Gestapo arrests be carried out. They didn't care about the prisoners after they were arrested because Himmler didn't care.

The directives about the Jews from Eichmann and [Major] Gunther were very clear. According to Himmler's order, dated the summer of 1941: all Jews were to be exterminated. Gestapo Headquarters raised the most serious objections when Himmler, on Pohl's suggestion, ordered the selection of those who were able to work. The Gestapo had always been in favor of the complete destruction of all Jews. They feared that every new work camp and every new group of a thousand Jews selected to work would survive and be liberated. No department showed more interest in the increasing death rate of the Jews and the actions against the Jews than the Gestapo office.

Contrary to this, Pohl was directed by Himmler to bring as many prisoners as possible to the arms factories. Pohl, therefore, put the greatest emphasis on getting all the prisoners that he could to the arms factories, including as many able-bodied Jews as possible. They were to be taken from the transports destined for the extermination camps. He also stressed that these workers be kept healthy, even though he had little success with that. The Gestapo and the Armaments Department were pulling in exactly opposite directions. However, Pohl seemed to be stronger because Himmler supported him. With more and more urgency, he demanded prisoners for the arms factories. Himmler was forced to do this because of his promises to Hitler. On the other hand, Himmler also wanted to have as many Jews as possible exterminated.

From 1941, when Pohl became in charge of the concentration camps, the Jews became part of Himmler's armaments program. The tougher the war became, the more relentlessly Himmler demanded the use of prisoners. The main body of prisoners came from the East, and later came the Jews. They were mainly sacrificed to the arms industry. The concentration camps were in the middle of a tug-of-war between the policies of the Gestapo and the Armaments Department. The Gestapo delivered the prisoners to the camps to be exterminated. It made no difference to them whether it happened by firing squad, gas, or by the horrible conditions in the camps. It was part of their plan not to improve conditions in the camps. At the same time the Armaments Department wanted to keep the prisoners alive to manufacture arms. Pohl, however, was influenced to such an extent by Himmler's constant demands for more workers that he actually furthered the goals of the Gestapo. By his determination to fulfill the large numbers demanded by Himmler, he caused uncounted thousands of prisoners to die in the work places. They died because almost all the basic necessities to live were lacking for such mass numbers of prisoners. At that time, although I sensed this connection, I could not and did not want to believe them to be true. Today I see the picture a lot more clearly.

These were the unseen, but true, factors underlying the operation and the philosophy of the concentration camps. Thus, the concentration camps were changed deliberately, and sometimes unintentionally, into large-scale extermination centers. The Kommandants received extensive composite reports from the Gestapo about the Soviet concentration camps. Escaped prisoners had made reports about the conditions and organization of these camps down to the smallest detail. They emphasized that by using forced labor methods the Soviets were annihilating entire nationalities. For example, if the inmates of one camp were used up during the building of a canal, they just shipped thousands of new kulaks or other political prisoners who, after a time, died the same way. At the time I wondered if the reports were meant to slowly prepare the Kommandants for their new tasks, or whether they were being used to desensitize them against the deteriorating conditions which were slowly growing in the camps. When I became chief inspector, I had to conduct unpleasant investigations in the different concentration camps, and even more often in the work camps. This was always unwanted by the Kommandants. I also had to relieve people of their commands and instruct new replacements, as in the case of Bergen-Belsen,

Until I was appointed, the inspector of the concentration camps did not pay any attention to this camp at all. Gestapo Headquarters considered this camp to be mostly for the so-called pampered Jews, and it was considered to be a transit camp. A grim, inscrutable man named Major [Adolf] Haas was the Kommandant and he ran the place the way he felt. Even though he had been executive officer in Sachsenhausen for a while in 1939, he nevertheless came from the General SS and had almost no idea of how to run a concentration camp.

He didn't do a thing to try to improve the condition of the buildings since the time it had been a POW camp for the army, and he made no attempt to improve the terrible sanitation problems at Bergen-Belsen. In the fall of 1944 he had to be relieved of his command because of his neglect of the camp and his involvement with women. I had to personally go there and transfer [Captain] Kramer from his Kommandant's position at Birkenau.

The camp presented a hopeless picture. The prisoner barracks and even the guard barracks were as totally run down as the work buildings. Sanitation conditions were much worse than at Auschwitz. As far as construction was concerned, nothing much could be done anymore, since it was the end of 1944. In spite of this, I was able to get an excellent building foreman from SS Lieutenant General Kammler, who was in charge of all construction matters for the Gestapo. All we could do was improvise and use makeshift methods. The sins that Haas had committed could not be corrected by Kramer, even though he did his best. This explains why Bergen-Belsen was instantly overcrowded when a large number of the prisoners were sent there from Auschwitz when it was evacuated [January 18, 1945]. The conditions were so bad that even I have to describe them as horrible, even though I had gotten used to quite a bit at Auschwitz.

Kramer was totally powerless to do anything. Even Pohl was shaken when he saw these conditions during our lightning tour through all the concentration camps as ordered by Himmler. Without hesitation, Pohl immediately took away a neighboring camp from the army in order to create some relief, but this camp was just as run down and in no better condition. There was hardly any water. The sewage just ran into the nearby fields. Because of this, typhus and spotted fever ran wild. Immediately, we started to build mud huts in order to alleviate housing conditions, but all of it was too little too late. A few weeks later the prisoners from the nearby underground factories were added to this camp. It was no wonder that the British found the dead, the dying, and those sick with diseases. There were only a few healthy prisoners left and the whole camp was in a condition which could not be surpassed by anything.

The war, especially the air war, had an increasing effect on all the camps. All the belt-tightening which became necessary only made the total situation worse. The hastily built work camps near the most important arms factories suffered the most. The air war and the bombing attacks on the arms factories caused countless deaths among the prisoners. Even though the Allies never bombed any camps, you should remember that prisoners were used in most of the important arms factories. They died like the civilian population. When the air attacks increased in 1944, not a day went by without receiving casualty figures from the camps caused by the bombing attacks. However, I could not even guess a total number, but it was in the high thousands.

I also lived through many bombing attacks and most of them not in safe "hero cellars." I experienced attacks of incredible destruction on the, factories in which prisoners were working and saw with my own eyes how the prisoners behaved; how guards and prisoners often died together, crouching in a protective ditch, and how prisoners even helped the wounded guards. During such heavy attacks everything was a blur. There were no more guards or prisoners; they were only people trying to escape the hail of bombs. Even though I was often buried alive, I remained unharmed through countless bombing attacks. I lived through the rain of bombs on Hamburg, Dresden, and the never-ending attacks on Berlin. I escaped certain death by mere chance in Vienna. During my official trips I survived many a low-level attack on the trains and cars in which I was riding.

Gestapo Headquarters and the Bureau of Economics were saturated with bomb hits, but they were constantly patched up again. In spite of this, neither Muller nor Pohl would leave their posts. Our country, at least the larger cities, had become the front line. The total number of victims of the air war will probably never be found. In my estimation there were probably several million.' The casualty figures were never made public. They were top secret.

I am constantly faulted because I did not refuse to carry out the extermination order: the horrible murder of women and children. I have already answered that question in Nuremberg. What would have happened to a squadron commander who would have refused to fly a bombing mission on a city, knowing full well that there were no arms factories, no essential factories, and no military installations; knowing full well that his bombs would kill mostly women and children. He would certainly have been court martialed. But the Allied interrogators and prosecutors would not accept this comparison. I believe that both situations are comparable. I was just as much a soldier and an officer as the squadron commander was, even though they do not want to recognize the Waffen SS as regular armed forces, but more like a party militia. We in the SS were as much soldiers as the army, navy or air force.

These constant air attacks were a tremendous hardship on the civilian population, especially the women. In many cases the children had been evacuated to remote mountain areas which were not threatened by air attacks. Life in the big cities was nothing but turmoil, not just physically, but the psychological effects were considerable. If you looked at the faces and observed the behavior of the people in the public air raid shelters, in the private shelters, and in the houses, you could see the fear of death in their eyes, especially when the explosions of the rain of bombs came closer and louder and how they clung to each other and looked to the men for protection as entire buildings shook or began to collapse. Even the Berliners, who are known for their toughness, became unnerved as time went by. Day after day, night after night, our nerves were tested in the basements. The German people would not have been able to stand this war of nerves, this psychological hardship much longer.

I have described the activities of Bureau D, Inspection of the Concentration Camps, at length in the accounts of the various directors and office chiefs. I have nothing to add to that.

Would the concentration camps have been organized differently with another inspector in charge? Probably not. Because no matter how ambitious and strong-willed he would have been, he would not have been able to stop the effects of the war, and no one would have been able to oppose or act against the hard will of Himmler or try to bypass him. Even though the concentration camps were created by the strong-willed Eicke, the hard will of Himmler was always the real power behind him.

The concentration camps became what they were solely because Himmler intended them to be that way. It was Himmler who gave the directives to the Gestapo because he was the only one who could do this. It was his instrument alone. I am firmly convinced that not a single important large Gestapo operation was started without Himmler's approval. In most cases he was also the originator and the cause. The entire SS was the tool with which Heinrich Himmler, the leader of the SS, made his desires reality. Even though from 1944 on there was a more pressing need, the war, it does not change this fact.

During my official tours through the arms factories where prisoners were working I got a good look into our arms production. I saw and heard many things from the men in charge of the factories which greatly astonished me, especially in the aircraft industry. I learned from Maurer, who often had to deal with armaments, about delays which could not be made up, about the production breakdowns, and about incorrect manufacturing designs which demanded retooling for months on end. I knew of arrests, even executions of important, well-known industrialists who failed. This gave me a lot to think about.

Although our leaders continually spoke of new inventions and new weapons, there was no evidence of this in the everyday situations of the war. In spite of our new jet fighters, the Allied air offensive was felt to be getting stronger. Against a stream of bombers containing 2,000 to 2,500 of the heaviest aircraft [a gross overestimate by Höss], we could only send up a few dozen fighter squadrons. To be sure, the manufacture of our new weapons was proceeding and was being used experimentally. But in order to win the war, we would have had to have an explosion of production. Wherever a factory was running full blast, it was leveled to the ground in the span of a few minutes. The shifting of the arms factories to underground facilities was vital for victory. This could have been completed by 1946 at the earliest. However, nothing would have been gained by this because the transports of the raw materials to the factories and the transports of the finished product from the factories were still exposed to enemy air action.

The best example was the V rocket production called "Mittelbau."

The bombers destroyed all of the railroad tracks which led to the underground caverns in the mountains. Months and months of painstaking work had been for nothing. The heavy V-I and V-2 rockets lay uselessly locked up in the mountains. Just as soon as temporary tracks were laid, they were destroyed again. But that's how it was almost everywhere by the end of 1944.

The Eastern Front "moved back" more and more. The German soldier in the East was no longer able to hold [the enemy advance]. The Western Front was also being pushed back. Hitler, however, talked only of holding firm at all costs. Goebbels spoke and wrote about the belief in the miracle. Germany will be victorious!

A lot of doubt stirred within me whether we could ever win the war since I had learned too much to the contrary. We could not win the war this way. But I could not permit myself to doubt our final victory. I had to believe in it, even though common sense told me that without question we had to lose. My heart was with the Führer and with our ideology. That couldn't perish.

My wife often asked me about this in the spring of 1945, when everyone already saw that the end was coming. "How is it possible for us to still win? Do we really have anything in reserve which is decisive?" With a heavy heart I had to tell her that she must have faith because I was not permitted to say what I knew. I was not permitted to discuss with a single person what I noticed, or what I had seen or heard. I was firmly convinced that Pohl and Maurer, who both saw even more than I did, had the same thoughts. But no one dared to talk about this with anyone else. This was not out of fear that we would risk being charged with talk of defeatism, but because none of us wanted to believe the real truth. It just couldn't be possible that our world would perish. We had to win.

Everyone continued to work with a tenacity as if victory would depend upon his work alone. In fact, when the Oder [River] Front was demolished in April [1945], we made every effort to keep the remaining arms factories going full blast with our prisoners. We had to try everything; in fact, we considered doing substitute armament works in the camp annexes. Anyone who neglected his job by saying there was no use anymore was severely reprimanded where we still had influence. In fact, Maurer wanted to bring a staff officer up on just such charges before an SS court when Berlin was completely surrounded and we were preparing to evacuate.

I have already written several times about the insanity of the clearing of the concentration camps. But the pictures which were conjured up by this evacuation order have made such an impression on me that I will never forget them.

When Pohl didn't get a report from [SS Major Richard] Baer about the evacuation of Auschwitz, he chased me to Silesia to check things out. Baer was the first person I found in Gross-Rosen who was there preparing to receive the prisoners. He did not know where the camp prisoners were. The original plan had been totally disrupted because of the Russian advance. I immediately attempted to drive to Auschwitz to convince myself that everything important was destroyed as ordered.! But I could only get as far as the Oder River near Ratibor because the advance of the Russian tank force on the other side had already circled around. On all the roads and streets of Upper Silesia to the west of the Oder River, I now found columns of prisoners who were suffering terribly as they tried to make their way through the deep snow. There was no food. In most cases the NCOs who were leading this parade of walking dead had no idea which direction they were supposed to go. All they knew was that their final destination was Gross-Rosen. How they were going to arrive there was a mystery to all of them. Using their own initiative, they requisitioned food from the villages, rested for a few hours, and then moved on again. There was no thought at all about spending the night in the barns or the school houses, since everywhere they were filled to the top with refugees. It was easy to follow the route of this ordeal of suffering because every few hundred meters lay the bodies of prisoners who had collapsed or been shot. I directed all the columns that I could reach to the west into the Sudetenland, so that they would not stray into that completely bottled up mess near the Neisse River. I gave the strict orders to the leaders of these columns not to shoot prisoners who were unable to march any further. They were to hand them over to the Volkstürm [local militia] in the villages.

During the first night on the streets near Leobschütz, I continued to find prisoners who were shot. Since they were still bleeding, they could only have been shot a short time before. As I stopped my car by one of the dead prisoners and got out of the car, I heard pistol shots very close by. I ran toward the sound. At that moment I saw a soldier park his motorcycle and then shoot a prisoner who had been leaning against a tree. I yelled at him and asked him what business he had there and what business the prisoners were to him. He laughed at me insolently, looked me directly in the eye, and asked me what business I had sticking my nose into this. Without hesitation I pulled out my pistol and shot him dead. He was a sergeant in the air force.

Now and then I also met officers from Auschwitz who had managed to get hold of a vehicle. I ordered them to go to the crossroads and to gather up the straying columns of prisoners and bring them to the West, by train if possible. I saw transports of prisoners frozen stiff in open coal cars; whole trains of railroad cars were standing abandoned on side rails out in the open without food or water. There were groups of prisoners completely on their own, whose guards had simply disappeared. They also were moving peacefully toward the West. I also met groups of British POWs with no one guarding them. They were determined not to fall into the hands of the Russians. I found SS soldiers and prisoners perched together on refugee wagons and found wagon trains of construction and farm vehicles. Nobody knew which direction to follow. They only knew the goal was Gross-Rosen.

The weather at the time was terribly cold with a lot of deep snow.

The streets were blocked by army columns, masses of refugees, and multiple auto accidents which were occurring because of the icy streets. The dead on the side of the road included prisoners, refugees, women, and children. On the outskirts of one village I saw a woman sitting on a tree stump rocking her baby and singing. The child had long since died and the woman was insane. There were large numbers of women torturously making their way through the snow with baby buggies piled high with their belongings. They had only one thought. Escape! Escape from falling into the hands of the Russians.

In Gross-Rosen everything was overcrowded. SS General Schmauser had already given the order to prepare to evacuate. I drove to Breslau to tell him what I had seen and to try to convince him not to evacuate Gross-Rosen. He showed me Himmler's radio message, which ordered him to make sure that no healthy prisoners remained in any of the camps in his district, and said that he was personally responsible for carrying this out. That meant that arriving prisoner transports at the Gross-Rosen railroad station were immediately sent on. But only a very few could be supplied with food. Gross-Rosen itself had nothing left

In the open trucks dead SS soldiers lay peacefully alongside dead prisoners. Those clinging to life sat on top of them chewing their piece of bread; horrible pictures, which are best not described.

I lived through the evacuation of Sachsenhausen and Ravensbrück, where the same pictures were repeated. It was only luck that the weather turned a little warmer and drier, allowing the columns to spend the night out in the open. But after two or three days there were no more supplies. The Red Cross helped by handing out food packages. There was no food to be gotten in the villages, since for weeks many wagon trains of refugees had passed through. In addition, there was the constant danger of attack by low-flying aircraft, which left no street uncontrolled anymore.

Until the very last moment I tried everything to bring some order into this chaos. It was all useless. We too had to escape. Since the end of 1944 my family had lived in the immediate vicinity of Ravensbrück, From there I was able to take them along with me as the Office of Inspection of Concentration Camps "relieved itself of duty." First we traveled north to the peninsula of Darss [on the Baltic Sea coast near Rugen], then, after two days, to Schleswig-Holstein, but always on Himmler's order. We could not understand why we had to remain with Himmler, and what kind of duty he still had for us to do. I had to take Mrs. Eicke, her daughter and children, and a few other families who were not supposed to fall into the hands of the enemy.

This flight was horrible because we had to travel at night without any lights while the streets were completely clogged with vehicles. I constantly worried about everyone staying together in the cars because I was responsible for the whole column. Using a different route, Glucks and Maurer drove to Warnemünde. In Rostock two large trucks containing all of our radio equipment broke down. By the time they were fixed, the anti-tank traps had been closed, and there they sat in the trap. During the day we charged from one wooded area to the next because low-flying enemy planes were constantly hacking away at this main retreat route.

In Wismar, Field Marshall Keitel himself was standing in the middle of the street looking for deserters.

While traveling we learned at one of the farms that the Führer was dead [April 30, 1945]. When we heard this, both my wife and I had the same thought: "Now we too must go!" Our world had perished with the Führer. Was there any sense for us to continue living? We were going to be pursued and hunted everywhere. We wanted to take poison. I had gotten some for my wife, so that she and the children would not be taken alive by the Russians, in case they broke through unexpectedly. For our children's sake we did not do it. For their sake we were willing to bear all that was ahead of us. We should have done it anyway. I have since regretted it many times. We all would have been spared a great deal, especially my wife and children. And yet what will they still have to go through? We were bound and chained to that world. We should have died with it.

Since her escape, Mrs. Thomson, our children's teacher in Auschwitz, lived with her mother in St. Michaelsdom in Holstein. This is where I now brought my family. I didn't know where the Office of Concentration Camp Inspection would be stationed at that time. I took my oldest boy [Klaus] with me. He wanted to stay with me because we still hoped for front line duty to defend the last unoccupied spot in Germany in its final hour.

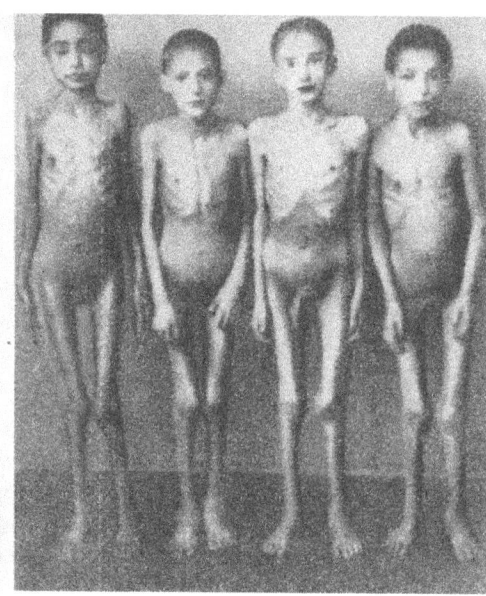

Dr. Josef Mengele and His Twins

XXIV
1945-47

We arrived in Flensburg to report for the last time. This is where Himmler and the government had moved. There was no more question of fighting. The order of the day was, "Save yourself, if you can." I will never forget the last meeting and farewell from Himmler. He was beaming and in a great mood; yet the world, our world, had perished. If he had said, "Well gentlemen, now it's over, you know what to do," I would have understood-that would have corresponded with what he had preached year in and year out, "Self-sacrifice for the ideology." But, instead, he gave us his last order: "Hide yourself in the army!"

This was the goodbye from the man I respected so highly, in whom I had placed such tremendous confidence, whose orders and sayings were gospel to me. Maurer and I just looked at each other in silence thinking the same thought. We were both old Nazis and SS officers who lived for our ideology. Had we been alone, we would have committed some kind of desperate act, but we still had to take care of our bureau chief, the officers and men of our staff and the vulnerable families. Glucks was already half dead anyway. Using a different name, we took him to the navy hospital. [General] Gebhardt took charge of the women and children who were destined for Denmark. The rest of the bureau submerged into the navy with fake papers. I took the name of Seaman Franz Lang and traveled with marching orders to the Naval Intelligence School on the Isle of Sylt. I sent my son back to my wife with a car and a driver. Since I knew a little about the navy, I wasn't noticed. There wasn't much work to do, so I had plenty of time to think over carefully what had happened. By chance one day I heard the news on the radio of Himmler's arrest and death by poison.

I too always carried my vials of poison with me. I was not going to take the chance of being arrested.

The Naval Intelligence School was dismantled and transported to the internment area between the Kiel Canal and the Schlei River. The British brought the SS soldiers of that zone to the school and interned them on the Friesian Islands. Because of this I was close to my family and was able to see them several more times. My oldest son visited me every few days. Since I was a farmer by profession, I was released very early and passed all the British checkpoints and through the employment office without any problems. I got a job on a farm near Flensburg as a laborer. I liked the work. I was completely on my own because the owner of the farm was still an American POW. I spent eight months there. I kept in touch with my wife through her brother [Fritz Hensel], who was working in Flensburg. I also learned from him that the British Field Security Police were looking for me. I knew also that my family was being carefully watched and that they constantly searched their house.

On March 11, 1946, at 11 p.m., I was arrested. My vial of poison had broken just two days before. The arrest was successful because I was frightened at being awakened out of a sound sleep. I assumed it was a robbery because there were a lot of them occurring in the area.

I was treated terribly by the [British] Field Security Police. I was dragged to Heide and, of all places, to the same military barracks from which I had been released eight months before by the British. During the first interrogation they beat me to obtain evidence. I do not know what was in the transcript, or what I said, even though I signed it, because they gave me liquor and beat me with a whip. It was too much even for me to bear. The whip was my own. By chance it had found its way into my wife's luggage. My horse had hardly ever been touched by it, much less the prisoners. Somehow one of the interrogators probably thought that I had used it to constantly whip the prisoners.

After a few days I was taken to Minden on the Weser River, which was the main interrogation center in the British zone. There they treated me even more roughly, especially the first British prosecutor, who was a major. The conditions in the jail reflected the attitude of the first prosecutor.

Surprisingly, after three weeks I was shaved, my hair was cut, and I was allowed to wash myself. My handcuffs had not been opened since my arrest. The next day I was taken by car to Nuremberg together with a prisoner of war who had been brought over from London as a witness in Fritzsche's defense. Compared to where I had been before, imprisonment with the IMT [International Military Tribunal] was like staying in a health spa. I was housed in the same building as the principal defendants [Hermann Goring, Rudolf Hess, Albert Speer, Julius Streicher, and others] and could see them daily as they were being led to court. There were daily inspections by the representatives of all the Allied countries. I was constantly displayed as a particularly interesting animal.

I had been brought to Nuremberg because Kaltenbrunner's defense attorney demanded me as a witness for his defense. I could never understand, and it is still not clear even today, how I of all people could help Kaltenbrunner's defense. Even though the prison conditions were good in every aspect and I now had time to read from an extensive library made available to us, the interrogators were really not pleasant. Physically there was no problem, but more so were the mental and emotional effects. I cannot really blame the interrogators-they were all Jews. I was for all intents and purposes psychologically dissected. That's how accurately they wanted to know everything-this was also done by Jews. They also left me with no doubt whatsoever what was going to happen to me.

On May 25 [1946], our wedding anniversary, I was driven to the airport with von Burgsdorff and Buhler and handed over to the Polish authorities. We flew in an American plane to Warsaw via Berlin. Although we had been treated very politely on the flight, I remembered my experiences in the British zone. I also thought of the hints about how I would be treated in the East. I feared for the worst. The expressions and gestures of the onlookers at the airport during our arrival also did not exactly inspire any confidence in me.

After arriving in prison several officials approached me immediately and showed me their Auschwitz tattoo numbers. I could not understand them, but I do not suppose they wished me well. However, I was not beaten. The imprisonment was very strict and totally isolated. I was often viewed and checked. The nine weeks I spent there became very difficult for me because there was absolutely nothing to keep my mind occupied. I had nothing to read, nor was I allowed to write.

I arrived on July 30 in Krakow with seven other Germans. We had to wait quite a while at the railroad station for a car. During that time a crowd had gathered and angrily cursed at us. Major Goth was recognized immediately. If the car had not arrived when it did, we would have been bombarded with stones.

During the first weeks' imprisonment was quite tolerable, but suddenly the prison caretakers were changed people overnight. From their behavior and conversation, which I could not understand but could figure out, I could deduce that they wanted to "finish me off." On a regular basis I received the smallest piece of bread and barely a ladleful of their soup. Never again did I get a second portion, even though each day there were leftovers. These were distributed in the cells next to me. Whenever a guard wanted to open my cell to give me some of the leftover food, he was immediately whistled back.

Here is where I learned the power of the prison caretakers. They had absolute rule. They confirmed to me again, clearly enough, my contention about the tremendous and often disastrous power which prisoner trusties can exert over their fellow prisoners. Here is where I also came to fully understand the three categories of guards.

H the prosecutor's office had not intervened, they would have finished me off, most of all mentally and emotionally. They almost had me at the breaking point. This was not feeble hysteria. I was almost totally finished at that time, and I can stand quite a bit. Life had often enough been hard for me, but the psychological torture of these three Satans was too much. I was not the only one who was mistreated like this. They also badly mistreated a few of the Polish prisoners. They have long since left this position and it is gratifyingly quiet.

I have to openly confess I never would have expected to be treated so decently and so kindly in a Polish prison as I have been since the intervention of the prosecutor's office.

XXV
Some Final Thoughts

What do I think of the Third Reich today? What is my opinion of Himmler? The SS? The concentration camps? And the Security Police? How do I now see all the events I have experienced?

I am now as I was then, as far as my philosophy of life is concerned.

I am still a National Socialist. A person who has believed in an ideology, a philosophy, for almost twenty-five years and who was bound up in it body and soul cannot simply throw it away just because the embodiment of that idea, the National Socialist state and its leaders, acted wrongly. In fact, criminally and through their failure our world collapsed and the entire German people have been plunged into unspeakable misery for decades into the future. I cannot do that.

From the discovered documents which have been published from the trial in Nuremberg, I can now see that the leadership of the Third Reich is guilty of having caused this monstrous war with all its consequences by their politics of tyranny. I can also. see that this leadership, by using extremely effective propaganda and through its use of limitless terror had made a whole nation submissive to such an extent that, with a few exceptions, the people followed in every way, wherever they were led, without criticism and without a will of their own. As far as I am concerned, the necessary expansion of the German living space could have been attained in a peaceful way.

I am firmly convinced that wars cannot be prevented, and that there will be wars again in the future. In order to veil the politics of tyranny, one simply has to use propaganda, by cleverly twisting all the facts, make the politics and the actions acceptable to the people. In order to prevent doubt and opposition from the beginning, a system of terror has to be created.

I believe that serious opposition should be conquered by the power of the superior idea. Himmler was a crudest example of the leader principle. Every German had to submit unconditionally and without criticism to the government since it alone was able to represent the true concerns of the people and to lead the people along the right path. Everyone who did not subject himself to this principle had to be removed from public life. For this purpose, Himmler created and educated his SS, created the concentration camps, the German police, and the Gestapo.

For Himmler, Germany was the only nation which had the right to exercise supremacy in Europe. All other nations were second rate. The nations with predominantly Nordic blood were to be treated favorably with the goal of incorporating them into Germany. The nations of Eastern blood were to be divided and suppressed into insignificance. They were to become serfs.

The prewar concentration camps had to become storehouses for the opponents of the state. These immediately became institutions of education for all types of asocials, and thereby served a useful purpose for the nation as a whole as a result of the cleaning up process. They had also become necessary in fighting and preventing crime. Because of the war, the concentration camps became extermination centers, directly or indirectly, for the nationalities of the conquered lands who had been fighting against the conquerors and oppressors. I have already expressed my attitude about the enemies of the state. It was wrong to exterminate the enemy nationals in any case. The resistance movement could have been reduced to insignificance if the population of the occupied countries would have been sensibly well treated, and only a few truly serious enemies would have remained.

Today I realize that the extermination of the Jews was wrong, absolutely wrong. It was exactly because of this mass extermination that Germany earned itself the hatred of the entire world. The cause of anti-Semitism was not served by this act at all, in fact, just the opposite. The Jews have come much closer to their final goal.

The Gestapo only carried out the orders of the extended police arm of Himmler. The Gestapo and the concentration camps were just the executive organ of Himmler's desires and Adolf Hitler's intentions, respectively.

How could it come to the atrocities in the concentration camps? I have already explained enough in these pages and in the personal descriptions. I never personally approved of them. I have never personally mistreated a prisoner, or even killed one. I have also never tolerated mistreatment on the part of my subordinates. Now; when I have to hear the descriptions of the horrible tortures as described during the course of this investigation that took place in Auschwitz and in other camps, I get cold shudders. It is true; I knew that Auschwitz prisoners had been mistreated by the SS, by the civilian employees, and not in the least by their own fellow prisoners. I used every means at my disposal, but I was unable to stop it. I was just as unsuccessful as other camp Kommandants, who had the same views as I did, and who were in camps which were much smaller and easier to oversee. One person is no match for the viciousness, depravity, and cruelty of a guard. The only way it could be controlled is if the guards are kept constantly in the view of the Kommandant. Generally, the worse the whole guard and the watch personnel were, the more the prisoners were mistreated. This was proven clearly enough in my present imprisonment. In the British zone, under the strictest constant surveillance, I was able to study enough of the three categories of guards. In Nuremberg individual mistreatment was not possible since all of the prisoners there were under constant observation of the jail officers.

It was only by luck that a third person walked into the lavatory at the Berlin airport during a stopover, thus preventing my being mistreated.

There was one, just one of the prison guards in Warsaw, who as soon as he came on duty in our cell block, ran from cell to cell, wherever there were Germans, and indiscriminately beat them. This happened in spite of the fact, as far as I could observe and judge from my cell, that the prison was run properly. With the exception of von Burgsdorff, who got away with only a few slaps in the face, every German there was beaten by this young man, approximately eighteen to twenty years old, out of whose eyes flickered cold hatred. He said he was a Polish Jew, even though he did not look like it at all. He certainly never got tired of beating us. Only when one of his colleagues on duty gave him a warning sign that someone was coming would he interrupt his activity. I am firmly convinced that none of the higher officials or the prison warden would have approved of his behavior. Several times I was asked by visiting officials about how I was treated, but I kept this secret because only one of them was like that. The other guards were more or less strict and unfriendly, but no one ever approached me.

So even in this small prison the warden could not prevent this behavior. How much more difficult was it in a concentration camp the size of Auschwitz. Yes, I was hard and strict. As I see it today, often too hard and too strict. Yes, I said many a bad word in anger over the deplorable

188

conditions, or the carelessness, and said many things which I never should have done. But I was never cruel, nor did I let myself get carried away to the point of mistreating prisoners. A great deal happened in Auschwitz, presumably in my name, on my direction, on my orders, about which I neither knew, nor would have tolerated, nor approved of. However, all this did take place in Auschwitz, and I. am responsible for it because according to camp regulations: the camp Kommandant is *fully responsible* for everything that happens in his camp.

I am now at the end of my life. Everything of importance which I experienced in my life, all the events which influenced me strongly, which touched me in some special way, I have laid down in these notes according to the truth and the reality as I saw it, and the way I experienced it. I have omitted a great deal that I felt was insignificant. Some of it I have forgotten, and I don't have clear in my memory anymore about a lot of events. I am also not a writer and never have been particularly skilled with the pen. I am quite certain that I have often repeated myself and probably I have not always expressed myself clearly enough. Also, I don't have the inner peace and balance to concentrate on such a labor.

I have written just as I remembered it, often mixed up, but without trying to be clever. I have written the way I was; the way I am. I lived a full and varied life. Fate led me through all the highs and lows of life. Often life dealt harshly with me and shook me, but I gritted my teeth and got through it. I have never given up. I had two guiding stars, my country and my family, which gave direction to my life ever since I returned from World War I, when I went in as a school boy and came out as a man.

My tremendous love for my country and my feeling for everything German brought me into the NSDAP [the Nazi Party] and into the SS. I believed that the National Socialist world philosophy was the only one that suited the German people. The SS was, in my opinion, the most energetic defender of this philosophy, and the only one capable of leading the German people back to a life more in keeping with its character.

My family was the second thing that was sacred to me. I am firmly anchored to it. Worrying about their future is always uppermost in my mind. The farm was supposed to be our homestead. My wife and I saw in the children our purpose in life. It was to be our life's task to enable them to get a good education and create a stable home life for them. And that's why now most of my thoughts deal mainly with only my family.

What will become of them? This uncertainty concerning my family is what makes my present imprisonment so difficult. As far as I am concerned, I have written myself off right from the beginning. I do not worry about this anymore. I am finished with it. But my wife, my children? Fate has played strange tricks on me. How many times did I miss death by a hair: in the last war, in the Free Corps battles, during work-related accidents, the car accident in 1941 on the Autobahn, where I drove into a tractor trailer with no lights. I was able to recognize it in a split second and was able to jerk the car aside. We ran into it sideways so that even though the car was squeezed together like an accordion, the three of us escaped with just cuts and bruises. Then in 1942 I had a riding accident where I wound up lying next to a stone just as the heavy stallion crashed down onto me and came away with only broken ribs. And again during air raids; so often I wouldn't have bet a dime on my chances, and yet I came through it all. Also, in the car accident just before the evacuation of Ravensbrück. Everyone thought I was dead; the way things looked I couldn't possibly still be alive. Then the vial of poison broke before I was arrested.

Everywhere fate has spared me from death only to do away with me now in such a shameful manner. How I envy my comrades who were allowed to die an honest soldier's death. Without realizing it, I became a cog in the wheel of the huge extermination machine of the Third Reich. The machine is smashed, the motor has perished, and I must perish with it. The world demands it.

I would never have allowed myself to open up about myself or to expose my most secret inner self had it not been for the humanity and understanding with which I have been treated. It has totally disarmed me. I never ever could have expected this kind treatment. I owe it to this humane understanding to contribute, as far as it is possible for me, and to shed light on events which needed clarification. I do ask, however, that when these notes are evaluated, all things concerning my family, and all of my tender emotions, my most secret doubts, not be revealed to the public. May the general public simply go on seeing me as the bloodthirsty beast, the cruel sadist, the murderer of millions, because the broad masses cannot conceive the Kommandant of Auschwitz in any other way. They would never be able to understand that he also had a heart and that he was not evil.

These notes comprise 114 pages. I have written all this down voluntarily and without being forced.

- Krakow, February 1947 Rudolf Höss

The Selection

XXVI

The Final Letters to His Wife and Children

11 April 1947

My dear good Mutz!

My path through life is now coming to a close. Fate has worked out a truly sad ending for me. Row fortunate were the comrades who were allowed to die an honest soldier's death.

Calmly and composed I look toward the end. From the beginning I was completely clear about the fact that I would perish with the world to which I had pledged myself with all my body and soul when that world was shattered and destroyed. Without realizing it, I had become a cog in the terrible German extermination machine. My activities in performing my task were out in the open. Since I was the Kommandant of the extermination camp Auschwitz I was totally responsible for everything that happened there, whether I knew about it or not. Most of the terrible and horrible things that took place there I learned only during this investigation and during the trial itself. I cannot describe how I was deceived, how my directives were twisted, and all the things they had carried out supposedly under my orders. I certainly hope that the guilty will not escape justice.

It is tragic that, although I was by nature gentle, good-natured, and very helpful, I became the greatest destroyer of human beings who carried out every order to exterminate people no matter what. The goal of the many years of rigid SS training was to make each SS soldier a tool without its own will who would carry out blindly all of Himmler's plans. That is the reason why I also became a blind, obedient robot who carried out every order.

My fanatic patriotism and my most exaggerated sense of duty were good prerequisites for this training. At the end it is difficult to have to admit to myself that I have chosen a very wrong path and, because of it, I have brought about my own destruction.

But what good does all the weighing and balancing do? Was it right or was it wrong? In my opinion all our paths through life are predestined by fate and a wise providence, and are unchangeable.

Painful, bitter, and heavy-hearted is the separation from all of you, from you dearest best Mutz, and from all of you, my dear good children, and that I have to leave you behind, poor unfortunates, in poverty and misery.

On you, my poor unfortunate wife, destiny has put the heaviest burden on us through our sad fate. For in addition to our unlimited pain of being torn apart, there is the burdensome worry about your future life and the worry about the children. But dearest, be consoled! Don't despair!

Time has a way of healing even the deepest, most serious wounds, which you cannot believe you can survive in the first painful moments. Millions of families have been torn apart or have been destroyed by this wretched war.

But life goes on. The children grow up. I only hope that you, dearest, best Mutz, may be given the strength and health so that you can care for all of them until they all can stand on their own two feet.

My misspent life places on you, dearest, the holy obligation to educate our children so that they have, in their deepest heart, a true humanity. Our dear children are all naturally good-natured. Nurture all of these good impulses in their hearts in every way. Make them sensitive to all human sorrow. What humanity is, I have only come to know since I have been in Polish prisons. Although I have inflicted so much destruction and sorrow upon the Polish people as Kommandant of Auschwitz, even though I did not do it personally, or by my own free will, they still showed such human understanding, not only by the higher officials, but also by the common guards, that it often puts me to shame. Many of them were former prisoners in Auschwitz or other camps. Especially now, during my last days, I am experiencing such humane treatment I never could have expected.

In spite of everything that happened, they still treat me as a human being.

My dear good Mutz, I beg you, don't become hardened by the heavy blows fate has dealt us! Keep your good heart for yourself! Don't be led astray by troubles or hardship and misery through which you are forced to endure! Don't lose your faith in humanity. Try, as soon as possible, to get away from those dreary surroundings. Start the proceedings to change your name. Take back your maiden name again. Now there should not be any more difficulties about that! My name is now disgraced throughout the whole world, and you, my poor ones, have suffered unnecessary problems time and again because of my name, especially the children, who will be held back from future advancement. Certainly Klaus would have had an apprenticeship long ago if his name had not been Höss.It is for the best that my name disappears with me.

I also received permission to enclose my wedding ring in this letter to you.

With sadness and happiness, I think of that time in the spring of our life when we exchanged the rings. Who could have guessed this kind of end of our life together?

"Days in the sun" were not granted us, but instead there were difficult toils, much sorrow, and worry. Only step by step did we get ahead. How happy we were through our children, whom you, dearest, best Mutz happily bore for us time and again. In our children we saw our life's task. Our constant concern was to create a home as a steady foothold for them, and to raise them to be useful human beings. Time and again during my imprisonment I have gone back over our life together, remembering all the events and happenings, over and over. What happy hours we were allowed to experience, but we also had to suffer a great deal of deprivation, illness, grief, and heartbreak.

I thank you with all my heart, my dear good friend, for all the goodness and beauty you brought into my life, and which you, at all times, shared bravely and faithfully with me, and also for your endless love and care for me. Forgive me, you good woman, if I have ever offended you, or hurt you.

How deeply and painfully I regret every hour that I did not spend with you, dearest and best Mutz, and the children because I believed duty would not allow it, or there were other commitments which I thought were more important.

A kind fate has allowed me to hear from you, dear ones. I received all eleven letters dated from December 31 to December 16. How happy I was therefore, especially during the days of the trial, to read your dear lines. Your care and love for me and the dear Smalltalk of the children gave me new courage and strength to withstand everything. I am particularly grateful, my dearest, for the last letter, which you wrote Sunday during the early hours. It was as if you had a premonition that these would be the very last words that reached me. How bravely and clearly you write about everything. But what bitter sorrow, what deep pain can be found between the lines. I do know how intimately both our lives are intertwined, how hard this having to leave one another is.

I wrote to you, my dear good Mutz, on Christmas, on January 26, and on March 3, and March 16, and hope you have received these letters. But how little can be said in writing, and especially under these circumstances.

How much has to be left unsaid, which cannot be done in writing. But we have to make the best of it. I am so grateful that I could learn even a little about you, and that I could still tell you, dearest, essentially what moved me.

All my life I have been a reserved person. I never liked to let anyone look into me, to see what moved me in my innermost soul, and I always settled everything inside myself.

How often have you, dearest, regretted that, and found it painful, that you yourself, who stood nearest me, could be only such a small part in my inner life. And so I dragged with me all my doubts and depressions for many years about whether what I was doing was right or wrong and whether the harsh orders given to me were necessary. I could not and was not allowed to express my opinions to anyone. You, dearest good Mutz, can now understand why I became more and more reserved, and more and more unapproachable. And you, dearest Mutz, and all of you loved ones, inadvertently had to suffer from that, and could not explain to yourselves my discontent, my absentmindedness, and my often grumpy manner. But that's the way it was; I regret it painfully. During my long and lonely imprisonment I've had enough time on my hands to think exhaustively about my life. I have thoroughly reviewed every aspect of my actions. Based on my present knowledge I can see today clearly, severely and bitterly for me, that the entire ideology about the world in which I believed so firmly and unswervingly was based on completely wrong premises and had to absolutely collapse one day.

And so my actions in the service of this ideology were completely wrong, even though I faithfully believed the idea was correct. Now it was very logical that strong doubts grew within me, and whether my turning away from my belief in God was based on completely wrong premises. It was a hard struggle. But I have again found my faith in my God. Dearest,

I cannot write more about these things. It would just lead to too much.

Should you in your misery, my dear good Mutz, find through the Christian faith strength and consolation, then follow the urge of your heart. Don't be led astray by anything. Also, you don't have to do what I have done. You should make your own decision about your Lord. The children will in any case, because of school, walk a different path than the one we have taken. Klaus may later wish to decide for himself, after he has matured, and maybe find his own way.

And so there is only a pile of rubble left from our world from which the survivors have to build a new and better world with great difficulty.

My time has come.

Now it is time to say the final goodbyes to you loved ones, you who were dearest to me in all the world!

How hard and painful this parting is.

You, dearest best Mutz, I thank with all my heart once more for all your love and care and for all that you brought into my life! Through our dear and good children I will always be with you, you my poor, unfortunate wife. I leave with confident hope that after all the difficulty and sadness, you, my loved ones, will be allowed to find a small spot on the sunny side of life, and that you will find a modest chance at life and that you, my dear good Mutz, will be accorded through our children a quiet and content happiness.

All my intimate good wishes accompany all of you dear ones on your life's journey to come. I thank with all my heart all of the dear, good people who stood by you in your hour of need and helped you, and I send my best regards.

My last dear greetings go to my parents, to Fritz and to all our dear old friends.

For the last time I send to you loved ones my regards, to you all my dear good children, my Annemausl, my Burling, my Puppi, my Kindi and my Klaus, and to you, my dearest best Mutz.

Oh you, my poor, unfortunate wife, most most dear and with a heavy heart.

Keep me in loving remembrance.

Until my last breath, I remain with all my loved ones.

Your Daddy

You, my dear, good children!

Your daddy has to leave you now. For you, poor ones, there remains only your dear, good Mommy. May she remain with you for a good long time yet. You do not understand yet what your good Mommy really means to you, and what a precious possession she is to you. The love and care of a mother is the most beautiful and valuable thing that exists on this earth. I realized this a long time ago, only when it was too late; and I have regretted it all my life.

To you, my dear good children, I address therefore my last (beseeching) request: Never forget your dear good mother! She has constantly taken care of you with such sacrificing love. Her life concerned only you. How much of the good things in life has she sacrificed for your sake? How she feared for you when you were ill and how painfully and untiringly did she nurse all of you. She was never at ease when all of you were not around her. Only for your sake must she suffer now all of the bitter misery and poverty. Don't ever forget this throughout your whole life.

Help her now to carry her painful fate. Be loving and good to her.

Help her as well as you can with your limited strength. In this manner pay her part of the thanks for the love and care she gave you during the days and nights.

Klaus, my dear good boy!

You are the oldest. You are now going out into the world. You have to now make your own way through life. With your own strength you must now shape your life. You have good aptitudes. Use them! Keep your good heart. Become a person who lets himself be guided primarily by warmth and humanity.

Learn to think and to judge for yourself, responsibly. Don't accept everything without criticism and as absolutely true, everything which is brought to your attention. Learn from life. The biggest mistake of my life was that I believed everything faithfully which came from the top, and I didn't dare to have the least bit of doubt about the truth of that which was presented to me.

Walk through life with your eyes open. Don't become one-sided; examine the pros and cons in all matters.

In all your undertakings, don't just let your mind speak, but listen above all to the voice in your heart. Much, my dear boy, will not be understood by you as yet. But always remember my last advice.

I wish you, my dear Klaus, all the luck in your life. Become a competent, straightforward person who has his heart in the right place.

Kindi and Puppi, You my big girls!

You are yet too young to learn the extent of the hard fate dished out to us. But you especially, my dear good girls, are specially obligated to stand at your poor unfortunate mother's side and with love assist her in every way you can. Surround her with all your childlike love from your heart and show her how much you love her and show her how much you want to help her in her need. I can only beseech you, listen to your dear good mother! She will now in her devoted love and care show you the right way and will bestow on you those lessons you will need for life in order to become good and capable human beings.

As fundamentally different as you two are in your character, you both, my dear [Puppi], and you, my dear Hausmiitterle, have, however, soft and feeling hearts. Retain these throughout your later life. This is the most important thing. Only later will you understand that and will you remember my last words.

My Burling, you dear little guy! Hang on to your happy child disposition.

The cruel life will tear you, my dear boy, soon enough away from your child's world. I was happy to hear from your dear mother that you are progressing so well in school.

Your dear father is unable to tell you anything more. You poor little guy have now only your dear good Mommy left who will care for you. Listen to her with love and kindness and so remain "Daddy's dear Burling."

My dear Annemausl,

How little was I permitted to experience your dear little personality.

Your dear good Mommy will have to take you, my dear Mausl, for us into her arms and tell you of your daddy, and how very much he loved you.

May you be for a long time Mommy's little ray of sun and continue to give her much joy. May you, with your sunny ways, help your poor dear Mommy through all the dreary hours.

Once more from my heart I ask you all, my dear good children, take to heart my last words. Think of them again and again.

Keep in loving memory,

Your *Dad*

[The following note was attached to the above letters and is the last thing that Rudolf Höss wrote.]

To the First States Attorney of the Highest National Court at *Warsaw*.

By way of the First States Attorney at the Court of *Wadowice*.

I most respectfully request that the enclosed last letter and the wedding ring be delivered officially to my wife.

I have submitted this request to the Highest National Court during my final summation.

Wadowice, on the 12th of April, 1947 [signed] Rudolf Höss

Unloading a Transport

Manuscript Page of Höss's Memoir

Part III
Profiles of the Camps

Sachsenhausen Prisoner Drawing

XXVII

Rules and Regulations for Concentration Camps

These rules for the camps were instituted in 1936 and were meant to be a draft only, and, as such, temporary.

Fundamental and detailed camp rules based on experience were supposed to be written later.

In this sense, I have written down the essentials of the camp rules and regulations to the best of my memory. Krakow, October 1, 1946 Rudolf Höss

Purpose of the Camps: The destructive, subversive activities of the enemies of the state shall be neutralized by putting them in protective custody in a concentration camp.

Asocial elements who had brought harm to the entire nation shall be rehabilitated to become useful people again by educating them to order, cleanliness, and regular work.

Incorrigible criminals who constantly had relapses into crime shall be excluded from the German people by being put away safely.

Organization of the Concentration Camps

I Kommandant's Office

Camp Kommandant Adjutant-Master Sergeant Mail Censorship Office

II Political Division

Director of Political Division Records Department

III Protective Custody Camps

Protective Custody Camp Commander Officer of the Day [Rapportführer] Block Leader

Labor Service Leader Kommando Leader

IV Administration Administrative Director

Prisoner Property Administration Camp Engineer

V Camp Doctor

VI Guard Troops Duty Officer

I Kommandant's Office

The *camp Kommandant* is responsible for the entire camp in every way.

His first duty is to guarantee the security of the camp permanently.

He is to be available at all times. Every important event in the camp must be reported to him immediately.

If he leaves the area of the camp, he must delegate in writing his deputy to take control of the camp. He then is fully responsible in the Kommandant's absence for the entire camp. The protective custody camp commander is always the deputy. Upon the Kommandant's return, he returns control of the camp, again in writing, to the Kommandant, If the Kommandant is away for more than twenty-four hours, he must have the approval of the inspector of concentration camps. The Kommandant must be constantly alert and must be able to handle any situation that may arise. His decisions should be clear and well thought out because the consequences often have great significance.

In case of an emergency such as an escape attempt or a rebellion, the entire Guard Battalion down to the last man is at his disposal. For the duration of the emergency, the camp Kommandant has full power to give all orders, and he determines the course of actions taken.

The officers of the guard companies are at that time subordinate to the Kommandant.

The Kommandant must lecture and instruct those officers and men who are subordinate to him about their duties and jobs, especially about camp security and how to deal with prisoners.

In order to put every prisoner to work, the Kommandant must create suitable work. He must oversee all jobs.

The Kommandant determines the duration of the prisoners' workday as well as the time to move out to the work sites and return to camp.

Inspections of the camp must have the authorization of Himmler or the inspector of concentration camps.

All inspections must be led by the Kommandant, unless he is absent, then his deputy must lead the inspection.

After the inspection is completed, those who inspected the camp must be sworn to keep secret all they saw.

The adjutant is the first assistant to the Kommandant and has a special position of trust. He must ensure that no important event in the camp remains unknown to the Kommandant.

The adjutant is the superior of all noncommissioned officers and men of -the Kommandant's staff. All of the incoming mail is presented to the adjutant who looks it over and then separates it for the different departments and units.

He handles all correspondence of the Kommandant's office with offices outside the camp and departments.

He signs F.A. or A.B. on all those documents which are not important or have a repetitious content.

He is the caseworker of the Kommandant's staff and proposes all nominations and promotions to the Kommandant.

He also works on disciplinary matters and watches over the Penalty Book.

He is particularly responsible for appointments and their dates.

All confidential matters are personally worked on by him and he is responsible for their safekeeping.

In case there is no officer or noncommissioned officer available to teach the ideology of the Third Reich, the adjutant must take care of teaching the Kommandant's staff himself.

All of the news organization of the camp comes under the control of the adjutant. He is responsible for the entire news mechanism functioning smoothly.

He is responsible for the arms, ammunition, and all the equipment of the Kommandant's staff. By continuously inventorying supplies, he has to ensure that everything that must be there-is there.

During the daily change of the guard, the officer of the day and the first watch commander report to the adjutant, present their duty reports for his information, and sign them.

As additional assistants, the adjutant may use the staff sergeant and several capable noncommissioned officers from the Kommandant's staff.

The adjutant is in charge of vehicle and driver readiness.

He is responsible for the orderly and correct issue of all orders pertaining to transportation.

The *director of the Mail Censorship Office* is subordinate to the camp Kommandant and is responsible for the dispatch of all mail in and out of the concentration camp.

For censoring the prisoner mail, he has SS men from the Kommandant's staff at his disposal.

The prisoner mail must be read painstakingly and in detail in order to prevent undesired communication *with or from* the outside. Objectionable mail is to be placed in the prisoner's file.

If there is any suspicion of actual dissemination of nonpermitted news about the camp or exchanged letters with families or similar offenses, the Kommandant can order surveillance of the mail of the identified SS families. This mail surveillance *has to be carried out personally by the director of the Mail Censorship Office.*

II Political Department

The director of the Political Department is always an official of the Gestapo or of the Federal Criminal Police Bureau [Kripo].

He is at the camp Kommandant's disposal and is responsible for the Political Department.

In carrying out his duties as an official of the Gestapo or the Kripo Main Office, whichever is responsible for a particular concentration camp, he may use suitable members of the Kommandant's staff as additional assistants.

The director of the Political Department conducts investigations of prisoners by order of the police departments, courts, and the Camp Kommandant.

He is responsible for the prisoner card index and the orderly entry of data in the prison files.

He is also responsible for registering new arrivals and setting up files for them. If any records are missing, he has to demand them.

It is his responsibility to verify the correct dates of prisoner transfers to the various police departments and court dates.

In order to make available directors' reports, he directs the appropriate files to the camp Kommandant and keeps track of the dates for appointments.

When a release has been ordered, he must notify the appropriate police department and carry out the release.

When a prisoner has an accident, he must carry out the investigation. If an unnatural death has occurred, he must notify the district attorney and demand that a coroner perform an autopsy. In all cases of death, he must notify the closest relative.

He must order the transport of the body to the nearest crematory.

If the family of the deceased prisoner wishes to receive the urn containing the ashes, he must direct this to be sent to the cemetery of the home town of the prisoner.

After a prisoner escapes, he must take all necessary steps to have the local police departments take immediate action.

Any change in the status of the prisoner, such as release, transfer, death, and escape must be reported to the appropriate intake officer.

Attached to the Political Department is the Records Department. Every prisoner is listed therein. There must be photographs taken, fingerprints, exact personal data, and complete descriptions for each prisoner, all of which must be included in the prisoner file.

III Protective Custody Camp

The *protective custody camp commander* is responsible for the entire area of the prisoner camp. By utilizing an appropriate surveillance system, he must at all times be aware of all the events occurring in the camp.

He must pay particular attention that the prisoners are treated strictly but fairly. He must report any mistreatment immediately to the Kommandant,

After carefully searching through the files, he chooses which prisoner becomes a block leader, Kapo, or other functionary, and installs them in their jobs. If a prisoner turns out to be unsuitable for the job, he must immediately relieve him of his duty. All new arrivals are to be immediately informed of the camp regulations.

Also it is his responsibility to instruct all released, all transferred, and all exchanged prisoners to keep the strictest secrecy as to what they saw and experienced while in the camp. He must carefully scrutinize the reports to the Gestapo and the Kripo headquarters. After listening to the block leaders, those prisoners not known to him are paraded before him so he can form a mental picture of the new prisoners.

Any punishment report must be checked over carefully and he must personally interview every prisoner. He makes his judgment about the prisoner and proposes to the Kommandant the length of time to be served by that prisoner.

By constantly checking the work sites, he must know how much work was accomplished.

He must use all measures in order to prevent a prisoner escape.

The prisoners who are suspected of escaping must be identified, marked, and must not be assigned to any work outside the protective custody camp.

Each time the prisoners march out of the camp to their various work sites or into the camp, he must be present.

He must immediately eliminate any adverse condition which may arise. Sick prisoners must be put in the hospital. He must pay particular attention to the utmost cleanliness and orderliness in the whole camp area.

Through periodic checks, he must convince himself that every prisoner receives the food he is entitled to. He has to watch over the preparation of the food by sampling the food.

Camp detention must always be checked by him.

All camp personnel in the protective custody camp must be present at lectures by the protective custody camp commander, especially those pertaining to the mistreatment of prisoners!

The *duty officer* is responsible to the protective custody camp commander for an exact prisoner count at roll call. He has to be apprised of any change in the protective custody camp.

He must ensure punctuality when prisoners are presented to the camp commander for roll call, or to the doctor, appointments at the Political Department and other departments of the Kommandant's office. He must also have the prisoners ready on time when their release or transfer comes up.

The duty officer is the superior of the block leaders, regulates their duties and watches over them. Block leaders not suited for this position must be reported to the camp commander for a replacement.

Any poor condition of the camp must be reported by him to the camp commander.

Any punishment ordered by the Kommandant or the camp commander must be carried out by him and a written report of it must be submitted.

The *block leaders* are responsible for a certain number of prisoners who are assigned to them. They are responsible for order and cleanliness in the assigned barracks and have to supervise the respective block elders, room elders, clerks, etc. They have to be able to give an opinion about every single prisoner assigned to them.

At the various work sites, they must perform control patrols in order to keep themselves informed of the work accomplished by the prisoners.

The *block leader of the day* supervises the main gate to the protective custody camp. During the marching in and marching out of the prisoners, he is responsible for an accurate count of the prisoner columns marching through. Those prisoners who move out without a guard have to be exactly accounted for in order to discover any possible escape attempt early enough.

Anyone not permitted to enter the camp, whether he is a member of the SS or a civilian employee, must be refused entry by him.

Any disagreements have to be reported immediately to the camp commander.

The *work Kommando leader* puts together the work Kommandos according to occupations and abilities and has to be ready when work Kommandos are demanded.

He selects the Kapos and foremen and recommends them to the camp commander.

On the day before a work Kommando is needed, he requisitions the necessary guards from the guard company. He has to take care in issuing the correct work orders and in the selection of the work Kommandos.

By constant controls of all of the work places he must be exactly informed about the progress of all work. If he finds any problems, he must report them immediately to the camp commander.

For major work projects, there are designated work Kommando leaders.

They are responsible for the entire work Kommando. Their job is to make certain the prisoners are working in their fields of expertise and that no stoppage of work occurs.

IV Administration

The *first administration officer* is responsible for housing, food, clothing, and wages for the Kommandant's staff, as well as the housing, food, and clothing for the prisoners.

He is advisor to the Kommandant in all economic matters and has to report to him all important events.

He must pay particular attention to the shelter, the clothing, and, above all, the food supply of the prisoners. He constantly checks and personally knows about the preparation of meals. The prisoners are to be adequately fed.

Problems which arise that the first officer cannot solve must be reported immediately to the Kommandant.

Special emphasis must be placed on always having a specified amount of supplies on reserve. There are officers and noncommissioned officers at the disposal of the first officer to help him.

The Department of Prisoner Property Administration is under the supervision of the first administrative officer. The prisoner property administrator is responsible for all the stored personal belongings of the prisoners.

Prisoner civilian clothing is to be free of all vermin and cleanly stored; the valuables are to be kept safely in strongboxes. There must be an exact accounting for all prisoner items, and the prisoner must countersign an itemized list. In case of death, all prisoner items are to be sent to the next of kin.

The money brought into camp by the prisoner or sent to him from the outside will be deposited to a special account by the Prisoner Money Administration. Every prisoner can draw up to fifteen marks per week from this account to buy things in the camp store. If so desired, every prisoner can check his account.

The prisoner property administrator is responsible for making sure the prisoner's insurance policy does not lapse.

Social security contributions are to be made by the administration.

Private insurance policies have to be paid for by the prisoner himself.

The *camp engineer* is subordinate to the *administration*. He is responsible for all the technical installations of the camp, especially for the daily testing of the security installations, such as the electrified barbed-wire fence, inside and outside camp lighting of the walls and fences, the spotlights, and the sirens. He is responsible for the water supply for the camp and also the drainage. He is in charge of the fire brigade and is responsible for their training and constant readiness.

He has to order all repairs to the camp area and supervise them.

For the various special fields of work, he has at his disposal trained noncommissioned officers.

V Camp Doctor

The camp doctor is responsible for the medical care of the whole camp and for all the sanitary facilities. He must supervise the hygiene of the protective custody camp with special care in order to prevent any contagious disease or epidemic from breaking out.

New arrivals are to given a thorough medical examination and if there is any doubt, they must be sent to quarantine for observation.

Those prisoners working in the prisoner kitchen and the SS kitchen are placed under constant doctor's observation for possible infectious diseases.

The camp doctor randomly checks the cleanliness of the prisoners. Those prisoners who report sick must be examined daily by the camp doctor.

Fakers who want to get out of work must be reported by the camp doctor for punishment.

In case it is necessary, the doctor must transfer sick prisoners to a nearby hospital for professional treatment.

Should a prisoner need dental treatment, a dentist is at his disposal.

Whether the dental treatment is necessary is the camp doctor's decision.

The camp doctor must continuously inspect the kitchen himself regarding the preparation of the food and the quality of the food supply.

Any deficiencies that may arise must be reported to the camp Kommandant.

Accidents are to be treated carefully in order not to lose the full productivity of the prisoners.

Those prisoners who are to be released or transported must see the camp doctor for examination.

Subordinate to the camp doctor are the attached doctors, dentists, and medics as well as prisoner health care workers in the hospital.

The camp doctor is the advisor to the Kommandant in all medical and sanitary matters.

All medical problems of the camp as they become known must be reported at once to the Kommandant.

All reports the camp doctor is required to submit to his immediate superior must first be submitted to the Kommandant for his information.

VI Guard Troops

The Guard Battalion is independent. The officer of the Guard Battalion makes available to the Kommandant the daily required number of officers, noncommissioned officers, and men for guard duty and to escort prisoners.

For the duration of their duty, the duty officer, the guards, and the prisoners are under direct orders and disciplinary powers of the camp Kommandant.

A contingent of guards must be in a state of readiness within the confines of the camp in case of an alarm and must be ready to take action immediately.

In case of an emergency situation, the entire Guard Battalion comes under the direct order of the camp Kommandant.

The guard battalion is to be painstakingly trained in a military fashion.

However, the safety of the camp takes preference over military training.

The officer of the guard company is responsible for the instruction of every officer, noncommissioned officer, and SS man extensively about his duties when guarding or escorting prisoners. He also must instruct in the use of weapons and about associating with prisoners, especially about the prohibition on mistreating prisoners. These points concerning the prisoners must be constantly stressed in the ongoing instruction by the company commanders.

In order to educate the SS man to his highest sense of duty, the toughest discipline against violations and offenses against the prevailing orders must be severely punished, especially guard violations, misuse of weapons, forbidden associations with prisoners, mistreatment of prisoners, carelessness and negligence in the guarding of prisoners.

If the punishment is beyond the authorization of the camp commander, the punishment reports must be immediately sent to the inspector of concentration camps.

The duty officer, who is changed daily and is in charge of the guards, is subordinate to the Kommandant. The duty officer's first line of responsibility is the security of the camp.

The duty officer is in constant control of all guards and sentries and their weapons. He repeatedly checks all security devices of the camp. Any defects must be repaired or reported at once.

He has to be present when the prisoners march out; it is his duty to send back any work Kommandos which do not have enough guards with them.

In case of danger, he must take the necessary steps until the arrival of the Kommandant or his deputy.

Camp Punishments

The following punishments are given to prisoners who violate order and discipline:

A. warning

B. punishment labor during leisure time

C. transfer to the punishment company for a certain time, up to one year

D. detention

E. hard detention with partial withdrawal of food

F. detention in darkness of up to forty-two days

G. corporal punishment of up to twenty-five lashes with a cane.

Punishments *a* are handed out by the camp Kommandant. Punishment *g* is given only by order of the inspector of concentration camps or Himmler.

The basis for a report for punishment can only come from a member of the SS or a prisoner functionary. The camp commander must immediately check into this punishment report and present it to the camp Kommandant. He alone decides and demands the appropriate punishment.

The application to administer corporal punishment can only then be made by the Kommandant: a) if with repeat offenders, all punishments which are under the Kommandant's authority have failed; b) if the violation or offence of the prisoner is such that punishments *a* through fare not enough for the misdeed committed.

To apply for further punishment, the correct form must be filled out in triplicate.

It must contain all the personal information about the prisoner to be punished; a short and clear description of the misdeed; and naming the time and place and the exact number of lashes proposed to the Kommandant.

The prisoner to be punished must be presented to the doctor with his forms. The doctor makes the decision if corporal punishment can or cannot be administered to the prisoner and attaches his decision to the form. Those over fifty years old, disabled war veterans, frail, and handicapped are excluded from corporal punishment.

After the Kommandant fulfills his responsibility by signing the form, it must be sent by the quickest way to the inspector of concentration camps for his decision.

If the petition is granted, the caning is to be carried out immediately in the presence of the Kommandant, the camp commander and a doctor. Two block leaders shall administer the punishment. The caning will be administered to the buttocks only.

For purposes of deterrence, the punishment can be carried out in front of the assembled prisoners.

After punishment has been administered, the camp commander, the doctor, and the two block leaders must sign all the forms in order to certify that the punishment has been carried out.

Work Deployment

The complete deployment of the labor service of the prisoners in a concentration camp is placed under the work Kommando leader. He in turn is responsible to Bureau D II of the Economic Headquarters for the proper deployment of all prisoners according to their professional background and their ability to produce.

All prisoners of a camp are to be in a so-called job, file which is kept and worked on only by the work Kommando leader.

Every month, D II must be notified how many prisoners of each profession are available. Prisoners who had an important and rare professional background must be reported by name, such as diamond cutter, optical lens grinder, precision tool maker, watchmaker, tool maker, etc. These prisoners are like a historic treasure, protected at all times. Their deployment is determined strictly by D II only.

Every work project, that means every prisoner work deployment, must have the approval of D II.

They also have to approve new work sites, as well as the existing work projects if they want to enlarge them. Outside firms such as arms factories, mining companies and other strategic firms that want concentration camp labor must apply through the proper channels, namely the armaments commander of D II. They then determine through the War Ministry the urgency of the proposal. In the meantime, the camp Kommandant and the work Kommando leader instantly determine the logistics of guarding and feeding these prisoners. Based on this, recommendations are then made to D II. Large work projects are checked over personally by the chief of D II. After D II presents its case, the chief of headquarters, Pohl, following established, prioritized lists, checks all aspects, and then makes contingents of prisoners available. Requests for prisoners are then received after applying to the camp Kommandant and work Kommando leaders or D II respectively, who either approve or refuse.

But it happened repeatedly that Himmler ordered the deployment of prisoners over the rejection of the camp Kommandant, the work Kommando leader and even D II because of its importance to the war effort or because it would lead to victory. This was done even though the housing and food were totally inadequate or the work was totally unsuitable to prisoners. Himmler got his way even over the objections of Pohl and paid no attention whatsoever to anyone. The work Kommando leader had a few noncommissioned officers at his disposal for carrying out his task. The overwhelming part of the "work," however, was carried out by prisoners, while the noncommissioned officers had their hands full just to take care of the guard duty. For example, the work Kommando leader had to reinforce the existing Kommandos daily or change them around according to the situational requirements. Since it was impossible to know among the thousands of prisoners who was suited for a particular Kommando, he had to rely upon the prisoners, who recommended suitable workers and, often on their own, brought the Kommandos up to strength or altered them. The same principle was followed in forming new Kommandos. It was only natural that the worst violations and the worst switches occurred during this process. It happened that there were countless good opportunities to escape, especially in the Kommandos outside the camp. It was also possible for prisoners who had friends in a desired Kommando to "change his profession," and so get into a more suitable or easy Kommando. In the same manner, the Kapos played their games to get the prisoners they wanted for their Kommandos, Of course, if there were prisoners they didn't like or want, the Kapos arranged for them to suffer punishment by being railroaded to a tough Kommando,

Originally every Kommando had to be supervised by an SS soldier and the work Kommando leader, who was supposed to be with them until the work detail was finished.

But long before the war, as the camp enlarged so did the number of work projects, thereby also increasing the need to guard the prisoners. The effect of all this led to an increase in the use of Kapos and foremen in the guarding and supervision of the labor details.

According to Himmler's order, all juvenile prisoners were to receive vocational training in a suitable trade. Special emphasis was to be placed on the training of stone cutters and construction workers.

The work Kommando leader had the job of guarding these apprentice training sites, and he was required also to have suitable teachers at his disposal.

These apprentices were also to receive better room and board. It was possible to do this in the older camps, but it was impossible at Auschwitz, because in that camp there was always a shortage of housing and increasing numbers all the time.

However, even in Auschwitz the apprentices received extra food rations. It was possible for the leader of the guard troop to supervise both the Kapos and prisoners depending on size and clear visibility of a work Kommando. If this was impossible, then the work Kommando within the chain of guards was strictly left to the Kapos and his foremen. As for the control of these Kommandos, only a few totally inadequate SS soldiers were available. The supervisory personnel furnished by the firms for whom the prisoners worked were undependable. These people also liked to leave everything to the Kapos and foremen to handle. This is how they became dependent on them. This dependence increased steadily, since they were no match for the shrewd and often mentally superior Kapos. This in turn led to a mutual cover-up of rampant negligence and abuse. Of course, the prisoners paid for all this to the detriment of the camp or to the firms deploying the prisoners. The camp commander constantly lectured the Kapos and foremen about not mistreating prisoners.

All violations were to be reported when the prisoners marched in after work. This was done by only a few Kapos, as most of them inflicted the punishment themselves according to the way they felt. If a Kapo was actually caught beating a prisoner, he himself was then subject to corporal punishment. But this did not deter the others from continuing the beatings. All that happened was that they became more cautious. Their abuses were naturally supported by men like Fritzsch, Seidler, Aumeier, and Palitzsch. Even among those SS noncommissioned officers and SS soldiers who controlled things, there were those who saw *nothing* when the Kapos beat the prisoners, or, in fact, even asked them to beat the prisoners.

The SS soldiers of the Kommandant's staff, the troops, as well as all bureaus who employed prisoners were constantly given lectures on how to treat prisoners, especially about the prohibition on mistreating the prisoners. I seem also to remember that some SS soldiers of the guard troop were brought before the SS court and received severe punishment for mistreating prisoners. Even though the SS guards had the authority to put prisoners on report who lagged in their work, they had no right to punish them for violations. If a prisoner committed an offense such as willful laziness, negligence, actual maliciousness in his work, or similar offenses, he was to be reported to the camp commander during the evening march into the camp.

In the same manner all the guard personnel at the arms factories and at other work sites were constantly reminded about the treatment of prisoners through printed pamphlets or in class lectures. Particular emphasis was placed on the fact that no one had the right to punish a prisoner or indeed abuse him.

If it was reported that in one plant, a prisoner was beaten, then an immediate investigation was ordered by either the Kommandant or the labor project leader. These investigations always were without results because the prisoners *never* remembered who had beaten them. To be sure, the director of the firm was notified in no uncertain terms that the prisoners would be withdrawn if any further mistreatment occurred; the result was that nothing happened there anymore. But it was not possible to eliminate these things altogether because of the constantly deteriorating situation. The replacement personnel in the factories became increasingly worse; the factory directors had lost control.

During his constant rounds the labor project leader had to pay particular attention to the treatment of prisoners by the factory personnel. However, this was an almost impossible task because there were so many factories and they were spread far and wide!

Listed below are the offenses which were punishable while the prisoners were at work:

Obvious laziness, shirking work, intentional negligence, or intentional sabotage, slovenly use of tools or machines, neglectful misplacement or loss of tools.

If a punishment report was made, it had to be from an authorized guard; an SS officer on control rounds; a Kapo; foreman; or the supervisory personnel of a firm, a factory, or a construction firm. After *the concerned prisoner* had a hearing from the camp commander, he *was punished accordingly by the camp Kommandant.*

It was the decision of the camp commander to prepare the proper punishment on the form sent on to the camp Kommandant.

The camp Kommandant had the authority to pronounce the following penalties:

Arrest up to forty-two days with intensifications, such as food deprivations, deprivation of the camp, darkened cell, and chains for the real troublemakers.

Penalty standing up to six hours with deprivation of one meal.

Transfer to the punishment company for a designated time.

Punishment by lashes with a cane could only be requested by the camp Kommandant and then only after certain criteria had been met and it is recommended by the camp doctor.

Permission to carry out corporal punishment for women was given exclusively by Himmler himself and for the men by the inspector of concentration camps.

Penalties 2 and 3 in the 1936 Camp Regulations were not in force until later, by Himmler's order, and were abolished again in the last years of the war.

The camp commander was fully authorized to hand out punishments during the absence of the Kommandant, providing the camp had been signed over to him in writing.

The camp commander could, at his own discretion, order a maximum of up to two hours of punishment drilling if a work Kommando did poor work.

In larger camps, the Kommandant could delegate the camp commander to administer penalty 2 to the prisoners.

The Non-Medical Activities of the SS Doctors in Auschwitz

Aside from the customary medical duties, the SS doctors of Auschwitz pursued the following activities:

According to Himmler's guidelines, they had to select males and females from the incoming transports of Jews who were able to work.

The doctors had to be present during the extermination process in the gas chambers to supervise the prescribed application of the poison gas Zyclon B by using the disinfection fixtures. Furthermore they had to make certain after the gas chambers were opened that the extermination process had been completely carried out.

The dentists continuously had to conduct spot checks to make certain that the prisoner dentists of the Sonderkommando pulled all the gold teeth from the gassed and dropped them into a special security container. Furthermore, they had to supervise the melting of the gold teeth and their safekeeping until delivery to the proper SS branch was made.

At Auschwitz-Birkenau, as well as the other labor camps, the SS doctors continually had to select those Jews who could not work any more and probably would not become able to work again within the next few weeks, and detail them to be exterminated. Also, those Jews who were suspected of having infectious diseases were to be exterminated. The bedridden were to be killed by injections; the others were to be exterminated in the crematories or in the bunker by gas. The injections consisted of either carbolic acid, Eipan, or Zyclon B.

They had to carry out the so-called secret executions. This dealt with the question of Polish prisoners whose executions were ordered by SS headquarters or by the Security Service of the General Government of Occupied Poland. Since these executions could not become public because of political and security reasons, they were to be masked as normal deaths using the usual causes of death in a camp. Healthy prisoners who were condemned to death were brought by the Political Department to the arrest Block II and an SS doctor liquidated him by injection. The sick ones were unobtrusively killed in the hospital also by injections. The doctor in question then had to write on the death certificate that the prisoner died from an illness which led to a quick death.

The SS doctors had to be present at executions ordered by the Summary Courts and certify that the executed was dead. The same applied to executions ordered by Himmler, SS headquarters, the Security Service, or by the General Government of Poland.

Prisoners who were to receive corporal punishment had to be examined for possible reasons which might prevent corporal punishment; the doctors also had to be present when this penalty was carried out.

They had to perform abortions on foreign women up to the fifth month of pregnancy.

Experiments were performed by:

Dr. Wirths: cancer research, examinations and operative surgery on those suspected of having cancer, or Jewesses having cancer.

Dr. Mengele: research on twins, examination of identical Jewish twins.

By non-SS doctors:

Professor Clauberg: sterilization research, injections to paste together the Fallopian tubes and thereby prevent offspring from Jewish women.

Dr. Schumann: sterilization research, to destroy the reproductive organs of Jewish women by X-ray.

Part IV
Profiles of the SS

BELSEN

Les fers aux pieds le
bourreau est tenu sous
bonne garde.

Josef Kramer Awaiting Execution

Profiles of the SS

Organization Schmelt

SS Brigadier General Schmelt, who later became a governing president in Oppeln, had been ordered back to Germany by Himmler after Upper Silesia was annexed. He was ordered to set up work sites for arms factories and army repair shops which would use foreign workers, especially Jews.

Schmelt created shops and small work camps in closed-down factories in the Silesian area and in the cities of Upper Silesia. After workers were done working, they returned to their homes or to the ghetto.

These work places and the arms factories were under the command of Schmelt, who also provided the guard details. In general, the guards came from the police and the SS. /he workers, other than those from the concentration camp, were paid a decent wage.   .

The revenues from this work were put into a special fund which the governor of Upper Silesia could use for other projects. I do not know how the money was used.

As far as I recall, Schmelt employed over 50,000 Jews. I do not know how many Poles and Czechs were included in this number.

When Himmler issued the extermination order in the summer of 1941, the entire Schmelt organization was forced to dissolve all work camps and work places. The Jews were supposed to be transported to Auschwitz. But because of the constant complaints from the army and from the arms factory managers to the Main Security Office and to Himmler himself, Himmler kept postponing moving Schmelt's work force.

It wasn't until 1943 that Himmler gave the clear order to close the work places and to transport the Jews to Auschwitz. The work camps, which were the most important for a decisive German victory, were put under the control of the Auschwitz camp administration or of Gross-Rosen, where the work was supposed to continue. The less-important work camps were dissolved and the workers were to be transported to Auschwitz. This program was carried out and completed in the spring of 1943. Schmelt'swork camps were run down, neglected, and almost totally without discipline. The death rate in these work camps was very high. The bodies of those who died there were just buried in the ground outside the camps. There was hardly any medical care. After the Ministry of Armaments repeatedly urged Himmler, Schmelt received permission to remove 10,000 Jews from the transports and to use them to fill up the work camps at the most important arms factories. The selection process was done in Bosel in Upper Silesia by an officer of the work selection force of D II and some of Schmelt's men. These men on their own authority, without informing anyone, and without orders from the Reich's Security Office, later stopped the transport trains to Auschwitz. They took the healthy Jews from the trains and exchanged them for their disabled workers and even dead ones. This created serious difficulties such as delayed trains running late, prisoner escapes, etc. This continued until my complaints finally moved the higher SS and police leaders to put an end to it.

Krakow, Nov. 1946
[signed] Rudolf Höss

Aumeier

SS *Captain Hans Aumeier* replaced Fritzsch and was the second officer to command the Auschwitz camp. Aumeier was from Munich and was an early member of the Party and the SS. Even before Hitler came to power, he had been working in the "Brown House" [Hitler's headquarters in Munich] in a fairly high position. When Dachau was created, he was one of the first SS men to be ordered there. Because his SS number was below 5,000, he soon became an officer; he was in the Office of Special Training in Dachau because of his previous basic training in the State Police. I was in this unit under his command for half a year. In 1935 Aumeier received his orders to become company commander at Esterwegen; then he went on to Lichtenberg and finally was posted at Buchenwald. In 1937 Eicke thought he was no longer useful in the Death's Head unit. He was supposed to be transferred to the General SS as a company commander. Eicke relented, however, and sent him to Auschwitz as camp commander in exchange for Fritzsch.

Aumeier was in many respects the opposite of Fritzsch. One could call him vigorous, almost restless, very easily influenced, good-hearted, eager to serve, and willing to follow any order.

And yet I can't explain why he had such a fear of being reprimanded by me. He had a fundamental flaw; he was too friendly and without a strong will of his own. His views were narrow; he easily lost sight of things. He did not have much foresight and so did not think ahead. He was rash and often acted unwisely without considering the results of his actions. He did not take responsibility and lacked initiative. He constantly had to be pushed. When Himmler visited in 1942 he remarked that Aumeier's brain was too small-Himmler had known him since 1928.

When Aumeier took command from Fritzsch, the situation was very bad. At the very beginning I told and showed him how deplorable the state of affairs in the camp had become under Fritzsch. I told him about Fritzsch's attitude and behavior. Because he was an old comrade of mine, I asked him to help me to eliminate the conditions created by Fritzsch and to stand by me as a true friend. I am firmly convinced that Aumeier really wanted to do that. However, he was not strong enough to go against the established routine and didn't want to be too tough right in the beginning with the officers of the day and the block leaders. He soon succumbed to the whisper campaign of the "good" comrades not to change the status quo. His misunderstood camaraderie, which soon brought him to the point that he went along with Fritzsch's old slogan: "Make sure the old man doesn't find out!" On the one hand, he did not want to be reprimanded for mistakes which came to my attention; on the other hand, he minimized the mistakes of his subordinates so they wouldn't be punished. And so he gradually fell into the same rut as Fritzsch. Other things contributed to this also. The cover-up continued even for the most serious blunders. With his limited mentality, he just couldn't change the way he had started, and this began to lead him more and more astray. He increasingly distanced himself from me because of fear, because of a bad conscience, and because of a false sense of team spirit with his comrades. However, he never was guilty of taking unauthorized steps, as Fritzsch did. But later on, he did many things in my name without consulting me or getting my permission. Aumeier also loved Eicke's outdated point of view concerning the treatment of prisoners. To him, they were without exception all "Russians" [a Buchenwald expression for prisoners]. Aumeier was much smarter than Fritzsch, and could not be caught as easily. And yet, he felt the Kapos and the block leaders had more power. In the meantime, the camp grew quickly: there was the women's camp, there was Birkenau, and added to that was the program of exterminating the Jews. This was much too vast for Aumeier's mental range. He became nervous and more and more careless. He began to smoke and drink more and more. He became increasingly irresponsible and was literally "bowled over" by this complex operation. He could not control this huge operation anymore. He tried to swim, but he was carried along by the current of events. *He* was incapable of mastering the terrible conditions and was unable to alleviate them. Sometimes it all came to a head and the camp Kommandant wondered how he was going to cope with all these things!

The abuses of the Kapos and the block leaders were in full bloom and now reached a high point. The tremendous growth of the camps brought incalculable complexity. As the number of prisoners grew daily, it was necessary to appoint new block leaders and new Kapos. To make matters worse, the worst creatures were picked for these positions. Aumeier had no knowledge of human nature at all. Anyone with a forceful manner was able to get his approval.

On a daily basis new officers of the day and block leaders had to be appointed from the troops; they were usually the least desirable. It was felt that they were just good enough for the camp. Aumeier was no match for this chaos. Even the officers, such as Schotte, Schwartzhuber, Hossler, and so on, who were delegated to him were unable to understand the whole situation. So everyone just muddled along to the best of his ability. I, however, had to oversee everything. It was a full-time job for most of the officers just covering up their mistakes and carelessness from me. The Kapos were also "trained" to avoid my finding out anything that was improper. In quiet moments I often talked to Aumeier man to man. I came right out and told him about the things that went on behind my back. He denied everything and said that I was too pessimistic and that I didn't trust anyone, and that everything wasn't as bad as I said. It was no use-not even tightening the discipline and demanding more from them. The cover-up just kept increasing.

Several attempts by Glucks to get rid of Aumeier in a nice way failed, as did the transfer requests, which contained in detail all the reasons to get rid of him. Finally, Glucks, who was pushed by Maurer, had to give in. He did not, however, remove him from concentration camp duty altogether, but appointed him Kommandant of Camp Vaiara in Estonia. In Glucks's view, Aumeier couldn't ruin anything there because it was off the beaten track, and Himmler never visited there. The only prisoners there were Jews! After the camps in the Baltic were closed, Aumeier came to Oranienburg and was put in charge of the work camps near Landsberg.

In January 1945 he became Kommandant of the newly opened concentration camp Grissi near Oslo in Norway. Aumeier was in a subordinate position in a rather easily controllable situation and was under strict supervision. He was useful, but in no way was he a capable officer in a camp as large as Auschwitz.

XI, 1946

H.

Baer

SS Major Richard Baer came from Bavaria and in 1933 became a member of the guard troop at the Dachau concentration camp. Later on he was also in other camps. In 1939 he went to the Death's Head Division [of the Waffen SS], where he remained until he was wounded. Since he was unable to return to the fighting troops, he was transferred to concentration camp duty at Neuengammen in 1942, where he became adjutant. In 1943, through Maurer's prompting, he was transferred to Auschwitz to become my adjutant. Three days later, however, he was called back again because Pohl wanted him as his adjutant. Pohl had again become tired of his adjutant and gave the order to find the best adjutant in all the Economic Headquarters. In Glucks's and Maurer's opinion, Baer was the best, subsequently he was stationed with Pohl, Baer soon learned how to gain Pohl's complete trust and confidence and was able to get himself into such a position of trust that no other adjutant had been able to do before. He skillfully led Pohl by the hand and influenced him. He knew how to get his ideas and opinions across to Pohl in such a manner that Pohl thought they were his own!

Baer was skillful, could speak well, and knew how to get his way.

He handled the various department heads and office managers as if they were his subordinates, always very skillfully, so as not to offend. The word soon got around that if you wanted to get something from Pohl, you had to get into the good graces of Baer, and it didn't matter what rank the person held. Because of all this, Baer became very spoiled, power hungry, and eccentric. He also started to spin his own webs. But Pohl had the greatest confidence in him and called him his friend! Attempts to call Pohl's attention to Baer's intrigues not only bounced off Pohl, but reflected badly on those making the attempt. Later Glucks and Maurer bitterly regretted having recommended Baer as adjutant and even later as the successor to Liebehenschel. When Liebehenschel had to leave Auschwitz, Baer was proposed as his successor. Baer realized that if he continued as he had been doing, he would one day run into conflict with Pohl, Baer preferred, therefore, to retreat to a safe position which at the same time meant a promotion for him and a chance to advance himself. He was promoted to major. It was amazing for anyone to be promoted to major after such a short time and at his age. This normally would have been strictly refused by Pohl, Incidentally, Baer behaved very rudely toward Liebehenschel and his second wife when he was transferred. Anyone else but Liebehenschel would surely have made Baer account for this. In June 1944 Baer assumed his position as senior officer and camp commander of Auschwitz I [the main camp]. I, myself, had the honor to install him and to show him how the camp was run. In his opinion, it was unnecessary because he had had enough experience in concentration camps. Anyway, I had very little time to make him acquainted with the existing indescribable conditions. He said he had seen everything for himself and would have no trouble managing things. In almost three weeks while I was in Auschwitz, he improved absolutely nothing and did not make any effort to do so. He had other interests. He often went hunting and fishing, or went for walks. Baer believed that he had worked enough when he was Pohl's adjutant, and that he was now in need of a rest. He also became arrogant and very unfriendly.

He did not care for the program against the Jews. He left all that tome.

He also did not involve himself much in the transports of able-bodied prisoners. He only got involved from time to time if Pohl had something important for him. In fact, I had to personally get involved with the federal train authority in order to untangle a tie-up of railroad cars and get them rolling again. In any case, it was an unpleasant working relationship. He hardly ever saw his other two camp commanders, Krause and Schwartz. They heard from him only through camp orders. He cared very little about the prisoners and had hardly any time for them. Because he was very moody, he constantly changed his point of view. As far as the prisoners were concerned, the officer of the day and the camp commander were responsible for them.

He looked at the orders and directives from Group 0 only if they interested him. He could afford to neglect these things without any repercussions. Glucks took no action against him and Maurer overlooked things after he received a few severe reprimands regarding Baer.

According to Pohl's orders the evacuation of Auschwitz was to be thoroughly prepared. I had to write the precise evacuation plan in great detail, which had to be observed. Baer had over two months' time to make all the preparations. He did nothing. The proof of this now came to light. When the evacuation order came from Maurer, Baer immediately climbed into the biggest and best car he could find and transferred himself to Gross-Rosen concentration camp so that he could "prepare things" there! The evacuation and the cleanup he left to Kraus and Hossler. He left it up to them to find a way to carry out all the orders. Had he planned and thought out the evacuation well, we would never have seen the conditions that existed on the streets and railways in Silesia and the Sudeten area four days later. I had been ordered there by Pohl to take action in case Baer couldn't solve the difficulties and because Pohl had received no reports from Baer. I no longer had authority in this situation, and I could only observe and report. When I returned, I reported to Pohl without coloring the facts. I also harshly criticized Baer and his behavior. Pohl became silent and did not say a word. A few days later Baer was appointed Kommandant in Mittelbau. Schwartz, who was originally scheduled to go there, was "honored" to command the sorry leftovers from Natzweiler. It became increasingly dangerous in Mittelbau as the air raids steadily increased in intensity. Baer sprained his foot and went to Steiermark [in Austria] to recuperate. Hossler was left behind and, according to his orders, had to fight his way to Bergen-Belsen. In short sketches, these were Baer's activities as camp commander at Auschwitz and Mittelbau.

XI 46 H

Bischoff

The second, but real building director of camp Auschwitz was SS Major Karl Bischoff. Bischoff was brought over from the air force by Kammler and was appointed construction chief in Auschwitz on November 1, 1941.

Bischoff had been active in the air force for many years when he built airports in France and Belgium in 1940-41. He was usually sent to places where progress was going slowly. Bischoff was a tough, headstrong and stubborn construction expert. He saw everything from the viewpoint of a builder. He was a workhorse and demanded that his subordinates give him their best. There was nothing he couldn't cope with when it came to the technical aspects of construction. He was a great organizer, but exceeded himself when it came to obtaining construction material of all kinds. Whatever could be gotten in Germany or from the occupied countries, Bischoff got it. He had several buyers constantly on the move.

From the very beginning he correctly assessed the terrible conditions at Auschwitz. He threw himself completely into his work until he dropped so that he could push Auschwitz's construction projects ahead.

Bischoff and I had many serious arguments because he could not see the need to modify the sequence of the projects. I was often forced to change plans because of unforeseen events. He could not see that or he would view it only from a technical standpoint as a builder. Another problem was his desire to have the prisoners at the different sites, which I refused for security reasons. One sore point between us was the use of civilian laborers. He believed that he could not do the work without them. But I had to refuse him because with the large number he demanded the work sites would be terribly difficult to see and guard. So there was friction between us which could not be resolved until Kammler took Bischoff aside and gave him hell.

But in spite of everything, Bischoff worked to build up Auschwitz as if he were possessed. For a time, he was on provisional duty to build Mittelbau. But he didn't rest until he was at Auschwitz again, in spite of the fact that he had great chances for promotion if he stayed at Mittelbau. No matter how much construction material Bischoff could get either legally or illegally, or from I. G. Farben, it was never enough to solve the problems in Auschwitz. All the department heads were furious with him because their projects were always last in line. He was constantly at war with everyone. He could never accept the fact that prisoner labor had to be used because he felt they achieved too little; no one could change his mind on that subject. He also demanded too much from the men. He was always complaining that there weren't enough prisoners working. He always blamed the poor work of the prisoners for the lack of progress in construction.

And, of course, he used this excuse to avoid meeting the deadlines. He did everything in his power for Auschwitz. No one else could have accomplished more.

XI 46

Burger

The chief of the Government Office D IV in the SS Economic Headquarters was SS Major Will Burger.

Burger came from Bavaria and was an early member of the Nazi Party and the SS. Like Maurer, he was an early member in the administration of the SS and was also an auditor on the Board of Examiners. Until the end of 1939 he was employed in various positions in the SS Economic Headquarters. When the Death's Head Division was formed, he was transferred to them. He was in charge of the battalion administration and later he was the D IV of a regiment. At the end of 1941, he was exchanged for Captain Wagner, who took Burger's place in the work operation. This is how Burger came to Auschwitz and brought with him all kinds of bad front-line habits, among others-heavy drinking. Burger was a competent worker and whatever he tackled was done well. But he had no concentration camp experience and had to learn the business. That, however, was not good for Auschwitz because precisely at that time the number of prisoners increased tremendously. Burger really tried hard to keep up. Because he had worked for years at the headquarters in Berlin, he had many friends there, and he was able to get a lot out of them. But because of the increasing numbers of prisoners, even he could not get what was needed for Auschwitz. In addition, the shortages caused by the war became considerable. Whether it was clothing, or food supplies, everywhere there were shortages and a decrease in rations. Burger made many improvements; he had learned this on the front lines. He also kept a sharp eye on things. But he could not be everywhere and his personnel were not much better than that of the concentration camp administration or those of the Kommandant. There were many duds among these officers, who were the cause of the deplorable conditions. This would not have happened if we had honest and hard- working noncommissioned officers. Canada [in the women's camp] was Burger's main area of responsibility. He constantly wanted to straighten things up by using force to get things working. But he never succeeded. In spite of the most cunning controls which he had put in place and even by his personally supervising everything, he still could not stop the stealing. Burger was also able to take action on his own, and this helped me a lot, even though we often disagreed on how to handle situations. Burger was hard, tough, and stubborn-the typical Bavarian. At the beginning of 1943, he was transferred by Pohl to be the D IV in Group D. This position had been vacant for quite some time; D I and their office had to take care of things. The rapid increase of concentration camps, however, made it necessary to have a D IV again. Burger managed to fit in quickly as D IV. Through his experience and knowledge about concentration camps, he helped all the concentration camps a great deal, at least as far as it was possible at that time.

In any case, during his many official trips he saw a lot that had to be done immediately and correctly done. He alleviated conditions where it was still possible. He also did a lot for Auschwitz because he knew that everything was needed there and that every form of help was most urgent there. No day went by that he did not bother the higher offices for help. And when Burger and I met at the house, we immediately began talking about help for Auschwitz. And yet everything was too late and ended up for nothing.

Because he drank a great deal and because he was too friendly with his comrades, he didn't rate very high with Pohl and therefore received no promotions. Since 1941 he was still a major.

XI 46

Caesar

SS Lieutenant Colonel Dr. [Joachim] Caesar was the director of the agricultural section of Auschwitz. Dr. Caesar had studied and was certified in agriculture. He had worked for several years at the Federal Institute of Plants, and was a plant expert. After Hitler came to power, Dr. Caesar was the mayor of Holstein. In 1934 he joined the SS School Administration and was soon in a leading position. He was responsible for the SS pamphlets that outlined conduct, and later on, for all the literature that was issued by the Indoctrination Office. At the beginning of the war, he created the first field library for the Waffen SS. They remodeled large buses and made field bookstores out of them in the shops at Concentration Camp Sachsenhausen. This is when I got to know Caesar much better.

He was conceited about his knowledge and ability. On top of all that he was dogmatic and did not allow any opinion but his own. He had a tremendous desire to show off and always wanted to play a controlling role. He was a typical example of the master race type and aloof from everything! This is the way he also treated his subordinates. Despite all this he was good-hearted and could occasionally be very friendly. There is one incident which highlights his whole outlook. When he was working with the motorized libraries, he often had business at Sachsenhausen. One evening we sat together in the officers' club in Sachsenhausen. At that time a large number of SS officers from the General SS were present who had been called up for service. These men had very important jobs at the federal level and in the economic offices. Caesar steered the conversation to Himmler's settlement program in Poland. Opinions about that really bounced around the room. Caesar completely believed in Himmler's plans and claimed to know them in great detail. He believed that the way Himmler wanted the Farm Settlement Plan implemented could not be done in the Eastern region. Only large, extended plantations with strong, farseeing, generous people could be best managed. These plantations were to be given to the master types [Herrentypen]. Only these aristocrats with the necessary prestige of large land ownership would be able to dominate the Slavic people of the East! Almost no one there would agree with him; most of them saw the Germanic farm population as the guarantee of the continuation and the spread of the German people.

In 1941 Caesar saw that he could not advance himself either in the SS School Administration or in his main office. Also he repeatedly had serious differences of opinion with his chief of staff and, therefore, started looking for a different field of work.

This is how Caesar got to be in Pohl's office. Lieutenant Colonel Vogel, who was the chief of the Economic Office, knew Caesar at the time, when Caesar was gaining experience on the farms. He introduced Caesar to Pohl. Pohl was immediately enthusiastic about his winning appearance and his mannerism. Through Vogel's proposal, Pohl saw immediately in him the man who was qualified to carry out Himmler's grandiose agricultural experimental plans at Auschwitz. And so Caesar came to Auschwitz as director of the agricultural operation with complete and important powers. His subordinate position to me, then and even now, was never made clear. According to him everything in the field of agriculture prior to him had been done wrong. He wanted to change everything around. Aside from basic orders and Himmler's plans, I let him alone. Our agricultural philosophies were far apart and for the most part conflicted. He was a theoretician; I was from the practical school. He was a passionate scientist about raising plants and the use of laboratories; I was interested in farming and raising animals using the old tradition and practical experience. In addition to all that there was our totally opposite view concerning all aspects of life. We could not agree on anything, even though there was no lack of good will on my part.

As I mentioned before, he was not popular with those who worked for him; not because he was too strict or asked too much, but because of his arrogant behavior. He thought everyone was stupid and that he was the only one who had the knowledge. In a strange way, he had a totally different attitude toward the prisoners. Because he was so good-hearted, he overlooked a lot concerning the prisoners and let them do what they wanted, especially the women prisoners. He had complete confidence in the Kapos. He constantly fought for the prisoners in the agricultural department to be governed by his rule. In a large part he prevailed upon Pohl to separate these prisoners and let them be housed at the farms. The prisoners who were in the plant-growing section were placed under "historical monument" protection. According to Pohl's orders, they had to be treated with kid gloves so as not to endanger Caesar's scientific work. Among these prisoners there were many women, mostly French Jewesses, who were academically trained. He treated them almost as colleagues. As a natural consequence, this led to the worst cases of lack of discipline. When the necessary punishments were carried out, Caesar took it very personally. He also was very successful in getting the best clothing for his prisoners. It was hard to distinguish the civilian employees from the prisoners in the laboratories, particularly as there were many Russian agricultural specialists and scientists working on the "Koc-Sagys" research project. He was able to get everything he wanted from Pohl because he knew how to convince Pohl about the tremendous importance of the science of raising plants. Included in this project was the much-needed ability to obtain natural rubber from dandelion-type plant families.

It was impossible to cut down on the German farming area, which in itself was not large enough, by planting experimental vegetables. Caesar couldn't see that as he was a theoretician. He was blinded by his ideas and couldn't see the everyday reality. Thus he never understood that the farm-building projects had to take second place to the critical general interests of the camp. Caesar's second marriage was a happy one, and there were children. He was divorced from his first wife because she did not want children. His second wife worshipped him and mirrored him in his manner-isms and his philosophy of life. A tragic fate took her from him. She died in 1942 from typhus. In 1943 he married his first lab assistant, who worked with him in the experimental works at Raisko, and she was a great help to him in all the important things. It was a continuation of the second marriage in that this wife also considered him a god.

As to the general camp interests, Caesar did not face the facts and turned a deaf ear to them. Stubbornly, he only saw his agricultural special interests and referred constantly to Himmler's orders, which stated that the agricultural experiments were to be pushed ahead to the fullest This, of course, also included any building that had to be done!

He didn't see most of the conditions in the camps and for the most part learned about what was happening from his men and the prisoners. He did not realize that the elimination of these conditions was more neces-sary than the most urgent agricultural building projects.

XI/46 H.

Eichmann

The director of the Jewish Department D IV B4 of the Federal Security Main Office was Lieutenant Colonel Adolf Eichmann.

Eichmann came from Linz. With Kaltenbrunner he was active in the then illegal SS in Austria; they knew each other and were friends. After Austria was annexed he became a member of the Secret Service and later on, the Gestapo. Finally, he arrived at Bureau IV of the Federal Security Main Office under Müller.

Ever since his youth Eichmann was concerned with the Jewish question and had a vast knowledge from studying all the literature about it, both pro and con. He spent quite some time in Palestine in order to learn from the source about the Zionists and the developing Jewish state. He knew the distribution of Jews and also the approximate numbers, which were kept secret even from the Jews themselves. He also knew the traditions and the customs of the Orthodox Jews and was also acquainted with the views of the assimilated Jews in the West. Based on his expertise he became the director of the Jewish Department.

I got to know him after I received the order from Himmler to exterminate the Jews. After that he came to Auschwitz to discuss all the details of the action to exterminate the Jews. Eichmann was a lively man in his thirties who always kept busy and was full of energy. He always came up with new plans and always looked for new ways, not just improvements. He was never at rest. He was possessed about the Jewish question and the Final Solution. Eichmann had to report continuously to Himmler directly and verbally about the preparations and the implementation of the individual roundups. Only Eichmann was in a position to furnish any information concerning the numbers. He could refer to almost everything from memory. His files consisted of a few pieces of notepaper with some unintelligible symbols. He constantly carried them around with him. Even his second-in-command in Berlin, Gunther, wasn't always able to give complete information. Eichmann was constantly on business trips and very seldom could be found in his office in Berlin.

In preparing for the Jewish roundups Eichmann had representatives in the designated countries. They knew these countries, and they had to get the necessary information for Eichmann. For example, Wisliceni was hard at work in Slovakia, Greece, Rumania, Bulgaria and Hungary. Negotiations with the various governments of these countries were carried out by diplomatic representatives of Germany or special envoys from the foreign office. If a government agreed to hand over the Jews, they designated a branch of that government as a center. This center was responsible for the gathering and handing over of the Jews. Eichmann discussed the details with the officials of these centers concerning the transportation of the Jews and also, based on his experiences, gave a great deal of advice on how to round up the Jews. In Hungary, for example, the minister of the interior together with the rural police carried out these roundups. Eichmann and his assistants observed the roundup operation, and they themselves participated if things were handled carelessly or if things dragged on too much. Eichmann's staff also had to have the transport trains ready and had to determine the train schedules for the Federal Ministry of Transportation.

On Pohl's orders I was in Budapest three times in order to determine the approximate expected numbers of able-bodied workers. There I had the opportunity to observe Eichmann in his negotiations with the Hungarian government officials and the Hungarian army. He carried himself in a resolute and correct manner. In spite of that, he was charming, obliging, popular, and welcomed everywhere. The many invitations from the heads of the various offices confirmed that. Only the Hungarian army did not like to see Eichmann. The army sabotaged delivering the Jews wherever they could, but in such a manner that the Hungarian government could not interfere. Most of the Hungarian population, especially in eastern Hungary, and the rural police had anti-Jewish feelings. This meant that in 1943 there weren't many Jews that escaped the roundups. It is possible that some were lucky and were able to escape over the Carpathian Mountains into Rumania

Eichmann was firmly convinced that if it were possible to destroy the biological foundation of Judaism by the process of total extermination, Judaism would never survive the blow, since the assimilated Jews of the West, including America, were not in a position to catch up to this tremendous loss of blood, nor did they want to. It was not expected that these Jews would have more than the average number of children. What convinced Eichmann even more of this view were the efforts of the Jewish Elders of Hungary, who continuously tried to get the families with many children to be exempt from the extradition of the Jews. Eichmann had many prolonged conversations with this Zionist leader about all of the important questions. Furthermore, it was interesting to hear that this Jewish leader knew all about Auschwitz, the number of Jews rounded up and the selection for extermination. Eichmann's business trips and his contacts with the bureaus in the various countries were also constantly under surveillance. The Jewish Elder in Budapest could tell Eichmann exactly where he had been and with whom he had negotiated. Eichmann was completely convinced of his task and had the deep conviction that this extermination process was necessary in order to preserve the German people from this desire of the Jews to be assimilated. Thus, he saw as his task and used all his energy to bring to reality the extermination plans of Himmler. Eichmann was also a determined enemy of selecting able-bodied Jews for work. He saw in this a constant danger to his Final Solution plans. He was afraid of mass escapes or other developing situations. He was of the opinion that the roundups of all Jews had to be carried out as quickly as possible and then just as quickly completed as one never knew about the outcome of the war. Knowing this attitude, I knew I could not get any help for Auschwitz from Eichmann. All entreaties, all complaints, and the most shocking proofs right there in the camp were not able to change his mind. He was always very quick to hide behind the order received from Himmler, which was to carry out the roundups as quickly as possible and not to let anything get in the way.

In spite of the fact that I had a good relationship with Eichmann as a comrade in arms, concerning this question we often had various differences [fights] with each other. I had to fight for each transport train that I wished to delay. Most of the time I lost. In fact, he often surprised me with unplanned transports. He just used every means to carry out the Final Solution of the Jews as quickly as possible. Every day that he won was important to him. He did not consider any difficulties at all. That he had learned from Himmler. The solution of the Jewish question was Eichmann's life mission.

XI 46

H.

Eicke

The first inspector of the concentration camps was SS *General Theodore Eicke.* It should be understood that except for Dachau he was the actual creator of the concentration camps. He gave it its shape and form. Eicke comes from the Rhine-Palatinate area, and he was in every theater of World War I. He was wounded several times and decorated. During the occupation of the Rhineland [by the French after World War 1], he was one of the leaders of the resistance movements against the French. He was sentenced in absentia by a French military court and remained in Italy until 1928. When he returned [to Germany], he joined the Nazi Party and became a member of the SS.

In 1933 Himmler transferred him from the General SS and appointed him the Kommandant of Dachau with the rank of colonel after his two predecessors were forced to leave. Eicke was a simpleminded, old-time Nazi from the street-fighting days. Everything that he did began from these ideas:

National Socialism has had to fight long and hard with heavy sacrifices to grab power for itself, and now it is imperative to use this power against all enemies of this new state. He considers all prisoners: ENEMIES OF THE STATE who must be kept safely locked up at all times, must be treated harshly, and annihilated if they resist. This is what he lectured about and how he educated his SS officers and soldiers.

In the early days of Eicke's time as Kommandant, the largest segment of the guard troops were former members of the Bavarian State Police, who also occupied most of the leadership positions. For Eicke the police alone were always a red flag, but especially the state police, which had made his life extremely difficult during the early years of struggle. In no time at all he substituted his SS troops for all the state police. Two of them were inducted into the SS, but the remainder of the "Laponese" [acronym for LandesPolizei], as they were called in camp jargon, were chased out of his camp. The prisoners were treated severely and harshly and were punished with beatings on the block for even the slightest infraction. These Whippings always took place in front of at least two companies of guards in order to "toughen up the men," especially the new recruits, as Eicke liked to express it. They had to witness these whippings as a regular part of their duty.

At that time the prisoners were almost all political prisoners: Bavarian Communists, Social Democrats, or members of the Bavarian Peoples Party. The conclusion of every Eicke lecture was, "There behind the barbed wire lurks the enemy and he watches everything you do. He will try to help himself by using all your weaknesses. Don't leave yourself open in any way; Show these ENEMIES OF THE STATE your teeth. Anyone who shows even the smallest sign of compassion for the ENEMIES OF THE STATE must disappear from our ranks. I can only use hard men who are determined to do anything. We have no use for weaklings." On the other hand, Eicke did not tolerate impulsive acts against the prisoners by his men. The prisoners had to be treated harshly, but justly. Only Eicke could decide if a prisoner was to be punished. He planned how the prisoners were to be guarded in the camp and was involved in every phase of prison life. Gradually he structured the whole concentration camp in such a manner that it later became the model for all future concentration camps. The guard troops he created were a hard, tough team who not only guarded the prisoners, but were also quick to use their guns when ENEMIES OF THE STATE tried to escape. Eicke punished the guards with extreme harshness for even the smallest infraction. But his men loved him and called him "Papa Eicke." In the evenings he would sit among the men in the mess hall or in their barracks. He would talk with them in their own language and concern himself with all their needs and cares. He gave them advice and taught them how they could be useful to him. He wanted tough, hard men who wouldn't be afraid to do anything when he gave them an order. He demanded that, "Every order must be carried out even if it is the hardest!" He demanded this and lectured about it during each briefing. Make no mistake. These lectures become engraved in every SS soldier. These ideas entered his flesh and blood and stayed there. The guards under Eicke's command later became camp Kommandants, duty officers, and other staff officers. They never forgot Eicke's lectures! To them the prisoners were and always remained ENEMIES OF THE STATE. Eicke understood his men. He knew how to handle them and how to educate them for the future.

In 1934 Eicke became the first inspector of concentration camps. At first he still operated out of Dachau, but later he went to Berlin to be near Himmler. With fiery determination he started to reorganize the existing camps: Esterwegen, Sachsenburg, Lichtenburg, and Columbia. Officers and men were constantly being transferred to other camps in order to bring to life the "spirit of Dachau" and become more like the Prussian military.

Himmler gave him a free hand to do as he wished because he knew that he could not find a more suitable man to trust with the camps. Himmler himself had often said this. This proved that Himmler had the exact same opinions and views as Eicke did concerning the concentration camps and the ENEMIES OF THE STATE. In Berlin Eicke came to the conclusion that the happy-go-lucky, fatherly Bavarian way of military training which included many parties and Bavarian beer drinking sessions was not enough to train a truly useful soldier who could be sent anywhere into action. So he looked for a Prussian drill sergeant and found him in the person of Police Captain Schulze, to whom he now gave the job of instilling the Prussian spirit into the easygoing Bavarians. His other responsibility was to educate the officers and men to the old Prussian military ways. There were terribly bad feelings in Dachau as this hated Prussian Schulze started out quite hard on the men and began to train them according to his ways. The veterans of Dachau never got used to it and opposed Schulze every day until after only one year they were able to get rid of him. Schulze was told the reason for his sudden demotion. Although he was an excellent officer and had achieved exceptional results in training the men, he never really was a National Socialist, nor was he an SS soldier, and, therefore, he did not know how to treat the men correctly. Even as inspector, and still later in his service career, Eicke was true to his habit of fraternizing with the guards and other low-ranking members of the Kommandant's staff without their superiors present. This is why he was so loved by his men and how he earned their loyalty. This became very noticeable in SS circles, which traditionally put a value on team spirit. All of this was really considered very important by Himmler. However, for the superiors and officers in charge, this habit of Eicke's was not pleasant. This is how Eicke learned about everything that happened in the camp. Nothing, even the insignificant, ever could be kept hidden from him. Furthermore, he was always informed about the behavior of the SS officers during and after their duty hours. To remark that the SS men abused these occasions with the worst lies about what went on goes without saying. Many SS officers had to justify themselves to Eicke about things which only existed in the fantasies of the gossiping SS men. But Eicke's purpose was achieved. He had all of the camps in the palm of his hand. Later on he ordered mailboxes to be placed in every camp which only he could open. The purpose: every SS man was now in a position to turn directly to him with requests, complaints, and suggestions. He also placed people he trusted among the prisoners in every camp who were totally anonymous and who informed him of all that was worth knowing.

From the time he became inspector of the concentration camps, Eicke placed special emphasis on ways to strengthen and increase the guard troops in all camps. Until the end of 1935, the financing of the camps was provided by each state of Greater Germany, but not the financing of the guard troops. Until then Eicke and his men were paid with monies from the Nazi Party, SS bank credits, and the mess hall profits. He finally was able to get permission from Himmler to let Hitler himself decide about the matter. Hitler gave Eicke permission to use federal funds to maintain twenty-five companies of soldiers, each consisting of one hundred men. Until further notice the funding of the camps themselves remained in the hands of the various states. Eicke now took the first decisive step to increase his guard detachments, later called the Death's Head units. In the meantime, the planning and preparation of the building of new concentration camps continued. The acquisition of suitable land and the financing of the construction caused great difficulties. Eicke's tenacity, however, and his endurance were successful in making them a reality. Sachsenhausen and Buchenwald were built. From the very beginning prisoners built these camps with their own hands under Eicke's direction. He alone ordered what construction was to be done and how. This caused tremendous friction with Pohl, who in the meantime was given the command over all SS construction. Pohl was also responsible for the financing of all construction. Camp Esterwegen was dissolved and transferred to Sachsenhausen, as was Berlin-Columbia. Sachsenburg, Lichtenburg, and Bad Sulza went to Buchenwald.

Lichtenburg then became a women's camp under Eicke's direction.

The following camps were built before the war: Flossenburg, Mauthausen, and Gross-Rosen. At first these were designed by Pohl to be just work camps for quarrying stone which the SS had purchased, but they soon became independent camps. These new camps were built by Eicke in a high-handed manner using all his experience and his philosophy. This caused an ongoing war with Pohl. Even then, Pohl wanted more barracks space built for the prisoners because he was able to foresee future needs, but Eicke was narrow-minded and unable to see into the future. Eicke also did not believe in enlarging the camp substantially.

When I was adjutant at Sachsenhausen in 1938, I witnessed the following: a new camp for women was being planned. Lichtenburg was not suited for a concentration camp and was too small. After searching around, Pohl and Eicke decided to use the land at the lake near Ravensbrück with Himmler's approval. The time came when more detailed discussions were held at the construction site between Pohl and Eicke. The Kommandant of Sachsenhausen, who provided the prisoners for the construction and also housed them at the site, was called in to these discussions. I also was included. At that time the question had not been decided as to how large the women's camp should be. Eicke estimated that the camp should be built for 2,000 women prisoners at most, but Pohl wanted to build a camp for 10,000. Eicke called him crazy, stating that the figure of 10,000 would never be reached. Pohl absolutely wanted to make provisions for increased construction even though his final estimate was not being taken into consideration. Eicke stubbornly held to his figure of 2,000; in fact, Eicke felt that even that number was too exaggerated. Eicke won! So the women's camp at Ravensbrück was built, hemmed in on all sides. Later it was continually enlarged with great difficulty, to the point where the guards could not get a clear view of the entire camp. Ravensbrück ended up housing 25,000 women. They were squeezed together in extremely overcrowded conditions with all the subsequent results.

Pohl was a much better planner. Eicke's thinking was always small and narrow-minded when it came to the question of concentration camp planning. It is his fault that the old camps could not be enlarged when the war caused this increased surge in the number of prisoners in the concentration camps because he could not see into the future. The penalty of the continued expansion of the camps was paid for by the prisoners being continually squeezed together into smaller and smaller places. I have already described the consequences of this in detail. It wasn't only the fact that it was impossible to enlarge the living quarters. In every camp, even under normal conditions, there was a very touchy situation regarding the supply of fresh water and the removal of waste water because the plumbing situation could not keep up with the growing needs of the ever-increasing size of the camps. This caused the deplorable state of affairs later. In contrast to his narrow-mindedness concerning the concentration camps, Eicke was tremendously generous in every respect when it came to his troops. The expansion of the Death's Head units had now become his main goal. The concentration camps, full of ENEMIES OF THE STATE, were just a means to an end for him. Using strong arguments, he constantly pointed out in later budget discussions the dangerous nature of the ENEMIES OF THE STATE, which made it necessary to continually expand the numbers of his guards. New barracks for the guards could never be too large or roomy enough for him. The furnishings could never be comfortable enough. Whatever space he saved, his troops received it tenfold. In order to obtain the necessary funds for outfitting his troops, he even got along with Pohl.

Eicke did not understand people. Again and again he was deceived by liars, sweet talkers, and people who knew how to be skillful and adept in dealing with people. He trusted these creatures. His judgment about people was also often subject to chance and his moods. If an SS officer got on his bad side, or if he couldn't stand him for whatever reason, it was best that this officer transfer as quickly as possible out of Eicke's sphere of duty. Eicke hoped to reeducate the officers and NCOs who were not suitable for duty in his unit. He either removed them from his command or he offered them a position in the concentration camps. Through Eicke's efforts the Waffen SS and the Concentration Camp SS were separated into different units after 1937. That is one of the reasons why the concentration camp staffs slowly came to be full of incompetent officers and NCOs. Eicke did not want to dismiss them from the SS because they had been in the SS for a long time or had been early Party members. It was then left up to various camp Kommandants to tolerate these people. They were constantly being transferred because it was impossible to find a suitable place of duty for them. Over the years most of them finally wound up in Auschwitz, which gradually became the personnel garbage dump of the concentration camps. If Eicke would have removed all of these incompetents from his command earlier, a considerable amount of the unpleasant and inhumane treatment would not have occurred in the concentration camps later on. This is how Eicke's policy affected the camps many years later.

Eicke's inability to understand people is also the reason that camp commanders like Koch and Loritz had his full confidence. He would not change his mind about them no matter how terrible the situation had become. They could do whatever they wanted in their camps. Eicke overlooked everything they did and never took steps against them even though he was constantly told about almost everything.

After the Waffen SS and the SS guards were separated, Eicke did not concern himself as much with the camps as he had before. He paid full attention only to the Waffen SS. Even though Eicke was responsible for directing the further development of the camps, he was concerned only about the external matters. He did not concern himself much about the internal matters of the camp. ENEMIES OF THE STATE had become his rut, even though this idea was obsolete, since only 10 percent of the inmates in the concentration camps were political prisoners. The rest were all professional criminals, asocials, etc. Eicke's directives and orders concerning prisoners have to be understood as being written from his office, based only on his experiences and viewpoints he had gained in Dachau. In spite of his tireless capacity for work, his flexibility, and his constant compulsion to improve things and look for innovation, he did not do anything new or revolutionary. He was unable to produce anything new concerning the concentration camps. He applied his mind and his heart to his troops.

His position as inspector of concentration camps was strictly only a framework. When Germany marched into the Sudetenland [Czechoslovakia, 1938], Eicke participated with the Death's Head unit of Upper Bavaria, which was the name later given to the Dachau guard units. The Fourth Regiment also participated in the occupation of Danzig [Poland, now called Gdansk]. Some of the formations of the Death's Head units were also involved in the Polish campaign. After the Polish campaign, Eicke received the order from Hitler to accelerate the formation of a Death's Head Division. He himself was promoted to lieutenant general.

At the beginning of the war all active Death's Head units doing camp duty were replaced by reserves from the General SS. This had already been a temporary practice during the occupation of Czechoslovakia. This caused many problems because the old reserve soldiers had no idea about guarding prisoners; also, many were physically unable to keep up with the strenuous duty. The professional criminals quickly took advantage of many of them. This condition caused lax work habits, help in escaping, and similar derelictions of duty. In order to carry out the assembling of the Death's Head Division, the entire Dachau camp was cleared; the prison population was transferred to Flossenburg and Mauthausen. After the Death's Head Division had been assembled and had left for maneuvers, the prisoners were returned. Even while the division was being assembled, Himmler issued the order that the current chief of staff of the inspector of concentration camps, Brigadier General Glücks, become inspector of concentration camps. The Death's Head Division took part in the French campaign and spent quite some time after that as the occupation force at the Spanish border. This did not change until the campaign in Russia, where they were constantly used at the hot spots. They were completely surrounded several times, as they were at Demians [France], and took incredible casualties.

Eicke's behavior during the assembly of the Death's Head Division was typical for him. Various departments of the regular army tried everything possible to delay the assembly and make it difficult. At one time the division was supposed to be motorized, then horse-drawn, then half-motorized again. With steeled calmness Eicke watched these maneuvers and still was able to accumulate the necessary weapons and equipment by stealing all the heavy artillery he finally obtained from transports that were destined for Rumania. Here is where educating his active guard soldiers into tough fighting soldiers really paid off. The achievements of the Death's Head Division were possible only because of the iron schooling and Eicke's close relationship with his men.In the spring of 1942 Eicke's plane was shot down during a reconnaissance flight near Kharkov [Soviet Union] as he was searching for the tank unit which his son-in-law commanded. Only a part of his uniform with the Knight's Cross with Oak Leaves and Swords was found. He died an honest soldier's death, which is what he had been seeking since the time his only son was killed in action.

After Eicke's death the Death's Head Division never really made any more outstanding contributions even though it saw action in the East until the end of the war. The unit was literally chained to Eicke's personality. While he was division commander he was hardly ever in touch with the concentration camps.

Only when on leave-he did live in Oranienburg-did he bring himself up to date from Glucks and Loritz. But he continued to honor the concentration camps with officers whom he could no longer use in his division. Glucks took them without protest. Most of these men were sent to Auschwitz. As a person, Eicke lived a very simple, withdrawn life and had a happy marriage with his very good wife. He had a son and daughter. He never felt comfortable in his official residence in Oranienburg, which was lavishly built by Pohl. He would have much preferred his modest apartment in Frohnow near Berlin. Eicke was hard, cruelly hard in his orders and against those who would not carry them out. Many an SS soldier, even a few officers, were demoted in front of the assembled troops, dressed in prisoner's clothes, and received twenty-five lashes. He even treated his own cousin this way. He had no human understanding for the prisoners as a whole. They were just ENEMIES OF THE STATE, even though he made special efforts for a few whom he knew more closely. He did everything for his SS soldiers; whether it was done out of camaraderie, or because it was expedient, I am unable to judge. Personally he was clean and totally honorable.

Nov. '46

Fritzsch

SS Captain Karl Fritzsch was the first camp commander of Auschwitz. Fritzsch came from Regensburg in Bavaria and was employed for years by the Danube Steamship Company. He was an early member of the Nazi Party and the SS. When the concentration camp at Dachau was first opened, he reported for duty to the guard troops there. Because he had such a low SS number, he was promoted to SS officer. Until 1935 he was a platoon leader in a machine gun company of the guard troops. After that, when he became too old for the guard troop, he was transferred to become director of the Mail Censorship Bureau. In 1940 he came to Auschwitz as the first camp commander.

Although he had been on duty in concentration camp service for more than seven years, I did not understand how the "old guard" walked all over him after the first eight days. Fritzsch was of limited intelligence, yet stubborn and always quarrelsome. He had to be right about all things. He wouldn't let anyone forget that he was an officer. The fact that he was the deputy of the Kommandant made him particularly proud. Right from the beginning I complained to the inspector of the concentration camps about Fritzsch because I knew enough about him when we were in Dachau together. His limited intelligence, his narrow-mindedness, and his stubbornness were reasons not to expect anything good from him. But Glucks ignored any complaints and said to try my luck for a while! And I later complained extensively; I was just as unsuccessful. "Fritzsch was good enough for Auschwitz."

Fritzsch made it a point to do everything the way *he* wanted to. He only obeyed my orders and directives when they coincided with *his* viewpoint. However, he never actually refused an order because he was afraid of the consequences. But he was clever enough to brush up or cover up when he gave contrary orders to my directives. If, in spite of this, his behavior was discovered, he was ready to maintain that he simply misunderstood my orders or that his subordinates went behind his back.

This last excuse was his favorite, and he always put the blame on his subordinates. Since I was away a great deal from the camp during the early days, he often used my absence to carry out the things that I had refused or even forbidden him to do. During that time, he became a master in camouflage where I was concerned. And he educated the whole camp to the motto, "Make sure the old man doesn't find out." That was his creed.

He had no understanding on how to deal with prisoners. He still had Eicke's teachings in his mind: "The enemies of the state have to be treated harshly!" He followed that motto and he also educated his block leaders to do so. Those prisoners he liked could do whatever they wanted, and he protected them. But, woe to those prisoners who got on his bad side! Fritzsch was also the protector of his Kapos and block leaders. If they were "aligned" with his ideas, he overlooked everything. Those who did not do as he wished or had tried to contact the Kommandant wound up by reason of a "crazy" punishable offense in the punishment company or were put into sick bay where they died either from spotted fever or typhus! I have often called Fritzsch to account, but he denied everything and felt grossly insulted and could not be convicted of his offenses. He was clever enough to always cover himself. And if an incident finally was reported to me, he just blamed one of his subordinates for it.

By this behavior he raised his men to be untruthful, particularly against me. The prisoners knew that by bypassing *him* it would lead to very bad results. And that's why no prisoner ever dared to come to me. Even when I tried to learn something from the prisoners directly, I always found resistance and evasive answers. The terror that was instituted by Fritzsch in Auschwitz could not be gotten rid of! This terror was handed down from the officer of the day, from the block leader to block leader, from Kapo to Kapo and so on. A bad inheritance with terrible consequences. But Fritzsch never took notice of the results. He wanted to be the ruler himself. He considered Auschwitz to be *his* camp. Everything that was done and was built was his "work" and "his idea."

It was difficult to work together with Fritzsch. I have tried time after time to point out his impossible behavior in a nice way. All for nothing. I was very strict with him officially, and I often bawled him out, but to no avail. On the contrary, he then became more stubborn and obstinate. In my absence he took liberties I could never approve.

He issued directives and orders in my name which were directly opposite to my views. I never could catch him nor did I have the time to spend on these disagreeable acts. I repeatedly pointed out very clearly to the inspector of the concentration camps how impossible it was to continue working this way-all without results.

Fritzsch remained at Auschwitz and worked the way he wanted. He considered the camp and everything connected with it as his complete personal field of activity in which no one had any say except him. He took no advice even from me and would not listen. He was in constant warfare with the building director, the administration, the doctors, and especially with the Political Department. With all the work I had, I was saddled with trying to settle all these arguments. Everyone in charge of a department constantly complained to me about the underhanded, malicious conduct of Fritzsch. Even though he was trying to be quite the good guy when he was off duty, he was no one's friend and was the opposite when on duty. Even today, I cannot remember any more details, but there were numerous little things which formed a regular chain of opposition. I also don't remember anymore which occurrence finally caused his transfer.

In any case it was the end of 1941 and our "working together" came to an end as Glucks finally had to admit that Fritzsch could not remain at Auschwitz.

Instead of removing him completely from concentration camp duty, he was transferred to Flossenburg and was exchanged for Aumeier. This occurred in spite of the fact that in my evaluation of him I persistently recommended not to put him in any concentration camp.

In Flossenburg he continued his activities just as before. It was easier to keep him under observation there because Flossenburg was situated on more open terrain, and it was smaller. But he wasn't there for long either. He was transferred again, to Mittelbau as a camp commander. But he had to leave there too because no one could work with him. Finally, in 1944 Glucks let him go. He came under the auspices of the main operations staff and ended up in the Moslem Division of the SS. Just imagine all the things that could have been avoided if Eicke had gotten rid of him for his incompetence when he was at Dachau.

Jan 1946

Globocnik

SS *Police Officer of Lublin:* SS *General Globocnik.*

Shortly after the beginning of the Russian campaign Himmler ordered a concentration camp to be built in Lublin. Globocnik had selected a site for the camp and Inspector of Concentration Camps Glucks appointed Globocnik to take charge of it. There already was a skeleton of a camp there and the former Kommandant of Buchenwald, Koch, was put in charge as camp Kommandant. At that time Globocnik promised Glucks tremendous amounts of blankets, sheets, clothing, and footwear. He also promised kitchen utensils and medical supplies for the concentration camp. After this Glucks came to Auschwitz and ordered me to select the items we needed and send a list to Lublin. With my administrative director, Wagner, I immediately drove to see Globocnik. After much haggling, we finally were able to dig up some useful items for Auschwitz. I can't remember the kinds of things or the amounts, but there were some medicines and medical instruments among them. Anyway, compared to Globocnik's promises the actual amounts were contemptibly small. Most of the items were confiscated from the Lublin area, delivered from all over and stored in a factory. This is how I got to know Globocnik. He acted incredibly important as he used Himmler's order to build new police bases in the newly conquered areas. He developed fantasy plans for bases extending as far as the Ural Mountains. No difficulties existed as far as he was concerned. He would just dismiss any objection with a sweep of his hand. He wanted to exterminate the Jews right then and there and save only those he needed for building the police bases. He wanted to truck the personal items of the Jews to a storage camp and use them for the SS. In the evenings by the fireplace he spoke about these ideas in his Viennese accent so casually that they seemed like harmless stories. I was somewhat shocked by Globocnik. According to Glucks's description of him, he was supposed to be tremendously capable and highly regarded by Himmler. My first impression was correct. Globocnik was a pompous ass who only understood how to make himself look good. The plans he presented of his visions were as if they were in large part already real. He wanted to do everything by himself, for only he knew the best way. It didn't matter if it was the extermination of the Jews, the resettlement of the Poles, or how all the confiscated goods from the Jews should be used. He knew how to tempt Himmler with these fantasy schemes. Himmler believed him and kept him long after a series of complaints just kept flowing to him. Some of those who complained were the SA governor general and the district governor. Globocnik became unbearable. I don't remember now what finally led to his being relieved of his duties. After Lublin he became a high-ranking SS officer and police inspector in Trieste. Whatever he was doing there is not known to me.

My second experience with him was in the spring of 1943 in Lublin.

I had to have a serious talk with him about the machines and tools sent to us from the local arms factory. This was after he was at armaments plants in Auschwitz. These machines were the worst junk, but he reported to Pohl that he delivered the most up-to-date machines. Because Globocnik himself had personally ordered these dirty dealings, he started to have second thoughts. But he soon shrugged it off and made it up to me by delivering five truly modern machines. My administrator, Mockel, had to account for the old machines. These deliveries were reported to Pohl as were the others. But they were almost never in service. He made great promises to make backup deliveries, but that never happened.

At this same time, it so happened that the chief of the Main Personnel Bureau, SS Lieutenant General von Herff, was in Lublin so that he could get to know the officers in Globocnik's area. On this occasion Globocnik showed him around making sure he saw all the model areas. First he showed him how he was using the personal items taken from the Jews in a former airplane factory; then he showed him the Jewish workshops where the most outlandish gadgets were manufactured, ranging from brush factories to foot mat weaving shops. All of this was so poorly made that you could only call it useless junk.

The Jews weren't really making these things, rather they were stealing them and fooling Globocnik into thinking they had made them. They had created so many checkpoints to prevent being exposed that they were carrying on their own businesses. I found this out later from Hoffle, who was his chief of staff at that time.

In addition to all this, Globocnik started his own organization-I forgot the name of it-that included all the old Polish businesses and even the former Jewish companies in his district. They were all in his organization; he was the head. His "company" was booming and made so much money that he exceeded any large firm that existed by a mile. When this underwent inspection, all the "companies" really were only one office where many charts and plans were hung on the walls, including his profit charts.

By his way of thinking, the Lublin concentration camp was also "his" concentration camp. He gave orders and directives which ran the exact opposite of those issued by the inspector of concentration camps or by Pohl. Consequently, they were always in a state of confusion. But Globocnik always got his way with Himmler by constantly referring to the important strategic position of Lublin. He also paid little attention to the directives of the Federal Security Main Office. He scheduled "his" police actions when it suited him. He carried out orders based on his judgment of those orders. He created prisoner work camps wherever he thought they should be without giving any thought at all to Pohl or D II, because it was "his" camp and "his" prisoners. He also considered Sobibor, Belzec, and Treblinka "his" extermination centers.

Eichmann knew Globocnik from the days when the Nazi Party was illegal in Austria and stated that he also had a very hard time with him. While I was fighting with Eichmann to slow down the transports to Auschwitz, Globocnik could not get them fast enough. He wanted to be at the top when it came to the numbers of exterminations without fail. An officer named Oldenburg, who had been in Hitler's chancellery and had created the extermination centers for liquidating the mentally ill before the war, was Globocnik's advisor.

Of the three extermination sites under Globocnik's command I only saw Treblinka during an inspection which I have previously described.

A training camp at Trawiaka was another of Globocnik's creations.

He wanted to create his own guard unit using Russians. It was approved by Himmler. Just as we had expected, these guard troops, which were called "protection personnel," were not very dependable. A company of them was put at my disposal at Auschwitz. After being there only a brief time, fifteen of them escaped with all the weapons and ammunition they could grab. During the pursuit they fought bitterly and three of my men died in these firefights. All but three of them were caught again. The company was immediately disbanded and divided up among the other concentration camps.

Globocnik's chief of staff, Hoffle, was supposed to assume command of the protective custody camp when Globocnik came to Oranienburg in 1944. Despite the shortage of qualified officers, even Glucks refused to appoint him because he had been too long in Globocnik's "school." It was from Hoffle himself that I learned about what Globocnik had done.

Globocnik wanted to create a large German settlement in "his territory" in the Zamosch area. He promised Himmler that within one year he was going to bring in fifty thousand new settlers as a pattern and example for the future, when huge settlements were supposed to be created further in the East. All the necessary things such as the cattle and the machinery were supposed to be supplied by Globocnik as soon as possible. However, the territory he had selected was still inhabited by Polish farmers. So he just evacuated them. He really didn't care where these people went. That was the problem of the Federal Security Main Office, or the local security in Krakow. The important thing to him was that the area become empty for the fifty thousand new settlers. Hoffle said that this new settlement was a complete catastrophe. The Germans who settled there were completely dissatisfied. None of the grandiose promises were kept. They suffered miserably in their new surroundings, constantly waiting for Globocnik's help.

In the summer of 1943 Himmler ordered him to Auschwitz in order to personally see the extermination process as it was performed there. He didn't think anything was special. According to him, his extermination centers worked much more quickly, and he threw numbers around of his daily accomplishments. I remember him saying that in Sobibor, for example, they processed five trainloads daily and that they collected valuables in the billions. His bragging was incredible on every occasion.

I was always under the impression that he actually believed and was firmly convinced about everything he said. From Eichmann I knew that for technical reasons only two trains could pull into Sobibor in anyone day.

After Austria was annexed into Greater Germany, Globocnik was made governor in Vienna. He made such a mess and caused such chaos that they had to recall him.

He was by and large a good-hearted person. The harm he caused was mostly from his pompous behavior, his feelings of self-importance, and his overbearing manner. I don't know if he himself stole anything during the utter confusion of Action Reinhardt as it was carried out in Lublin. I never heard anything about him concerning this either. I personally don't think he was that sort of person, but many of his officers and men enriched themselves considerably. The special SS court was constantly busy, and there were quite a few death sentences carried out.

It actually became a mania with Globocnik to confiscate everything and to channel it into SS accounts. He wanted to funnel incredible amounts of wealth to Himmler. He wanted to beat Pohl in the ability to create wealth for the SS by using all of his businesses. He pursued this goal without scruples. He didn't worry whether his actions were right or wrong. This, of course, carried over to his officers and men. Since there were almost no controls, many of them started their own personal roundup actions and did their own confiscation of valuables. In quite a few instances they started a thriving trade or stole whatever they could lay their hands on.

Globocnik's staff was the elite of losers. But they understood full well that they had to make themselves irreplaceable and well-liked by Globocnik. This wasn't hard to do since Globocnik was a poor judge of character. When violations had to be covered up, he good-heartedly did so, not just to protect his men but also so nothing would reflect on him. And Himmler believed his protest of innocence and that his territory was "in exemplary order" and was achieving extraordinary results.

Krakow. Jan, 47 Höss

Glucks

The second inspector of the concentration camps was SS General Glucks. Glucks came from Dusseldorf and had lived in Argentina for several years before World War I. When the war broke out, he smuggled himself aboard a Norwegian ship through British control points and reported for duty in the armed forces. He was an artillery officer for the entire war. After the war he was liaison officer with the Armistice Commission. He later became a member of the Free Corps in the Ruhr area. He was a clerk for a business when Hitler took power in 1933.

Glucks joined the Nazi Party and the SS in the early days. For several years he was chief of staff Group West of the SS, then he led a battalion of regular SS in Schneidemuhl. In 1936 he joined Viecke as chief of staff of concentration camp inspectors. Glucks was the typical bureaucrat and had no sense for practical things. He believed he could direct everything from his desk. He was hardly noticeable as far as the concentration camps when Viecke was chief. Even though he accompanied Viecke now and again to various camps, he really never noticed anything and he never learned what to look for. Since he was only chief of staff he didn't have much influence with Eicke because Eicke took care of almost everything with the Kommandants during his inspections. But Eicke held him in high esteem, and as far as personnel matters were concerned, Glucks made all the decisions, much to the disappointment of the staffs of the Kommandants.

Several of the Kommandants tried to prevent Glucks from having all that influence, but his position with Eicke was unshakable.

As I mentioned earlier, when the war broke out the active guard soldiers were transferred to the front lines and were replaced with reservists from the General SS. New units of the Death's Head Division were formed from the younger age groups of the SS. At first they were supposed to be supplements to the police and also the occupation troops. Eicke became inspector general of the Death's Head units and the concentration camps while Glucks was his chief of staff. When Eicke was given the job of organizing the Death's Head Division, the post of inspector general was taken over by the Command Bureau of the Waffen SS, so Glucks became inspector of concentration camps. He was subordinate to the Main Command Bureau of the SS, which later became Operations Main Office. In 1941 the Inspectorate of the Bureau of Concentration Camps became Administration Group 2 in the Army Administration Main Office.

Himmler never really trusted Glucks and quite a few times had intended to use him in another position. But Eicke and Pohl always spoke up for him, and this is how he remained inspector of the camps.

After Glucks became inspector nothing at all changed in the camps.

Glucks believed that anything that Eicke had ordered could not be changed, even if it was completely out of date. He didn't want to rock the boat, but more so he didn't want to ask Himmler to change anything. He also thought that his position as inspector was only temporary. He did not think he was authorized to make even the smallest change about the concentration camps without Himmler's permission. All requests for changes from the Kommandants to Glucks were denied without his even considering them, or if they were sent in writing, they were answered as evasively as possible. During the entire time he held office he had a pathological fear of Himmler. If Himmler called him, Glucks became confused; and if he had to see Himmler in person, he was no use to anyone for days before the meeting.

When Himmler demanded reports and position papers he fell completely apart. This was very surprising because normally nothing could disturb his even-tempered nature. Therefore, he avoided everything that could possibly lead to a meeting with Himmler, or, worse, possibly lead to a rejection or even a reprimand from Himmler.

He didn't take the things which occurred in the camps seriously, as long as they didn't have to be reported to Himmler. Prisoner escapes upset him and gave him sleepless nights because they had to be reported to Himmler. Every morning the first question was, "How many took off?" Auschwitz along with others caused him the most worries. This constant fear of Himmler naturally influenced his whole attitude about concentration camps. So it became, "Do what you want. Just don't let Himmler find out." When he became subordinate to Pohl, he breathed more freely. Now a stronger person was put between Himmler and the Kommandants and he took the heat.

Even then, his deep fear of Himmler never left him because, as before, he still had to appear before Himmler or answer Himmler's questions. Pohl saved him many times. Glucks only inspected the camps if there were necessary reasons, or if Himmler or Pohl urged him to do so.

When he inspected a camp, he saw nothing, and he even said so.

He was happy if the Kommandant didn't drag him through the camp too long. "It's always the same in every camp. What I'm not supposed to see, I won't see. Everything else I saw so many times already that it isn't interesting anymore." He preferred to sit in the officer's club of the camp and talk about every topic except the problems that bothered the Kommandant.

Glucks had an uncontrollable sense of "Rhineland" humor and looked at everything from the bright side of life. He made the worst things appear ridiculous and cracked jokes about them. He remembered absolutely nothing and made no decisions. You couldn't even get angry at him; such was his nature.

He never took me seriously. He believed I over-exaggerated my worries and needs about the camp, and he was astounded when he discovered that Pohl and Kammler agreed with me. Yet he never gave me help. He could have been such a great help by transferring the inefficient and un- suitable personnel out of Auschwitz. But because of the other Komman- dants, he didn't want to do that. "Don't rock the boat! Keep the peace in the Office of Inspection of the Concentration Camps. Glucks's inspections of

Auschwitz they were of no value and always ended without any changes. He really didn't like Auschwitz at all. Everything was too spread out, too complex, and caused too many difficulties for him. And besides that, the Kommandants had too many requests and complaints.

Twice he wanted to remove me or appoint a higher-ranking officer over me, but he really didn't have the courage to do it because of his fear of Himmler. Another reason was that the number of escapes was low at Auschwitz, and high in other camps, for which Himmler gave him a lot of grief. Auschwitz was a constant thorn in Glucks's side because it made him uncomfortable and because Himmler had such a deep interest in Auschwitz.

From the beginning of the extermination of the Jews, he didn't want to have anything to do with Auschwitz. He didn't even want to hear about it. He could never understand that his lack of interest was the very reason that the catastrophic conditions developed later on. He was unable to handle any of the difficult problems in the camps and was of no help in finding solutions to the problems. He left it up to the Kommandants to find a way to solve their problems. "Don't ask so many questions!" was the frequent comment during his conferences with the Kommandants. "You know much more than I do about these things." He often asked Liebehenschel just before a meeting, "What should I say to the Kommandants again? I don't know anything!" And that was the inspector of all the concentration camps, the supervisor of all camp Kommandants. He was supposed to give direction and set the course for the Kommandants whenever difficulties arose, manyof which developed because of the war alone. Later they did turn to Pohl for help; this made Glucks very angry at them.

Glucks was too soft and did not want to hurt any of his subordinates, especially when it came to his old comrades and SS officers who were his favorites. He gave into them much too easily. Because of his good heart, he saved SS officers who should have been brought before an SS court long before, or should have been removed from camp service. His good heart overlooked many of the sins of his staff.

After Liebehenschelleft for duty in Auschwitz, Maurer became Glucks's deputy and I became director of inspections. That's when Maurer and I began cleaning house in the staff positons by getting rid of the excess noncommissioned officers and lower staff officers who had been listed as indispensable. This, of course, caused many arguments with Glucks. Maurer finally threatened to go to Pohl, and Glucks gave in reluctantly.

He let Maurer gradually take control of this very loose way of doing things. Glucks's main worry was Himmler, although he did try to slow Maurer down when he thought Maurer was too strict with the men. Glucks had not been healthy for years. He was often absent from duty for weeks on end and never slept well. He ruined himself by taking many different medications.

He was really finished in 1944 when the constant air raids hit the Berlin area. As the front lines came closer and closer, his worsening health showed the effect. The only time he felt any relief was when he was drunk!

He lived a very simple life-withdrawn. He never invited anyone to his house when he was in Oranienburg. His wife was just like him. They had no children

As far as the prisoners who served as barbers, gardeners, and craftsmen were concerned, he had close relationships with them and was good-hearted and generous. He never witnessed an execution or a beating. Permission to administer a beating was left for the most part to his deputy.

Glucks was the exact opposite of Eicke in every respect. Both of them were extreme, and this made the development of the concentration camps a real tragedy!

Grabner

SS *Second lieutenant and Detective Secretary Maximilian Grabner* was in charge of the Political Department of Concentration Camp Auschwitz from 1940 until November 1943. Grabner was an Austrian from Vienna. He was a professional forester. Before Austria's annexation he was already very active in the illegal SS. He came to the Federal Police through the Security Service. Grabner was appointed as head of the Political Department of Auschwitz when it was being built in Katowitz. Grabner did not understand concentration camps and knew even less what the Political Department was supposed to do. I really had a difficult time with him in the beginning. He was very nervous and sensitive. Whenever he made a mistake and it was pointed out to him, he always felt he was being picked on. At first he made so many mistakes that I requested he be transferred and someone else take his place. Dr. Schafer was the director of the Federal Police then; he told me he could not send me a better officer. So Grabner remained at Auschwitz. He gradually got used to the job because I was able to give him some help by adding some NCOs to his staff. These men had experience from other camps because they had worked in the political departments before.

Grabner was a hard-working person, but he was very absentminded and inconsistent. His greatest mistake was that he was too good-hearted to his comrades. Out of a false sense of camaraderie he often did *not* report the countless excesses and fights among the SS officers and men to protect them from punishment. Because he was so shortsighted, Grabner had to carry the blame for the excesses, which got out of hand. More than anyone, he was supposed to report all the violations of camp regulations and orders to the Kommandant. This was part of his job. But he only reported the rule breakers that he knew I already was investigating because he was afraid he would be reported for not doing his duty. Because he had been a detective before, he was smart enough not to get caught. He came running to me daily with little problems to show how well he was carrying out his job. And if I gave him a clue about some activity, he pursued it conscientiously and skillfully until he had the results. Grabner was well-informed and knew everything that was going on in the camp, but he could not report on a comrade unless there was no other choice and he was forced to.

In the beginning he was constantly at conflict with the camp officers.

He never failed to stress the dominating role of his department as coming first, and he mixed this in with pure camp problems. But these differences were settled with his comrades during their drinking parties, which cemented the friendships all the stronger-much to the detriment of the camp Kommandant!

Although Grabner wanted to play an important role in the camp, I don't think that he would take any unauthorized actions on important matters. He was too much of a policeman and too shrewd. Without help from others, he could not do anything and every accomplice was a threat to being discovered. Despite months of searching, the very smart Fact-Finding Committee of the High SS Court couldn't pin a thing on him.

By the way, Grabner was especially eager to kill all the efforts of the committee. It is possible that Grabner was often negligent, but I don't think he intentionally wanted to cause the deaths of the prisoners. I don't think he was capable of that.

Because of his dual assignments with the State Police Headquarters and with the camp Kommandants, his authority and his duties were not quite clear. The limits of his duties could not be defined and there was no real control over his activities. He would always flop from one to the other when justifying his activities. I absolutely did not concern myself with the interrogations and examinations of the Federal Police, which were ongoing activities in Auschwitz. Grabner often reported about these interrogations to me and also when each investigative committee arrived in Auschwitz. He always reported any special order from the Federal Police Headquarters if he could get ahold of me. These orders varied so much and were so numerous that Grabner was actually busier with Federal Police matters than with the camp itself. This was particularly true when it came to the resistance movement. Camp matters and Federal Police matters often mixed with each other so that you could never find a clear line of separation between the two. Grabner's reports were always full of mysterious words which he chose to make it difficult to understand what he was trying to say. He was always saying how great his workload was and how diligently he was pursuing them to me and to his coworkers. He made sure to point out how important a person he was.

As the numbers of prisoners grew rapidly so did the problems in the Political Department. Like everyone else in the camp, Grabner had only a few competent coworkers.

As the workload increased continually Grabner received some SS men who were simply drawn from the troops. These were the men they wanted to get rid of. Most of them were not suited for this kind of work, and they joyfully let the prisoners do the work. They were used more and more for the less important work.

The work places were crawling with female Jewish prisoners, and Grabner assured me that they were doing only the less-important jobs. But the truth was that the leading prisoner groups in the camp became accurately informed about all the important matters occurring in the Political Department. Because there was an active connection between these groups and the resistance movement, many of the actions of the Federal Police became meaningless. The Jewish female "coworkers" were able to get decent-looking clothing for themselves, and when an SS soldier stubbornly blocked their path, they simply worked on him with their beautiful eyes until they got what they wanted. The Political Department had become too complex and too large for Grabner. The process of extermination required that a Federal Police official be there. At Auschwitz-Birkenau we needed at least one commissioner and three secretaries. It was almost impossible to get a replacement for Grabner. The scarcity of personnel was even greater in the Federal Police than in the concentration camps.

Grabner was also responsible for the crematories and the strict adherence to all orders pertaining to them. But the NCOs who were on duty in the crematories let the Kapo and the prisoners do all the work. This gruesome duty affected the workers to such an extent that they usually drank themselves into a stupor and the work became increasingly neglected. There could be no relief for them because the secrecy involved dictated that no others be assigned. Grabner was also responsible for carrying out the execution orders of Himmler, or the Security Service, or those ordered by the Summary Courts who had condemned them to death. The daily contact with death and the overload of responsibility of this kind of work actually dulls the senses and would, in any case, have broken a stronger man than Grabner.

In the summer of 1943 Grabner had completely collapsed, but he didn't want to admit it until an illness and the SS court brought him down.

XI/46

Gravits

SS *lieutenant General Dr. Dr. V. Gravits' was the surgeon general of the* SS *and chief of the* SS *Main Medical Office.*

I have known the doctor since 1938. He inspected Sachsenhausen several times when I had a tour of duty there. The camp hospital was equipped with the most modem equipment, and the entire hospital area was well-furnished. This is why he liked to bring doctors, medical commissioners, and classes from Berlin to show off the facilities. He also brought medical classes from the army to Sachsenhausen.

Gravits was a lively and vigorous man, very talented, and full of practical knowledge. He was interested in everything. From my observations in

Sachsenhausen and even later in Auschwitz, he was a very observant person. He was able to see his doctors for what they actually were, and no one could fool him.

I cannot recall the times, but he inspected Auschwitz twice. He wanted to see *everything,* and I made sure that he did. I showed him the worst abuses, the overcrowded hospital, the morgues, and even the temporary sewage treatment plants in Birkenau.

He saw the entire process of the extermination of the Jews, including the burning of the bodies in the pits and the crematories. He saw the lack of medical supervisors, as well as the insufficient supply of food for the sick and the general condition of the prisoners' health. During both inspections he promised to do his best to remedy the situation, but nothing ever happened. Even *he* couldn't help.

In addition to the many honorary positions he held, he was also president of the German Red Cross. As far as I know he was very active in this organization.

Anything to do with the SS Medical Corps was consolidated into the Central Health Office, which he had created. The highest medical officers of the Waffen SS, General Dr. Mugrowski and his Hygienic Institute staff were also located there along with others. Mugrowski was in charge and responsible for all hygienic matters, as well as preventive measures in all medical areas of the Waffen SS. During the war the concentration camps became his main field of work. His biggest problem was and remained Auschwitz. From 1940 on he came to Auschwitz many times.

He saw the whole camp develop and wrote reports to Himmler stating that he refused to accept any responsibility if the camp was not loosened up and the flood of incoming prisoners stopped. It was no use; everything stayed the same. Even when Mugrowski gave good advice to the Building Department and made many practical improvements, they were not enough to improve the basic conditions in the camp. His Hygienic Institute in Raisko helped a great deal in combating epidemics and in continuing the controls of the sanitary installations. If I remember correctly, the Zyclon B gas was manufactured by the Tesch and Stabenow firm until 1942 in Hamburg. This is the gas that was used for disinfection and also for the extermination of the Jews. It was procured by the administration from Tesch and Stabenow. From 1942 on, all poison gas was purchased for the SS by a central authority. Mugrowski was in charge of the Hygienic Department and he alone was responsible for the shipments of gas. So he was the one who continually had to get the gas for the extermination of the Jews. Tesch and Stabenow was able to deliver the needed amounts of gas by railroad on time until1943. But after 1943 the increasing Allied air raids made this impossible. Consequently, Auschwitz was forced a few times to use trucks to get the gas from the manufacturing plant in Dessau. According to a British public prosecutor in Munich who brought indictments against Tesch arid Stabenow for delivering the gas to Auschwitz, according to the books of that company a total of 19,000 kilograms [41,800 pounds] of Zyclon B gas had been delivered to Auschwitz.

To continue, the main medical department responsible for the camps was attached to the Office of Camp Hygiene. The head of this department was Medical Quartermaster SS General Dr. Blumenreuter. The gold from the teeth of the exterminated Jews had to be delivered monthly to this office. Whatever was done with this gold, I never did find out.

The same thing was done with all the valuable medical supplies taken from the Jewish prisoner transports.

The surgeon general and the president of the Red Cross were, I believe, informed in detail about these shipments.

Mugrowski also observed how the gold teeth were removed from the gassed corpses and how the gold was melted down by the dentists.

The ambulances were for use by the garrison doctor, and he was authorized to issue orders for their use. Because there was a constant shortage of trucks in Auschwitz, the garrison doctor had no choice but to use the ambulances for shipments to other camps. It gradually became the custom that all necessary trips for the garrison doctor were carried out with the ambulances. So, not only were the sick driven from camp to camp, but the dead also. Medicines, bandages, and surgical equipment were all transported in the same ambulances. The doctors and the medics drove them to their duties on the ramp and to the gas chambers. The Jews who could not walk were driven from the ramp to the gas chambers in ambulances. If no trucks were available, the standby ambulances were used. Because the medics were the ones who threw the gas into the gas chambers, they would be driven with their cans of gas to the gas chambers using the ambulances when no other trucks were available. They just hitchhiked a ride with the doctors who were going there anyway.

As time went by the ambulances were used for all kinds of purposes because no other trucks were available. No one ever gave a thought that they were profaning the symbol of the Red Cross when the ambulances drove to the gas chambers loaded with those who were to be gassed and the gas itself. No doctor ever objected to this. Even the ever-sensitive Dr. Wirths never brought this subject up with me, and I myself never gave it a thought either.

Krakow. Jan. 47 H.

Hartjenstein

SS *lieutenant Colonel Hartjenstein* had first served in the regular army and transferred to the Waffen SS in 1938. I have known him since then. At first he was a platoon leader, then a company commander of the guard troop at Sachsenhausen. For a time, he was Kommando leader of the work camps in Niederhagen and Wewelsburg. In 1940 he came to the Death's Head Division, where he was given different duties by the various departments. Because Eicke could not find any more assignments for him and because he repeatedly failed as a unit leader, he finally ended up assigned to concentration camp duty, as was the usual case. Glucks sent him to Auschwitz with praise for him as an outstanding guard troop leader. Hartjenstein replaced SS Major Gebhardt, who had really compromised his position.

Hartjenstein used his experiences from the front lines immediately to begin to whip this disorderly bunch of guard troops into shape and to bend them to his will. He wanted to have strict military order. He especially wanted to train and educate the officers. His main job of guarding the prisoners and camp security were not considered especially important to him. He believed that this was going to be very easy. He started in a very arrogant manner, and it continued that way.

All his grand intentions slowly vanished when he was faced with the terrible conditions in Auschwitz. As always, the number of guard troops was never enough to do the job of guarding the prisoners going to their work details outside the camp. To make matters worse, Hartjenstein wanted to free up entire companies from guard duty so they could perform field drills and basic training. He never could understand that it was necessary to have the whole roster of the guard battalion on duty. This was the cause of our disagreements right from the beginning. He couldn't understand that camp security and guarding the prisoners came before military training. He constantly criticized me for not understanding the military aspects of the guard battalion. The other thing we argued most about was who had the disciplinary powers. If I caught an officer or an SS soldier breaking guard rules or some other violation against camp security, I punished the man myself. If I thought that Hartjenstein's punishment was too easy, I turned the man over to the SS court. Hartjenstein was always against this and arrogantly told the SS soldiers who were involved that he would get them off because the punishment was too harsh. "The Kommandant had no heart for his soldiers!" So he systematically created a wedge between the troops and me. All my protest against his practices failed. While he wanted to be the independent regimental commander, I wanted to build fewer but stronger companies. It didn't matter if they consisted of 150 or 250 men. That way I could save on administrative personnel and free up more men for guard duty. He absolutely wanted to have twelve companies in order to show the need for a regiment and then divided them into battalions. Over my -objections, he succeeded in convincing Glucks and got his regiment. He also got a few more officers which Glucks had refused to give me for the camp.

Hartjenstein trained his officers so that their first obligation and love was to the regiment; the camp came second. I desperately needed those officers to supervise the work Kommandos which were spread far from the camp. I could get them sparingly, since they were needed for regimental service. He had an understanding with his comrades and camp officers that any violations by officers or soldiers would first be reported to him, and if he thought it necessary he would then report it to me. He expected me to report any violations by the administrative personnel to him. It goes without saying that with an attitude like that most of the violations were covered up.

Hartjenstein loved to celebrate with his officers. Because I had little time and also was little inclined to join in, he took advantage by convincing the officers of his views and to turn them against me. All this in the name of "camaraderie"! It is understandable that the entire service suffered from these intrigues. There were constant disputes about construction matters.

He could not see that it was much more important to improve the camp, especially the sanitary conditions, as far as the building program was concerned. He absolutely could not understand that it was necessary to speed up construction in the prisoner camp in order to ease the terrible conditions of the prisoners. Later, when he was Kommandant of Birkenau, he felt the bitter results of his attitude.

Hartjenstein was too shortsighted, narrow-minded, pig-headed, and two-faced. He worked tirelessly against my orders and directives behind my back. I told Glucks often enough about this and even proved certain accusations to him-without success. Glucks always felt that it was my fault that I couldn't get along with any of my officers. Hartjenstein never complied with my demands to have continuous training on how to handle the prisoners using real-life examples. He said that he could never get all his regimental officers together and besides, you couldn't expect the men to be at instruction after they had put in fourteen or sixteen hours on duty. Another thing he didn't do was to instruct the guard troops about the most important things before they went on duty. The officers didn't like this either because they had to get up too early, but they were very busy during the evenings having regimental parties-to practice camaraderie!

The troops had absolutely no understanding of the camp as a whole, although I always made it clear enough at the officers' meetings and pointed out the state of distress in the camp. There were a few officers who took their jobs and duties seriously and who taught their men and tried to educate them. Hartjenstein didn't like to see this and got rid of them at the first opportunity.

I would rather not say anything about him as camp commander of Birkenau, since I had no personal observations of him then. He hardly cared about the camp itself. He was busy enough during his six months just creating new administrative staff positions. After Birkenau he was Kommandant of Natzweiler concentration camp. He evacuated that camp so poorly that all the important things, especially the secret papers, fell into the hands of the French. In February Pohl released him for front line service after he saw the mess he made at Natzweiler.

Hartjenstein was *the right officer* for a concentration camp!

XI 46 Höss

HIMMLER

I already had a passing acquaintance with the leader of the SS, Heinrich Himmler, which dated back to the years 1921-22, when I repeatedly had business with Ludendorff as a courier for my Free Corps. General Ludendorff was the patron and secret leader of all the underground military and paramilitary organizations, which used political names as a cover. The reason for this was that all military organizations were forbidden by the Treaty of Versailles. Hitler was also a member of a Free Corps in Bavaria and that's how I became acquainted with him in Ludendorff's apartment. Later, in 1930, I became more closely acquainted with Himmler during a convention of the Artaman Society in Saxony. Himmler was the leader of the organization in the Bavarian district. The Artaman Society's goal was to help guide young, idealistic Germans of all parties and all persuasions back to the country and to settle the farmlands. Many of these people were without work because of the tremendous unemployment in Germany. The goal was to help them find work again. One of the ways to achieve this was by parceling out the land of large estates which were in tremendous debt; another way was by gradually moving into the Polish area of West Prussia and Posen. At the convention, however, Himmler was talking about the conquest of further areas of Eastern Europe by force. The idea behind this thought was brand new for all of us. Judging from the overall political conditions at that time, this did not appear practical in the foreseeable future. Himmler was irrevocably convinced that this would soon happen. I discussed this idea with him for a long time without being able to agree with him. As far as I was concerned, these goals were considered too high.

Himmler was a passionate farmer. He had studied agriculture for several years, had a degree in agriculture, and was later the chairman of the board of the Organization of Agricultural Graduates.

Originally the SS was created purely as a protective organization within the framework of the SA [Sturmabteilung-storm troops] for the purpose of protecting Hitler and other high Party officials. The organization was never supposed to have more than ten percent of the total SA in the larger cities. In the early years it was composed of experienced soldiers who were early Party members. The further development and the rise of the SS, the idea and finally the power which the SS later on represented is solely attributed to Heinrich Himmler's inflexible will, which was to create for our leader, Adolf Hitler, a mighty instrument of power. It was to be in a position to bring to reality the idea of National Socialism among all phases of life and to be strong enough to break all resisting opposition. Only by considering this can his personal rise to power and in the final analysis the power of the SS be understood.

Himmler was perhaps the most loyal and unselfish follower of Adolf Hitler. I have never heard a single word, not even from his worst enemies, that he in any way made any personal gain or that he abused his power for personal reasons. His personal reputation was clean. He lived a simple, modest life and worked constantly, filled with new ideas and improvements in the service of the idea of National Socialism. Every other trend or thought or political view he automatically denied for the German people, and labeled these damaging and corrupting to the nation. He also wanted to educate his creation, the SS, to this way of life. All his orders and lectures are based on this line of thinking. His fundamental principle was loyalty to Adolf Hitler and therefore loyalty to the idea of National Socialism. He knew no compromise or different interpretation. The first public stir was created by his "Order Concerning Engagements," which was issued prior to Hitler coming to power. From this order on, no member of the SS could get married without obtaining Himmler's personal permission. Those who were already married had to ask retroactively for this permission. In both cases the man and the woman of this union had to obtain proof of unbroken ancestry dating back to 1800, and the officers even had to go back as far as 1700. Furthermore, health certificates concerning inherited diseases, proof of potency for men, and the ability to bear children for women had to be presented. It goes without saying that one had to have a clean record with the police.

Large, clear photographs and resumes completed the documentation.

Any SS who wanted to get married in spite of Himmler's refusal had to leave the SS. According to Himmler, a healthy family with lots of children was the nucleus of a new nation and the renewal of the German race. Racially valuable families were to be supported in every way. The creation of the Department of Race and Settlement, Lebensbom, which was the program of homes for pregnant mothers, and the kindergartens were an extension of the "Engagement Order." Later on even promotions were dependent on the number of children, and the age of the parents. Older, unmarried SS men were given the order to marry by a certain deadline. Childless couples could easily obtain divorces or were ordered to adopt children from Lebensbom.' Once he had an idea he carried it out to the full extreme, even if it was unpopular. This is shown by the great stir he caused with his proclamation to all members of the SS and the Gestapo, particularly the unmarried, at the beginning of the war under the motto:

"Create children, so that the loss of blood will not deplete the German people." It was a tragedy that his marriage was childless. He adopted several children, but for him this was just a substitute and gave him no real satisfaction. He placed great value on racial selection, particularly in the officer corps of the SS and later the Gestapo. Meticulous selections for the officer candidate schools were made. Bitter experiences, however, have shown that the certified "racially valuable" were in no way the same as a "valuable person"!

Himmler's old friend and best helper, and in many cases also his inspiration, was the secretary of the Reich Chancery, Martin Bormann. He was instrumental in the realization of Himmler's ideas and especially later, in the general development of the power of the SS. They had known each other since 1924. Both were passionate farmers and they had many other common interests. Bormann's fundamental principle was to remain in the background and make decisions anonymously. He found Himmler to be just the right man to help his plans become a reality. Each complemented the other; but Bormann was the dominant one, and it was Bormann also who had the greatest influence on Hitler. It was at this time, when Bormann was [Rudolf] Hess's chief of staff, that he was spending more time with Hitler than he did Hess. From 1938 on he was constantly with Hitler, and in the later years no one, not even the highest Party leader, could even see Hitler without Bormann's permission. I have known Bormann personally since 1922, and I was the one who brought Bormann into the Party.

The following incident will prove my contention that Bormann was in many ways the stage manager.

In the spring of 1935, I and a few comrades from the time of the Mecklenburg Free Corps were guests at Bormann's house. At the time he lived in Pullach near Munich. Adjacent to his property was a large, newly built school for the Jesuits. Bormann told us that this school was completely modem in its furnishings and was organized in an exemplary manner. During our visit we observed a group of these Jesuit students running to their stadium. They were all selected: tall, slim, and yet strong-looking figures all seemingly of the same type. They could have been inducted immediately into the first company of Hitler's personal SS guard. Bormann now began talking about the Jesuits and their principles of education. Their main principle was "to unconditionally subordinate their own will to Jesuit ideas." Bormann maintained this should also be fundamental for the SS, if it were to become the sword of National Socialism. Soon afterward one could read in the SS newspaper, *Black Corps,* an article which expressed the above ideas almost exactly. The writer was anonymous. From that time on, one could see time and again articles in the brochures of the SS and in the lectures of the SS instructors expounding the necessity of this principle. In later orders Himmler expressed himself openly and stressed more and more the necessity of this principle: unconditionalsubjugation of one's own will to the ideas of National Socialist philosophy for each member of the SS. "Führer, give the order-we obey!" was not just an empty phrase for all of the SS. Himmler educated the SS, particularly the officers, to carry out this concept no matter what. Years and years of schooling in the SS finally created the SS soldier and especially the SS officers who blindly and tenaciously would obey any order from Himmler or Hitler without any thinking on his part. The shrewd propaganda of Joseph Goebbels- completed the education of the true National Socialist! The ideas of the Jesuit school combined with Hitler, Goebbels, and Himmler finally bore their fruit.

Shortly after Hitler's takeover in 1933, the first units of the Waffen SS were formed. In Berlin it was named the "Leibstandarte," Hitler's Praetorian Guard. Elsewhere in Hamburg, Ellwangen, Munich, and Dresden, elite regiments called "Political Support Troops" were formed from volunteers from the General SS. These battalions were forerunners of the later Waffen SS Divisions. In concentration camps the guard battalions steadily grew.

Himmler laid the cornerstone to the tremendous power which the SS had later. Now he went about finishing and expanding this instrument of power in the most covert way.

On June 30, 1934, the SS suppressed and wiped out the "planned insurrection of the SA." Chief of Staff Rohm and the higher leaders of the SA were killed. The SS became an independent organization. Again Himmler is the stepfather. The SA never recovered from this blow. Its second chief of staff, Lutze, was not a man who could stand up to Himmler.

Himmler became chief of the German police of the various German states. In setting up the Gestapo [Geheimnis StaatsPolizei-the Secret State Police], he created an inner political instrument of power. Under the direction of Heydrich and together with the "Nachrichtdienst" [intelligence agency] of the Security Police [SD], all of Germany was covertly but constantly spied on. Masked in the background stood the concentration camps.

On May 1, 1933, all Communist and Socialist Workers' unions were smashed and from that time on, there was no possibility for any resistance movements to rise again. They were ripped out by their very roots. All of this happened because the freethinking leaders had been arrested and put into concentration camps.

Himmler now set about to reorganize the police. The German police, no matter if they were state or local police, were for the most part Socialists or leaned toward democratic ideas. This was in contrast to the army, which was totally apolitical. Himmler now removed all the politically suspect or untrustworthy elements from the main body of the police forces and secretly substituted SS officers. From the first graduating class of the Officer Candidate School Tolz, half went to the police. The merging of the SS and the police was now completed. Later this led to the founding of the RSHA [Reichsicherheitshauptamt], the Security Ministry.

The secretary of the interior, [Wilhelm] Frick, was an old man without backbone. He and his whole office were headed by the state secretaries and ministry directors, who were anything but National Socialists. All members of the executive department of the interior were opposed to the head of the German Police, which was, of course part of the Department of the Interior. Frick had to go. Himmler became secretary of the interior and cleaned house. Oh! -not with force! No, very quietly and secretly. First this government president disappears, then that local official, and so on. In a short time, the inner administration was completely filled with Nazis. The Secret Service was very busy at that time.

Himmler became more and more unpopular among the masses of the people, mainly because of an extensive, horrible whispering campaign. They called him "Cheka Chief" [Cheka; Soviet secret police] and head of the mysterious concentration camps.

Hitler broke the Versailles Treaty and reinstituted the armed forces of Germany. Division after division was formed from the so-called 100,000-man army, which was all that was allowed by the Versailles Treaty. Every officer candidate had to go through a twelve-year service, which was planned and thought out to the smallest detail, and every one of these candidates later became an able company commander.

The crack Praetorian Guard, Hitler's personal SS regiment, became stronger, and the "political elite regiments" became the best-trained military regiments. In the concentration camps the guard battalions grew into active fighting regiments. This is how the First Division of the later Waffen SS came into existence, equipped with all possible technical units. The army tried in vain to halt this development and worked to counteract it with all its power. But Hitler ordered the continued expansion of the Waffen SS in the ratio of one SS unit for every six army units. Many problems arose with the army because of this. Himmler alone was unable to accomplish this since he was unwilling to quarrel with the high-ranking generals.

It was Bormann who came to the rescue and forced a truce. The generals sensed from the very beginning that the SS was their adversary, one which would later on destroy their plans to gather power for themselves. But the secret war with all the delaying tactics of suppression went on. The reactivated officers of the old imperial army were reactionary, conservative, and dreamed about their power positions in the old imperial Germany and the privileges they had. The ideas of National Socialism are totally alien to them, but most of all they vehemently rejected Socialistic ideas. They tried to prejudice their younger subordinate officers and most of all their soldiers against National Socialism. Himmler knew about all of this down to the smallest detail. He repeatedly spoke with Hitler to have these dangerous elements removed from the army. Even Bormann's assistance was no help. Hitler believed the success of the new state in all areas would eventually convince a large majority of the army of the correctness of the National Socialist ideas, and thereby nullify the efforts of the small reactionary minority. The attempt on Hitler's life in 1944 was only possible because Hitler never truly believed there was serious opposition in the army. This in spite of the fact that time and again proof was presented to him by Himmler and Bormann. Hitler wanted no interference in the rebuilding of the new armed forces and expressly forbade Himmler's Gestapo to interfere in any branch of the armed forces. The Security Ministry was at all times fully aware of all plans about the destruction of Nazi power among the circles of the reactionary officers. This almost openly conducted sabotage by these men in the later years of the war played a clear role in the armaments industry and even the conduct of the war itself. Hitler did not want to believe this. Because Himmler was not allowed to act, the activities of these men began to be increasingly felt. I ask: Would the war have gone differently, if all this obstructionism could have been brought to an end?

When Himmler became the commander of the Reserve Army after the attempt on Hitler's life in 1944, it was too late. With great emphasis and interest, Himmler accelerated the buildup and expansion of the Waffen SS. At the beginning of the war two powerful divisions were ready. Units of the Waffen SS had already participated in the annexation of Austria and Czechoslovakia. Death's Head units also participated in the occupation of Danzig [Gdansk, Poland] and the Sudetenland. The Waffen SS was totally composed of volunteers from all walks of German life. Hitler attached great importance on careful selection. [Himmler] repeatedly inspected the units, ruthlessly eliminated inept commanders, and made sure that capable experts were recruited from the army and the police. They received the best training according to the latest military knowledge. Most of the SS soldier's day was taken up with indoctrination into Nationalist Socialist ideas. Because of this mental saturation, the political soldier was created: the fighter who would summon all of his strength to give his all to the very last for the Nazi philosophy, which he now represents. Only because of this hard training is it possible to understand the tremendous feats accomplished in the various theaters of war, whether in the West or the East, by the divisions of the Waffen SS that grew out of these early regiments. Up to this point accomplishments of this type by soldiers had never been heard of and were incomparable to anything before.

As far as the public was concerned, Himmler remained completely in the shadows during the expansion of the SS. Himmler's plans were carried out by Jüttner, who was the chief of the SS Staff Headquarters. He was an outstanding member of the General Staff of the old army.

During the war the volunteer divisions of the so-called "BeuteGerma-

273

nen" [foreign nationals of German origin] came into existence in all occupied countries. No country and no race of people was overlooked by Himmler. His propaganda drums beat everywhere: Norwegians, Danes, Dutch, Flemish, Walloons, French, Spaniards, furthermore Mohammedans of the Sandschakund of Yugoslavia, Hungarians and Rumanians, Ukrainians, Latvians, Estonians, Laplanders, Finns, Swedes, and added to these contingents from all groups of German descent were fighting in the Waffen SS. All performed magnificently under great leadership. In the last years of the war, however, many of these volunteer units failed. Spirit alone is not always enough. Good leadership and careful training are the most important prerequisites for the success of a mission. Casualties among the Waffen SS were very high, as they were always used at the hot spots in any campaign. After the disaster at Stalingrad, where large parts of the army broke down and failed, the Waffen SS was to be the "fire brigade," and come to rescue the situation. But there just were not enough SS divisions left since the best had to fight the invasion in the West. Through Himmler's initiative, the "Dirlewanger" unit was created. Originally the commander of this unit took on only poachers and those who had broken the forestry laws. These volunteers came from the jails, prisons, and even the concentration camps. They wanted to fight on the front lines. Later they also took criminals convicted of assault, and others who had committed crimes which were not exactly dishonorable. Finally they took criminals who had already served time and political prisoners from the concentration camps. General Dirlewanger personally selected these men from those proposed by the camp Kommandants. They were dressed in uniforms of the Waffen SS and were used to fight the partisans on the Western Front. Many former prisoners fought bravely, received decorations, and were promoted. They were, however, not really a reliable and trustworthy unit as a whole. There were many deserters among the "politicals." The unit suffered high casualties, and Himmler ordered a continued stream of "volunteers" from the concentration camps. The prisoners saw their chance to escape the continually worsening conditions in the camps, and the number of volunteers grew steadily, but only about one in ten could be used.

The real goal of Himmler's work was definitely the resettlement and colonization of farmlands. He believed that the only way the German people would secure permanence was by an overwhelming number of farmers who owned enough land and were on a sound economic footing. These were his goals long before the Nazi Party took power. He never denied that the only way this could be achieved was to take land in the East by force. Because of his initiative the preparation of the German settlement in the Polish areas of Bessarabia and Wohlnya took place.

He became national commissioner for the consolidation of German nationhood and thereby created the official organization for planning and execution,together with the German Central Agency, which was responsible for the welfare of the German ethnic resettlers, carried out further resettlement during the war years. The main task of this department was to confiscate and admininster all the conquered land and soil in the occupied countries. Those properties and real estate holdings which personally interested Himmler were to be confiscated and made ready for resettlement. A central clearing office was created to take care of the relocation of the evacuated population who had originally owned the lands. I am not really acquainted .with Himmler's resettlement plans, but I know about the plans concerning the Bohemia and Moravian districts [Czech territory] and the plans to force the Polish people further to the east. This was done to create a cohesive German core area and, furthermore, to create a continuously connected German settlement area in the Baltic states from Lithuania to Livonia and a large area in the so-called "Black Earth" zone.

Only by using force against whole nations could Himmler see the possibility of expanding the German living space and thereby secure the future of the German nation. Himmler summoned up all his strength for these settlement plans and pushed as hard as he could wherever possible to. bring these plans into reality.

A law was passed to "prevent congenitally diseased offspring." Himmler was the chief architect of this law. With this law the health of the German people was in large measure secured for the future. The purpose of this law was to "clean up" existing conditions, namely: the incurably mentally ill who had inherited this from their parents, and later the professional criminals. They were to be exterminated and designated as "a life worthy of annihilation." This order originated in Hitler's Chancellery. Himmler stood behind it. The cover name used for this operation was "Transport Organization for the Common Good." A number of doctors and agents in Hitler's Chancellery conducted the selection in the institutions and also later in the concentration camps. Some of the concentration camps had to furnish able-bodied block leaders to do the work involved in the cremations. The killing of those selected was carried out in some of the insane asylums, which were evacuated for this reason. The method used was carbon monoxide administered through the showers and bathhouses. One of these doctors, Dr. Schumann, later conducted experiments at Auschwitz using X-rays to sterilize people. One of the agents of Hitler's Chancellery was later in charge of the Globocnik death camp [Majdanek], which exterminated Jews. Long before the war began Himmler was given full authority by Hitler to use every possible means to carry out all these measures to ensure the basic requirements for the security of Germany, even if those measures conflicted with the existing laws of the country. Hitler's secret decree was not even known to the inner Party members until much later. At the beginning of the war, the results of this decree began to be felt. In order to scare off sabotage during the outset of the war, even the slightest rule breaking was immediately punished with the death penalty on Himmler's order. This also applied to all draft dodgers, especially the Jehovah's Witnesses. The execution orders came from the Gestapo office and read as follows: "John Doe is to be shot immediately by order of Himmler," without any further grounds or any explanations. The execution was always carried out in the nearest concentration camp. A press release to the public stated that John Doe had been executed because of either draft dodging or sabotage. Himmler wrote the press release. There was never a verdict from any court for any of these executions. These executions took place based only on the investigation by the Gestapo and Himmler's decision with the help of Hitler's decree.

I also know of executions of SS members who had been guilty of service-related offenses. In these cases, Himmler was pitiless and absolutely rejected any extenuating circumstances brought up by others. After the SS became independent and grew to enormous numbers, Himmler created the SS court. Under this SS jurisdiction Himmler wanted to protect the laws of the SS concerning honor, loyalty, sanctity of a person's private possessions, truthfulness, etc., and be able to punish those who broke these laws. Until then there were no laws on the books concerning these idealistic values. Furthermore, the SS jurisdiction was to elevate discipline and gentlemanly behavior in the General SS units.

The verdicts handed out by these SS courts, later called "Field Court

Martials of the SS and the Police," were extremely harsh, in accordance with Himmler's will. To be discharged or even kicked out of the SS in peacetime was such a disgrace that it was previously unheard of. These former SS were unable to get any work anywhere in Germany, other than as very low-paid, unskilled laborers. Any social advancement was impossible for them. Verdicts from the field court martials were the same. Rarely had any revolutionary tribunal throughout history handed out so many death sentences than the field court martials of the SS and Gestapo. During the course of the war even Himmler became fed up with the many death verdicts because he had to approve each one, and thus instituted the so- called rehabilitation units at the front lines, "ascension squads" or "suicide squads," as they were called. One of their jobs was to find mines in the enemy minefields, or they were used as rear guards, where chances of survival were almost zero. Very few survived these rear guard duties with their lives and limbs. But if they did they were considered exonerated. The death sentence was categorically handed down for homosexual activities, desertion. cowardice in the face of the enemy, and refusal to obey an order. Other crimes were having intercourse with Jews or blacklisted racial members, and later the taking of Jewish property [of those gassed in the concentration camps]. Guards who were lax in their guard duties in the concentration camps were also severely punished. This crime could even be applied to those commanders and staff officers in whose concentration camps there were relatively many SS court verdicts handed out. This meant they also were lax in their guard and supervisory duties.

The SS had punishment camps in Mazkau and Dachau. These were comparable to prisons and jails and were greatly feared. That's where the SS and Gestapo were sent to do their time. In Himmler's point of view, those sentenced by an SS court could never be punished hard enough. Since these camps were soon overcrowded, the largest part of those sentenced were sent to the front to the suicide squads. Those sentenced also had the option of being sent immediately to these suicide squads. This request was usually granted.

Himmler also created a court of honor. One of the fundamental laws of the SS concerned a man's honor and was considered inviolable. This court of honor had to settle violations against the law of honor or had to make decisions as to how violated honor could be reestablished. The higher officers of the General SS and the active officers of the Waffen

SS each received a sword of honor and rules of honorable conduct. This speaks very clearly about Himmler's attitude on the question of honor and his pitiless inflexibility in these matters.

Himmler's attitude about the concentration camps and his views about the treatment of prisoners was never made clear because his opinions changed from time to time. There never were any policies about the treatment of prisoners or about the questions concerning this matter. Over the years his orders caused countless contradictions because of his changing attitude. This could also be noticed during his inspection tours of the concentration camps. One could never pin him down to a clear policy about the treatment of prisoners. One time he decreed, "Strictest, merciless treatment of prisoners without consideration," then next he decreed, "Gentle treatment, watching carefully over the prisoners' health conditions and trying to educate them with rehabilitation and discharge in mind." Another time, "Increase the work day to twelve hours and the harshest punishment for laziness," the next, "Increase in prisoner privileges and construction of brothels to voluntarily get higher work quotas performed; supplementary food for prisoners has to be curtailed in order not to deprive the surrounding, hard-working civilian population of their necessary food supply," then next, "The camp Kommandant has to do everything in his power to see to it that the rations allocated by the Ministry of Food will be increased for the prisoners and to add to that supply by gathering edible things growing in the wild." Then, "In view of the importance of defense contract plans there can be no consideration given to the health of the prisoners; they must be used to the utmost to get as much work out of them as possible." Then again, "So that prisoners can be deployed as long as possible in the arms factories, any unreasonable demands by the foreman to work harder must be vigorously opposed." His orders were always changing!

This also could be felt in the penalties. One time he complained there was too much corporal punishment. Another time, "Discipline in the camps has become very lax, drastic steps must be taken, and there must be harsher punishments. "

Here is just one example:

In 1940 Himmler suddenly drove up to Sachsenhausen Concentration Camp. Just as he was approaching the guard post, a group of prisoners were casually pulling a large wagon past him. Neither the guard nor the prisoners noticed Himmler sitting in the car, so the prisoners didn't take their caps off, which is what they were always supposed to do when passing any officer. Himmler drove directly through the guard post and right up to the administration building. I was just about to leave to go into the camp since I was the officer in charge at that time, and I was able to report to him on the spot. "Where is the Kommandant?" was his first angry question after a short greeting. The Kommandant, SS Major Eisfeld, appeared after a while. In the meantime, Himmler had entered the camp. Himmler snapped at the Kommandant that he was used to a different kind of discipline in a concentration camp. "The prisoners don't even salute anymore!" he barked at the Kommandant. Himmler dismissed the Kommandant's answer and did not talk to him anymore. He inspected the arresting rooms briefly, where a few special prisoners had been brought just before he had arrived; then he drove off immediately. Two days after that Eisfeld was demoted from his post; Loritz was brought back again and became Kommandant. Previously Loritz had been at Dachau and then later district leader of the General SS in Klagenfurt. Himmler had removed Loritz from Dachau before because he was too harsh with the prisoners and also because he cared little about the camp itself. In 1942, on Pohl's suggestion, Loritz was again removed from Sachsenhausen, for the same reasons.

The development of the war forced the use of all available workers for the arms industry. A considerable reserve of workers could be found in the concentration camps working in nonessential jobs.

Himmler promised Hitler the use of the SS and the prisoners to bring about a defense industry effort that would lead to victory. From that time on there was only one motto for Himmler: "Ruthless deployment of all available prisoners." He also instructed Eichmann to speed up his campaign against the Jews. Himmler told the arms industry: "Build work camps and demand work forces from me via the Mobilization Ministry. There are plenty available." He is practically promising tens, even hundreds of thousands of prisoners from campaigns which hadn't even been completed and for which an estimate of the final outcome couldn't even be guessed at. Neither Pohl nor Kaltenbrunner dared to dissuade Himmler from this bragging promise to furnish any number of prisoners needed. Each month reports were worked out down to the smallest detail clearly showing the condition of the prisoners, their exact numbers, and where they were deployed for work. Himmler knew exactly what the situation was, yet he pushed and demanded, "Defense! Prisoners! Defense!"

On Himmler's orders the greatest care had to be observed concerning the families of the prisoners, regardless of the reasons of arrest. The families of the prisoners were not to suffer any want because their breadwinner had been arrested, and they were amply assisted. When a German prisoner was handed over to a concentration camp, he immediately had to fill out forms which clearly showed his financial and economic situation. At that time the director of the political branch had the duty, if the prisoner so desired, to notify the proper authorities in the district where his family lived to make sure the family suffered no hardships. After four weeks he had to report that the family had been taken care of. If this report was not made, then the appropriate local branch of the Gestapo or the criminal police became involved. The prisoner was also required to report to his superiors if he heard that things were bad at home from the letters he received, or that the aid was inadequate. I also know of cases where Himmler personally saw to it that gifted children of prisoners received scholarships to attend national political education institutions. In peacetime no prisoner could be released until his economic security was guaranteed. After his release the prisoner was said to be rehabilitated and, therefore, should suffer no disadvantage or harm in making a living. His imprisonment was not listed anywhere except in the files of Himmler's office. Only out of dire necessity could the local police or Party officers get this information from Himmler's office, and even then they had to have a very good reason. Quite often, however, it happened that overzealous and hateful citizens who wanted to prove they were 100 percent Nazis, and malicious and petty low-ranking Party officials made life very difficult for the released prisoner. It also happened that the ex-prisoner in his need turned to his former concentration camp for help. When Himmler learned of cases like this, he took really drastic measures. Even Pohl was now as infected as Himmler was for more prisoners working to produce more weapons. Pohl persuaded the Kommandants, the camp inspectors and the administration of all the camps to use all their power and strength and do everything possible to deploy prisoners for the weapons industry. But then it became apparent that even though the arms industry still needed enormous additional numbers of workers' the construction of the workers housing stalled these efforts. The Organization Todt [federally conscripted work force] was now brought into the picture and had to construct camps for the industrial defense workers. This organization in turn demanded prisoners because they didn't have enough workers. But where were we supposed to house these new prisoners? Day and night Maurer went on inspection tours and was forced to deny emergency housing because there was a lack of even the most basic necessities. This in turn caused a delay in deployment. Himmler was livid and appointed a fact-finding committee giving them special powers to ferret out the guilty ones. Auschwitz was crammed to the limit with prisoners who were waiting to be transported to the industrial defense camps. Yet Eichmann kept the transports coming, overcrowding Auschwitz even more. The transfer of workers to the most important defense plants naturally progressed very slowly. At least two years had been wasted. Himmler then appointed Dr. Kammler the commissioner of this project. Kammler, however, was not a magician. Weeks, even months passed by without any noticeable progress. The constant air raids on Germany slowed, blocked, and crippled everything for months. Himmler continued to push; his promises [to Hitler] were really bothering him.

In Auschwitz thousands of able-bodied workers became weak and died before they even saw a job in a defense plant. In very poorly constructed, makeshift camps, the prisoners literally became human wreckage before they ever got a chance to do any work which could have contributed to victory. They traveled to the concentration camps in order to be made healthy and be able to work again. But in reality the conditions in the camps were already subhuman because of the war. This constant inflow of prisoners only made these conditions worse and led to total debilitation; as a consequence, they fell prey to one of the many rampant epidemics.

Himmler knew all about this, either through his personal inspections or through oral and written reports of all the officials involved or through their offices. He didn't pay any attention to any of this. He felt that this was the problem of the various offices in charge of the camps. Let them find the solutions. He categorically demanded again and again, "More prisoners, increased production, forced deployment!" He threatened everyone who delayed the SS court!

My personal contacts and meetings with Himmler during my membership in the SS were as follows:

In June 1934 at Stettin, he inspected the Pomeranian SS. Himmler asked me if I wouldn't like to serve in the General SS in a concentration camp. Only after considerable reflection with my wife, because we had planned to settle down and get a farm, did I decide to accept. This gave me a chance to become a soldier again. On December 1, 1934, the inspector general of the concentration camps, Eicke, summoned me to Dachau.

In 1936 there was the main inspection of all the SS installations including the concentration camp at Dachau. All the political leaders of the district and the nation, all the SA and SS generals, were there, led by Himmler. At that time, I was the duty officer and represented the Kommandant, who was absent. Himmler was in a great mood and the inspection went without any problems. At that time everything truly was in the best order at Dachau. The prisoners were well-fed, clean, and decently clothed, had good housing, and most of them worked productively in the shops. The prison infirmary was practically empty. The total number of prisoners, approximately 2,500, were housed in ten brick barracks. Hygiene was adequate in the camp, and there was plenty of water. Prisoners changed their personal clothing once a week, bed-sheets and blankets once a month. A third of them were political prisoners; two-thirds were in protective custody: asocials, work dodgers, homosexuals, and about two hundred Jews.

During the inspection Himmler and Bormann addressed me and asked if I was satisfied with my assignment and how my family was. A short time afterwards I was promoted to second lieutenant. As was his habit, Himmler selected a couple of prisoners and asked them the reason for their imprisonment in front of all the bigwigs. They happened to be a couple of Communist leaders who quite honestly remarked that they were Communists and intended to remain so. A few were professional criminals who minimized their records quite a bit. However, quick reference to their actual records freshened their memories considerably. This behavior was typical of many professional criminals, and I have witnessed this very often. Himmler ordered that those who had lied be given punishment details for several Sundays. Then there were a few asocials who were constantly spending their entire wages on alcohol and let public welfare take care of their families. There was also a Social Democratic minister from Brandenburg, Dr. Jasper, and also some Jewish emigrants who had returned from Palestine who answered all the questions asked of them with their well-known, ready wit.

The next time I met Himmler was in the summer of 1938 in the Sachsenhausen Concentration Camp. The minister of the interior, Dr. Frick, inspected the concentration camp for the first time. Accompanying him were all the mayors and police chiefs of Germany's largest cities. Himmler led the tour and made all the commentaries. At that time, I was the adjutant of the camp commander and spent the entire inspection tour near Himmler. I had a good chance to observe him closely. He was happy and quite satisfied to be able to finally show the minister of the interior and the gentlemen of the inner administration of the nation one of the mysterious and notorious concentration camps. Himmler was bombarded with questions. Very calmly and with great charm, often quite sarcastically, he answered all of them. Embarrassing questions about the number of inmates and others he was able to sidestep very charmingly. All numbers concerning inmates or prisoners in concentration camps were treated top secret according to Himmler's orders. As far as I know Sachsenhausen had at that time about four thousand prisoners, mostly professional criminals. They were housed in clean wooden barracks, half for sleeping, half as living quarters. The food was known to be good and plentiful. Clothing was adequate and clean since we had very modern laundry facilities. The infirmary with its treatment rooms was exemplary, and the total number of sick prisoners was low. All installations of the camp were shown except for the cell block, which was never allowed to be shown to any outsiders because most of them were Himmler's special prisoners in protective custody. I am convinced that nothing escaped the critical eyes of these experienced government and police officials. Frick showed great interest and remarked during dinner that it was actually a shame that he had not visited a concentration camp earlier and that only then, in 1938, did he do so for the first time. The inspector of the concentration camps, Eicke, explained about the other concentration camps and their idiosyncrasies.

Even though he was pressed for time and was constantly bombarded with questions, Himmler found time to have a personal talk with me and especially inquired about my family. He never failed to ask about my family on any occasion, and one had a feeling that he didn't do this out of politeness.

The next encounter, in January 1940, I have already written about.

That was the incident with the prisoner group which did not salute.

In November 1940 I gave my first oral report to Himmler about Auschwitz. Major [Heinrich] Vogel was there also. I described in detail and depicted the deplorable state of affairs starkly, which at the time was a sensitive subject to bring up. Compared to the catastrophic conditions of the later years, these were minor. He made very few comments and only remarked that as Kommandant it was actually my job to alleviate these conditions. Besides, there was a war going on, and it was necessary to improvise. Even in a concentration camp one could not live as if it were peacetime. The soldier at the front lines had to do without a lot of things, so why not the prisoners? When I repeatedly brought up the danger of epidemics because of the inadequate hygiene facilities, he cut me off in a short manner:

"You are too pessimistic!" Only when I started reporting about the overall picture by using maps and diagrams did his interest become aroused. His whole attitude changed immediately. He became very lively and started planning, issuing one directive after another, or made notes about all the things that needed to be done on the estates around Auschwitz.

Auschwitz was to be "the" experimental agricultural station for theentire East. The possibilities which existed here had never been possible in Germany itself. Certainly there were enough workers available. Every necessary agricultural experiment was to be tried out there. Huge laboratories and plant cultivation departments had to be built. Cattle breeding of all types and breeds of animals was to become important. Major Vogel was supposed to immediately recruit the necessary experts. The marshlands were to be drained and developed. A dam was constructed on the Weichsel River. Compared to all these difficulties, the deplorable conditions in the camp were nothing. In the near future he was going to see for himself what Auschwitz was like. He continued with his agricultural planning even down to the smallest details and stopped only when his adjutant called to his attention the fact that a very important person had been waiting for a long time to see him. Himmler's interest in Auschwitz had been aroused, but not to get rid of the terrible conditions there or to prevent them from happening in the future, but rather to increase them by his "I don't see anything" attitude. My fellow officer Vogel was enthusiastic about the agricultural research stations being planned on such a large scale. I confess that even I, a farmer at heart, was also infected by all this. As a camp Kommandant, however, I sawall hope of ever making Auschwitz healthy and sanitary vanishing. There was still a vague hope in my mind because of the announced visit of Himmler in the near future. I was hoping that during his personal inspection of the camp he would be influenced to alleviate the obvious shortcomings and deplorable conditions. In the meantime, I worked hard to improvise in order to prevent the worst from happening, but it wasn't of much use since I could not keep up with the constant growth of the camp and the steadily rising number of prisoners. No sooner had a barracks been filled-normally they housed about two hundred-than another transport would arrive with a thousand prisoners standing on the ramp. All my protests to the various departments of the SS administration in Krakow and elsewhere were in vain. The answer was always the same: "The roundup actions ordered by Himmler have to be carried out!"

Finally, on March I, 1941, Himmler appeared in Auschwitz. With him were District Party Leader Bracht, governors, and the high-ranking SS officers and political leaders of Silesia, leading corporate officers of the I. G. Farben industry and the inspector of the concentration camps, Glucks. Glucks had arrived earlier and constantly warned me not to say anything that would displease Himmler! And yet, everything that I had to report was unpleasant. Using maps and diagrams I explained to Himmler the situation as it was when I became Kommandant, the expansion made since, and the present conditions. Naturally, I couldn't really talk openly about the defects and flaws that really bothered me in the front of all the outsiders present. But I completely made up for this later when I was in the car driving through the camp with just Himmler and Schmauser. The hoped-for results failed to materialize. Even as we walked through the camp and I quietly pointed out to Himmler the worst conditions, like the overcrowding, the lack of water, etc., he hardly listened to me. When I begged him time and again to stop the new transports, he actually barked at me and bluntly refused. I could not expect any kind of solution from him. In fact, the exact opposite happened. After dinner in the SS messhall, he really got started telling me about the new tasks being designed for Auschwitz. He talked about expanding the prisoner of war camp to hold 100,000 prisoners. When we were out in the surrounding area, he discussed this and pointed out the approximate area that he wanted me to use. The district leader objected to that, the governor tried to point out the shortage of water, and they all tried to block this move because of the sewage contamination of the watery marshes. Himmler just smiled and disposed of their objections saying, "Gentlemen, this project will be completed; my reasons for this are more important than your objections!" Ten thousand prisoners were to be ready when needed for the construction projects of the I. G. Farben industry. The concentration camp at Auschwitz was to be enlarged to a peacetime capacity of thirty thousand prisoners. Himmler also said that he intended to move some of the important arms industry into this area. Space was to be left open and ready for this project. In addition to this, don't neglect the experimental agricultural stations and the farms. All that was to be done despite the well-known scarcity of building materials. The district leader pointed this out. Himmler answered: "And for what purpose are the brick factories which were confiscated by the SS, and for what purpose does the cement factory exist? There just has to be more work done, or the concentration camp will just take over these factories and run them themselves!

"Draining marshes and providing water supplies are strictly a question of technology, which is a matter to be solved by the experts, but are not reasons for rejections. The enlargement of the camp is to be accelerated with all means available. You will just have to make improvements as you go.

"Epidemics which occur must be contained and ruthlessly fought against. But the camp categorically cannot be closed to new arrivals. My orders for police roundups must be continued. I do *not* acknowledge the difficulties in Auschwitz!"

Shortly before he left Himmler visited my family and ordered me to remodel and enlarge my house to be able to host representatives who would visit. He returned to his old, charming self and became very talkative, even though he had been very brusque and harsh just moments before at the meeting. Glucks was devastated because of my constant objections and complaints to Himmler. He also was unable to help me. As far as my requests for change in personnel, transfers, etc., he also could be of no help since he had no officers or NCOs who were any better than what I had. He could not expect other camp Kommandants to exchange good men for inferior ones. "It is probably not going to be as bad as I anticipated, and I'm sure you'll master these problems!" That was the end of my conference with my superior officer. This is how Himmler's inspection ended which I had looked forward to with great hopes! No help from anyone or anywhere! I was supposed to wrestle with this problem by myself and solve it on my own. Grimly I went to work. I gave no quarter to any

SS soldier or any prisoner. The existing facilities were to be used to their very limits. Almost all my time was spent on the road locating, purchasing, stealing, or confiscating all sorts of materials. I had to help myself, and I did it thoroughly! Thanks to my good connections with industry I was able to gather together tremendous amounts of materials.

In the summer of 1941 Himmler summoned me to Berlin to give me the disastrous and harsh order for the mass annihilation of the Jews from all over Europe. This resulted in Auschwitz becoming the greatest killing institution in history. This also affected the thousands upon thousands of non-Jews who were supposed to stay alive. They, in fact, died in epidemics and from illnesses caused by the overcrowding of the able-bodied Jews. The overcrowding of the Jews selected to work was the catastrophic reason for all our woes, illnesses, epidemics, inadequate food supplies, inadequate clothing, and the lack of even the basic hygienic facilities. Himmler, and Himmler alone, bears the guilt for this, since he constantly refused to acknowledge any reports from anyone about these conditions and refused to do anything about them. He did not remove the cause of these conditions by stopping the transports and also created no remedy. I have already given the details of this horrible order in a previous writing. As he gave this order, Himmler was unusually and uncommonly serious and tight-lipped. The entire meeting was very short and strictly businesslike.

The next meeting was in the summer of 1942, when Himmler visited Auschwitz for the second and last time. The inspection lasted two days and Himmler looked at everything very thoroughly. Also present at this inspection were District Leader Bracht, SS General Schmauser, Dr. Kamm-ler, and others. The first thing after their arrival was a meeting in the officers' club. With the help of maps and diagrams, I had to show the present condition of the camp. After that we went to the construction head-quarters, where Kammler, using maps, blueprints, and models explained the planned or already progressing construction. He did *not,* however, keep quiet about the difficulties that existed which hindered the construction. He also pointed out those projects which were impossible not only to start, but to finish. Himmler listened with great interest, asked about some of the technical details, and agreed with the overall planning. Himmler did not utter a single word about Kammler'srepeated references to the many difficulties. Afterwards there was a trip through the whole area of concern:

first the farms and soil enrichment projects, the dam-building site, the laboratories and plant cultivation in Raisko, the cattle-raising farms and the orchards. Then we visited Birkenau, the Russian camp, the Gypsy camp, and a Jewish camp. Standing at the entrance, he asked for a situation report on the layout of the swamp reclamation and the water projects. He also wanted a report on the intended expansion projects. He watched the prisoners at work, inspected the housing, the kitchens, and the sick bays. I constantly pointed out the shortcomings and the bad conditions. I am positive he noticed them. He saw the emaciated victims of epidemics. The doctors explained things without mincing words. He saw the over-crowded sick bays, and the child mortality in the Gypsy camp and he also witnessed the terrible childhood disease called noma [a gangrenous mouth disease in children weakened by disease and malnutrition]. Himmler also saw the overcrowded barracks, the primitive and totally inadequate toilet and wash facilities. He was told about the high rate of illness and the death rate by the doctors and their causes. He had everything explained to him in the greatest detail. He saw everything in stark reality. Yet he said absolutely nothing. He really gave me a tongue lashing in Birkenau, when 1 went on and on about the terrible conditions. He screamed, "I don't want to hear any more about any existing difficulties! For an SS officer there are no difficulties. His task is always to immediately overcome any difficulty by himself! As to how? That's your headache, not mine!" Kammler and Bischoff got the same answers. After inspecting Birkenau, Himmler witnessed the complete extermination process of a transport of Jews which had just arrived. He also looked on for a while during a selection of those who would work and those who would die without any complaint on his part. Himmler made no comment about the extermination process. He just looked on in total silence. I noticed that he very quietly watched the officers, the NCOs and me several times during the process. The inspec-tion continued to the Buna Works, where he inspected the plant as thoroughly as he had done with the prisoner workers and how they did their jobs. He saw and heard about their state of health. Kammler was told in no uncertain terms, "You complain about problems, but just look at what the I. G. Farben plant has accomplished in one year in spite of having the same problems as you!" Yet he said nothing about the fact that I. G. Farben had thousands of experts and approximately thirty thousand prisoners available at that time. When Himmler asked about the work quotas and the performance of the prisoners, the spokesmen for I. G. Farben gaveevasive answers. Then he told me that no matter what, I had to increase the prisoners' output of work! Again it was up to me to find a way to accomplish this. He said this in spite of being told by the district leader and by I. G. Farben that soon the food rations for all prisoners were to be considerably decreased; even though he saw for himself the general conditions of the prisoners. From the Buna Works we went to the sewer gas installations. There was no program at all because the materials were not available. This was one of the sorest points at Auschwitz and was everyone's main concern. The almost untreated sewage from the main camp was draining directly into the Sola River. Because of the continuing epidemics raging in the camp, the surrounding civilian population was constantly exposed to the danger of epidemic infections. The district leader quite clearly described these conditions and begged Weise to remedy this situation. Himmler answered that Kammler would work on the matter with all his energy.

Himmler was much more interested in the next part of the inspection, the natural rubber plantations Koc-Sagys. He was always more interested in hearing positive reports rather than negative ones. The SS officer who ~as able to give only positive reports and was clever enough to show even the negative things in a positive light was both lucky and enviable.

On the evening of the first day of the inspection tour, all the guests and camp officers of Auschwitz were present at a dinner. Himmler asked all of them to introduce themselves before dinner; to those he was interested in, he asked about their families and the various duties they performed. During the dinner he questioned me more closely about some of the officers who caught his special attention. I took this opportunity and explained my needs concerning staffing. I stressed in detail the large number of officers who were unable to run a concentration camp and their poor leadership qualities concerning the guard troops. I also asked him to replace many of them and increase the number of guard troops. "You will be surprised," he answered, "to see how you will have to deal with impossible leadership types. I need every officer, NCO, and soldier that I can use on the front lines. For these reasons it is impossible to increase your guard units. Just get more guard dogs. Invent every possible technical way to save on man- power to guard the prisoners. My deputy of the dog squad will soon acquaint you with the modem, up-to-date deployment of guard dogs to illustrate how the number of guards can be reduced. The number of escapes from Auschwitz is unusually high and has never before happened to such a degree in a concentration camp. Every means," he repeated, "every means that you wish to use is perfectly all right with me to prevent escapes or attempts! The epidemic of escapes at Auschwitz must be stopped!"

After dinner the district leader invited Himmler, Schmauser, Kammler, Caesar, and me to his house near Katowice. Himmler was also supposed to stay there because on the following day he had to settle some important questions concerning the local population and resettlement with the district leader. Even though he had been in a very bad mood during the day and had hardly talked with civility to any of us, during the evening he was just the opposite in our small circle. He was in a very good mood that evening; charming and very talkative, especially with the two ladies, the wife of the district leader and my wife. He discussed every topic that came up in conversation: the raising of children, new houses, paintings, and books. He told about his experiences with the Waffen SS divisions at the front lines and about his front line inspection tours with Hitler. He carefully avoided mentioning, even with a single word, anything that he had seen during the day or any matters concerning official business. Any attempt by the district leader to bring business into the conversation was ignored by Himmler. We broke up quite late. Himmler, who usually drank very little alcohol, that evening had a few glasses of red wine and smoked, which was another thing he didn't usually do. Everyone was captivated by his lively stories and cheerfulness. I had never seen him like that before.

On the second day Schmauser and I picked him up at the district leader's house, and the inspection continued. He looked at the original camp, the kitchen, and the women's camp. At that time the women were located in the first row of barracks, numbers 1 to 11, then next to the SS Headquarters building. Then he inspected the stables, the workshops, Canada, and the DA W [German armaments factories], the butcher shop, the bakery, the construction units, and the planning board for the troops. He examined everything thoroughly and saw the prisoners, asked about their reasons for being there, and wanted an accurate count.

He did not allow us to lead him around. Instead he demanded to see the things he wanted to see. He saw the overcrowding in the women's camp, the inadequate toilet facilities, and the lack of water. He demanded to see the inventory of clothing from the quartermaster, and saw that everywhere there was a lack of everything. He asked about the food rations and extra rations given for strenuous labor down to the smallest detail. In the women's camp he wanted to observe the corporal punishment of a woman who was a professional criminal and a prostitute. She had been repeatedly stealing whatever she could lay her hands on. He was mainly interested in the results corporal punishment had on her. He personally reserved the decision about corporal punishment for women. Some of the women who were introduced to' him and who had been imprisoned for a minor infraction he pardoned. They were allowed to leave the camp. He discussed the fanatical beliefs of the Jehovah's Witnesses with some of the female members. After the inspection we went to my office for a final discussion. There, with Schmauser present, he told me in essence the following: "I have looked at Auschwitz thoroughly. I have seen everything as it is: all the deplorable conditions and difficulties to the fullest, and have heard about these from all of you. I cannot change a thing about it. You will have to see how you can cope with it. We are in the middle of a war and accordingly have to learn to think in terms of that war. Under no circumstances can the police actions of the roundups and the transports of the enemy be stopped-least of all because of the demonstrated lack of housing which you have shown me. Eichmann's program will continue and will be accelerated every month from now on. See to it that you move ahead with the completion of Birkenau. The Gypsies are to be exterminated. With the same relentlessness you will exterminate those Jews who are unable to work. In the near future the work camps near the industrial factories will take the first of the large numbers of able-bodied Jews; then you will have room to breathe again here. Also, in Auschwitz you will complete the war production facilities. Prepare yourself for this. Kammler will do his very best to fully support you concerning the construction program. The agricultural experiments will be pushed ahead intensively, as I have the greatest need for the results. I saw your work and your accomplishments. I am satisfied with them and I thank you. I hereby promote you to lieutenant colonel!"

This is how Himmler finished his important inspection of Auschwitz.

He saw everything and understood all the consequences. I wonder if his

"I am unable to help you" statement was intentional. After our meeting and discussion in my office, he made an inspection of my home and its furnishings. He was very enthusiastic about it and talked at length with my wife and the children. He was excited and in high spirits. 1 drove him to the airport; we exchanged brief goodbyes, and he flew back to Berlin.

The war was approaching its end. As the Russian offensive approached in January 1945, Himmler was forced to make a decision. Should the concentration camps be evacuated, or should they be left to the enemy? Himmler ordered the evacuation and wanted the prisoners moved to concentration camps closer to Germany. This order was the death sentence for tens of thousands of prisoners. Most of them died in death marches or in commandeered open railroad cars during transport. The temperature was below zero [Celsius], and the snow was very deep. They were transported without any hope of food or clothing. Most of the prisoners did not survive these conditions. The arrival of the survivors in the receiving camps also increased the already terrible, inhuman conditions there. There were so many corpses that it was difficult to bum them. But the order stood: "The camps are to be evacuated as the enemy approaches." One exception was made. Pohl and the Gestapo office urgently petitioned Himmler to leaveCamp Buchenwald to the enemy, but only after the most prominent and important prisoners were evacuated. It was totally impractical to march over a hundred thousand sick and disabled prisoners from Buchenwald through the densely populated German state of Thuringia. For all practical purposes the railroad could not be used because of enemy air raids. Reports came to Hitler that after the Americans liberated Buchenwald, prisoners were said to have armed themselves and raped and pillaged the city of Weimar. When Hitler heard this, he ordered that all the able-bodied prisoners be evacuated without exception as soon as the enemy approached the camps. Soon after that all inmates of the concentration camps and the work camps were on German highways marching to the next concentration camp. The result was unbelievable chaos everywhere. Radio messages still kept coming, but there was no longer any way to have any semblance of order in this chaos.

Near Sachsenhausen I personally tried to have this insane order rescinded. I frantically tried to get through to Himmler with the help of Muller and the Gestapo office. Himmler did not change the order! He gave specific instructions to clear out even the very last of the concentration camps. To where? He didn't say! In addition, there was the threat that any camp commander who disobeyed this order was to be executed. Representatives of the International Red Cross were constantly at my side and wanted to put the camps under the protection of the Red Cross. Himmler refused. Now there was no more hope of saving the prisoners. Only a few highways and roads were available. These were clogged with retreating army units and refugees. Everywhere one could see these prisoners staggering along and misery abounding. There were provisions for perhaps two or three days; then nothing. The Red Cross was constantly on the move to help with food packages, and tried to prevent the worst from happening. I myself was on the road day and night trying to find work camps to assemble the prisoners and to find food and help for the sick. The enemy, hunger and illness, however, were faster than I could be. The columns of misery were overrun by the enemy. Thousands of dead and sick lined the roads they traveled. In the evacuated camps, there were thousands of dead and dying, and those for whom we could no longer provide. This was the end of the concentration camps, and this was the shocking and horrible picture seen by the enemy as they marched in. All because of Himmler's insane evacuation order! I met Himmler for the last time on May 3. Following his orders the remaining officers from the Inspectorate of Concentration Camps had followed Himmler to the city of Flensburg. Glucks, Maurer, and I reported to him. He had just come from a meeting with the remaining members of the Reich government. He was vibrant and in a terrific mood! He greeted us and immediately gave us the following orders: "Glucks and I will escape over the Green border to Denmark disguised as army corporals cut off from their units and there disappear. Maurer and the rest of the officers from the inspectorate are also to fade into army units. All further arrangements will be made by Colonel Hintz, the chief of police in Flensburg." Himmler shook our hands and dismissed us. Professor Gebhardt and [Brigadier General Walter] Schellenberg from the Reich Security Office were with Himmler at the time. According to what Gebhardt told Glucks, Himmler intended to disappear into Sweden.

It was Himmler's will to create the SS as a powerful and invincible organization which would guarantee the protection of the future National Socialist state. He repeatedly demanded toughness, self-discipline, and commitment of the whole person to the point of totally ignoring one's own self and without any personal considerations. Your own will had to be subordinated and subjugated to all the demands of the ideals of National Socialism. During peacetime he constantly tried to clean out the undependable and incompetent elements from the SS by using continuous indoctrination courses and seminars which for the most part filtered out the officers of the General SS. Later, even the NCOs and the SS soldiers were to be screened to identify the useless members. The officers who failed these tests could never again be promoted and the best thing for them to do was to voluntarily resign from the SS. All officers up to the age of fifty had to earn the physical fitness medal. Every officer was supposed to be able to ride a horse, fence, and drive a car. Just before the war Himmler wanted to create an SS sports medal. To earn this medal one had to achieve not only certain goals in athletics, but also demonstrate proof of personal bravery such as parachute jumping, lifesaving in the water, and in other ways. As far as the members of the Waffen SS, that is, the General SS units, were concerned, their training and duty created by itself the necessary toughness in the men. Their officers were even more rigorously trained in toughness.

All SS education and training was geared totally to becoming hardened and to self-discipline. The selection of new recruits had Himmler's special attention. The new recruits were to be constantly tested and screened. The demands were to be made increasingly tougher and more difficult. Only those who proved to be equal to the almost inhuman and hardened demands, both physically and mentally, were to be inducted into the "Order of the SS," and then only after a long and arduous time of testing. By being assigned to the main part of the service and by taking the many courses at the SS academies, the SS officer was supposed to accumulate the necessary experience and general knowledge to such a degree that he would be able to be assigned anywhere in any important post in the future German state.

The above descriptions are told by me from memory and are in no way complete. Surely I have forgotten a great deal. These portrayals can give an approximate picture of the influence of this man, who probably played the most fateful role in the Third Reich. These accounts obviously cannot be totally objective since I was personally involved with all of these things. But this is how Isaw the leader of the SS: Heinrich Himmler, and how he appeared to me!

Krakow, November, 1946   Rudolf Höss

KAMMLER

The *chief of the "C" office in the Economic Headquarters was* SS *General Dr. Engineer Kammler.*

In 1941 Kammler was appointed to the Economic Headquarters to take over all SS construction projects. He was an old-time Nazi Party member and SS soldier. He had fought in the Free Corps and was later in an army cavalry regiment. He later studied the building industry and became director of construction with the air force when it was being formed. Himmler sent for him because he knew him from the old days. Kammler came with Goring's approval to the Army Supply Headquarters. At that point the SS construction industry was split into many separate projects and was restrained because it fell into many jurisdictions. Although Pohl was the director of the Office of Building and Maintenance, he lacked a qualified expert. He found what he needed in Kammler.

By natureKammler was open-minded and overflowing with great ideas, but in the air force he became even more liberal. Pohl really liked him and gave him a free hand, but reserved the final decisions to himself. At that time the SS was at full strength: barracks training areas, research institutes, rebuilding of the terrible old offices and finally the concentration camps, which had become very run down. Kammler appeared at Auschwitz with urgent orders from Himmler to build up the camp. My construction chief at the time was Schlachter, who, even though he was a nice enough fellow, was nonetheless a very narrow-minded person. He was one of a kind. In peace time Schlachter had been an architect in Württemberg in a farm area. He lacked bold ideas. Kammler recognized this immediately and promised me a suitable man from the air force, who turned out to be Bischoff. He arrived October 1, 1941.

Kammler began setting up the major building plan for Auschwitz-Birkenau following Himmler's improvement order of March 1, 1941. It

295

was decidedly generous. Kammler took into consideration all my experience in this field and also laid out the sequence of the projected construction. He had a complete understanding of the important questions, namely irrigation and water drainage, which had to be done quickly. He brought along a water specialist precisely for that purpose. Kammler also put urgent allotments at my disposal. He did everything to help me, but the effects of the war were already being felt. Despite the top-priority designation, the most-needed construction materials just could not be obtained in the quantities needed. Construction in Auschwitz was always sheer torture. Each time it looked like progress was being made, it had to stop because no supplies were available. And it was always the most needed that was missing. Kammler helped by taking materials from other construction sites to push Auschwitz ahead. But it was like a drop of water on a hot stove; there just was never enough. The effects of the war were too much.

Kammler also saw the miserable condition of the camp during the later years. He improvised, improved, and imported skilled workers and experts in construction. But all his efforts were useless because he could not keep up with the flood of prisoners sent to Auschwitz, much less plan for them. Kammler did his best and took every opportunity to improve the construction problems in Auschwitz-Birkenau. He understood everything and helped where he could, but in the end he was as powerless as I was.

Kammler also helped in the other concentration camps as well as he could. He diverted a considerable amount of construction material needed for the war. This can be told today. But then? Had Himmler found out, he would have brought Kammler before the SS court. Kammler knew quite well that only healthy prisoners would do well for the war factories. They had to be fully useful physically and able to perform the job. Besides that, he needed them for the backbreaking daytime work. Kammler often discussed with me questions concerning the prisoners. He also spoke several times with Himmler when the right occasion arose. But Himmler just shrugged it off saying it was not his concern, even after Kammler told him that half-dead prisoners could not produce a single SS weapon.

Kammler was supposed to build, build, build for the war production, for the troops, for the police whose projects Kammler had to take over also, for the concentration camps, and for the special jobs Himmler gave him, and then again for the war production, and then when he had to move the shafts in the mines. As far as the numbers of workers are concerned, there weren't many available from the minister of labor, Sauckel, but prisoners-there were an abundance of them; but in what condition! With them Kammler was supposed to achieve the impossible-"Something that has never been done before," as demanded by Himmler. According to Himmler the V rockets were to be produced in large quantities by prisoners! Kammler wasn't easy to bring to his knees but through such demanding orders he often lost courage. He produced and produced; he used up countless construction chiefs and coworkers. It wasn't easy to work for him. He demanded too much work from a man.

Kammler had incredible powers over the mining operation. He had his own police force with special courts which proceeded rigorously and without mercy against any delay. It made no difference if the delay was caused by saboteurs, directors, engineers, construction chiefs, skilled German workers, foreign workers, or prisoners.

Himmler demanded the completion dates be strictly adhered to since he had told Hitler that the projects would be completed on that date. Kammler was often in very tight situations as far as time was concerned, but thanks to an incredibly tough will and his powers of creativity, he was able to keep up the mining operation, even though almost two years had been lost. By then the air raids, had started, just when the mining production had barely begun. The air raids made all attempts to work just an illusion. Kammler had remarkable achievements in the production of the V-I and the V -2 rockets, and received orders to deploy these weapons. Kammler took soldiers and officers from all branches of the armed forces and created the V-I Division. They launched as many rockets as could be manufactured. This number decreased, however, from day to day because either the factories that made the parts were under air attack or the transportation routes were being bombed. In the area of Mittelbau where most of the V weapons were produced there were thousands of completed or half-finished V rockets lying around. This just plugged up everything. Of the finished rockets only a small number reached the launch sites because the railroads were under daily air attacks from enemy bombers.

On Kammler's orders, *railroad brigades* were formed. These consisted of 500 prisoners each and were transported in specially equipped freight trains to the bombed areas, where they quickly began to repair the damage.

These work details had special tools and made remarkable achievements. The prisoners were carefully selected and lived on these trains, which were much better than living in the camps. But they also were in constant danger because of the bombing, and they suffered very high casualties. The same thing happened to the troops guarding them. The war had truly become *total!* The construction brigades also had to thank Kammler for their fate. These prisoners were in Kommandos of up to 1200 men strong and were deployed in larger cities in the West and in Berlin. They had to clear away the bomb damage at vital sites as quickly as possible. They also had to clear the mountains of rubble from the transportation lanes.

In the beginning of 1944 Kammler received orders to build a headquarters for Hitler in the rocks on the maneuver grounds in Ohrdorf in Thuringia The construction deadline was so short that there was hardly time to finish planning it. Himmler had ordered that for this project only prisoners be used for reasons of secrecy. There were supposed to be thirty thousand prisoners used for this project. It was possible to get that number by using mostly Jews from Austria who had "backed up" there. Most of them arrived in a completely rundown condition. And it worsened by living in tents, dugouts, provisional barracks, wearing their totally ragged clothing and not getting enough to eat. After working hard for a few days or a few weeks they died.

The deployment of prisoners ordered and repeatedly inspected by Himmler caused thousands and even more thousands to die without accomplishing anything useful. The construction project was never finished,

Kammler was saddled with this mess, and he did all he could to alleviate the worst of the conditions. The blame for all this lies fully on Himmler's head because if his promises to Hitler, which could never have been carried out, and also his "I don't want to see anything" attitude toward the problems. Kammler was tireless when it came to work. He had many good ideas; he was firmly planted in reality and was able to assess the damages well. He was able to see through all his coworkers and, of course, demanded every last thing from them. He hoped to achieve the impossible by force and finally had to admit that the war was stronger than he was. He lived a very simple, humble personal life and had a good family.

XI 46   Höss

Liebehenschel

SS *lieutenant Arthur Liebehenschel* came from the province of Posen. He served twelve years in the army and then joined the SS. In 1934 he was adjutant in the concentration camp Lichtenburg, where he became seriously ill. In 1936 he came to the Bureau of Concentration Camp Inspections in Berlin, where he worked under Colonel Tamaschke in the Political Department. After Tamaschke left, Liebehenschel became the director of that department, which later was known as Bureau D I, after which he was transferred to Auschwitz in November 1943.

He was a quiet person and was very good-natured. He also had to be very careful because he had a very bad heart.

Liebehenschel lived through the entire development of the concentration camps under Eicke, from his desk, of course. He knew the basics and the entire organization of the concentration camps from the correspondence, and from the orders and directives by Eicke, who always worked on the most important things himself. Later, when he worked for Glucks, he became more independent and handled most of the correspondence on his own. He also took care of the orders and directives to the Kommandants and, through Glucks, signed everything.

He hardly knew the camps from a personal perspective, even though he was in one or another of the camps a few times. Glucks repeatedly wanted to send him into the camps as his representative but he always managed to get out of it.

He was in Auschwitz only once and that was before he was transferred. This is why neither Glucks nor Liebehenschel knew anything about the grim reality of the concentration camps. Sadly, the orders and directives regarding the camps, which often were of far-reaching importance, originated from the view of a desk-far removed from reality. As Glucks's deputy, Liebehenschel each day received all the incoming mail for the concentration camps and distributed it. He saw most of the correspondence that was prepared for Glucks's signature. Thus he saw all the correspondence to and from the camps and routed much of it himself because he influenced Glucks easily. Liebehenschel never had much use for Auschwitz because it forced him into an entirely different routine than that of the other camps and caused too much commotion. There was always something going on in Auschwitz, and the Kommandant wanted too much help and too many improvements. Besides that, Himmler was always worrying about Auschwitz. Liebehenschel could have done many things for Auschwitz. Later on he was sorry, when he had to swallow the bitter pill, when he became Kommandant of Auschwitz.

I became acquainted with Liebehenschel during a visit in Dachau, but by living together for two years in the SS settlement at Sachsenhausen I got to know him better. Although we were together quite often, we really didn't become close. We were of different temperaments and our interests were too far apart. Liebehenschel was a creature of habit who did not want to disturb his daily quiet and ordinary lifestyle. He preferred to meet things as they came. However, his divorce shattered his quiet manner of living. For years he had not gotten along with his wife, who was very quarrelsome and petty. He got to know Glucks's receptionist and in her he found himself a woman who understood him and didn't mind his idio-syncrasies. Finally, there was the divorce and he could not stay in the inspection office. That's why he was transferred to Auschwitz." He personally would have preferred a different camp. Shortly after he became Kommandant he married again and even had a child from this marriage. There were four children from the first marriage and after the divorce he was given custody of the oldest boy, who came to live with him at Auschwitz. When Lublin was later evacuated, his son fell into the hands of the Russians and he is most likely dead.

Liebehenschel was transferred to Auschwitz because of his divorce and he felt that Glucks and Pohl treated him indifferently. He also expected a promotion to colonel.

When he took up his position at Auschwitz he felt he was shunned by God and man and he was also quite deteriorated physically. His heart problem had become worse and he looked for his salvation in champagne, but it wasn't noticeable while he was on duty.

When Auschwitz was divided into three camps, Pohl decided that Liebehenschel would be in charge of the garrison and also be the Komman-dant of the original Auschwitz camp, which now numbered about eighteen thousand prisoners. Liebehenschel felt that it was unfair that he should be given the smallest camp. Besides that, he lost money because Pohl dropped the factory director's bonus. Then too Liebehenschel also lost his chief of office allowance and the minister's allowance, which was paid to all members of headquarters staff. In addition to all that, his divorce demanded support of his first wife and three children because he was the guilty party and on top of all that he was starting a new marriage. It is easy to see that he was experiencing serious financial difficulties.

With all these burdens he took up his new job at Auschwitz.

Since he had always been in a position of authority, he thought he would just come in and play camp Kommandant. In his opinion I had done everything absolutely wrong, and he proceeded to change everything from the way it had been done. His adjutant, Zoller, whom he had brought along from Mauthausen, showed him the mistakes made by the previous Kommandant.

Just then the Special Commission of the SS Court suddenly appeared on an official visit to search for those SS members who had stolen prisoner belongings from the Reinhardt Action. At the same time Grabner was arrested because he arbitrarily had prisoners executed without any authorization.

Liebehenschel always welcomed these investigations because he believed them to be proof of how wrong things had been managed in Auschwitz. He was unable to make any improvements in his whole sphere of command.

He appointed SS Sergeant Hofmann as his camp commander. Hofmann was no match for the hard-boiled old-timers among the prisoners.

In a short time they were walking all over him and they did whatever they wanted. Liebehenschel had no idea of how to run a camp and let Hofmann do whatever he wanted and so was very popular with all the prisoners. He also gave speeches to the prisoners in which he promised that now everything would get better and that he would change the murder camp to the way a concentration camp should be run.

He gave his word of honor to the prisoners that no more selections would be made for the gas chambers. A few days later when a truck loaded with prisoners selected from sick bay drove to the gas chambers, the word went through the camp like a bullet, "There goes the word of honor of the Kommandant." He constantly did such stupid things and he wasn't even aware of it. Soon he realized that in the light of reality, a concentration camp took on a different appearance than from behind a desk, especially Auschwitz. And this, in spite of the fact that Sachsenhausen was practically at the front door of the headquarters in Oranienburg. But from headquarters and from behind the desk one sees everything differently; mostly better!

At Auschwitz Liebehenschel was almost always in his office, dictating order after order and writing reports. He had conferences with his garrison officers for hours on end while the general condition of the camp declined. But he did not see this.

During the early part of his new marriage it came to light that his second wife had been accused by the Security Service to have associated with Jews for quite a long time, even after the Nuremburg laws went into effect. These facts became known in Auschwitz and Liebehenschel became intolerable.

Pohl made short of this matter and transferred him to Lublin in June 1944. He didn't like that at all, since his second wife lived in the town of Auschwitz. Liebehenschel was on more official trips to Auschwitz than actually in Lublin. He escaped another almost certain transfer because of his behavior when Lublin was evacuated. Away from Lublin he finally got beyond the close reach of headquarters and ended up with Globocnik in Triest. They were fighting bandits there. This is the same Liebehenschel who couldn't harm a fly.

XI/46

H.

Lolling

The *chief executive officer of D III was* SS *Colonel Dr. Enno Lolling.* Dr. Lolling had been a medical officer with the navy during World War I. Untill939 he had a country practice in Mecklenburg as a general practitioner. Because he was a member of the SS he was drafted into the Waffen SS and was posted in the concentration camps. At first he was in Dachau as camp doctor and then he became the chief doctor of the Office of the Inspector of Concentration Camps. When Pohl took over the camps Lolling also became the chief of medical services of headquarters.

Dr. Lolling was an older man, tired and spent, who used morphine and liked to drink. He never achieved anything special on his own during his entire time in office. He just drifted along with events and went on a great number of inspection trips to all the camps. He had no understanding of the medical needs and he never really saw the state of health of the prisoners. He never saw the medical and sanitary conditions as they really were in the camps. When epidemics broke out or when Pohl pointed out the deplorable state of affairs he awoke and-wrote reports! It was the only thing he could do. He demanded report after report from the camp doctors, read them carefully and then wrote voluminous reports to Pohl and the surgeon general of the SS. He described very conscientiously all that he had read in the camp doctors' reports. But he scarcely made any notable recommendations in order to improve things or to institute preventive measures. Pohl and Glucks had tried repeatedly to get rid of him when he first began his duties. For a long time he was on leave with the intention of dismissing him. His morphine addiction had become well-known. But because the surgeon general couldn't find a better doctor, Lolling stayed at his post. Most of the capable SS doctors were at the front lines, or in the SS hospitals, and the shortage of doctors was already a problem even before the war. So everyone put up with him and tolerated his "peculiarities." No one took him seriously, not headquarters, not the home office, much less the doctors who knew him. He tried very hard to be a strict boss, which made him only more ridiculous. His orders were obeyed to the point where his subordinates found they made sense. He was also very easy to fool on inspections, especially if they gave him a lot to drink, which happened quite often.

He inspected Auschwitz more than the other camps, but I cannot say that anything was ever done based on his extensive inspections. The improvements which were made were done by the doctors themselves. Dr. Wirths had often bitterly complained to me that he received no help and no understanding from Lolling.

One of Lolling's jobs was to oversee the experiments done with the prisoners. Although he knew everything from the reports he read, he himself witnessed none of them. He also saw none of the terrible excesses which occurred because there was no supervision. As the war went on, there was an increasing shortage of doctors. The surgeon general could only send those doctors to the camps who could not be used at all on the front lines, or those who were old, or those who had unpleasant habits. All of them were not fit to serve anywhere except in the concentration camps. By using only these totally unfit characters, the sanitary and medical conditions of the camp were not improved. Lolling removed these "impossible doctors" only when the situation became unbearable or when they caused visible damage.

Lolling completely ignored the complaints about the medical and sanitary conditions. He insisted on the authority of his position as surgeon general, and was very stubborn about this. He always made certain that everyone knew his rank. As director of inspections I later heard this often enough, and I wasn't happy when I had to accompany him on official trips.

The man in his position should have been a man full of energy, with farsightedness, knowledge and ability. But in the highest echelons this requirement could not be seen. Had they filled the position with a man of these qualities much could have been avoided.

XI 46   H.

Maurer

The *office director of D II in headquarters was* SS *Colonel Gerhard Maurer.*

Maurer was a businessman by profession and had been an old Party and SS member. He came from Saxony. Before 1933 he was chiefly occupied as the treasurer of his home garrison. In 1934 he came to Munich to work in the SS administration. Pohl put him in the auditing department. As an accountant he attracted Pohl's attention. When the Central Administration of SS Commercial Enterprises was created they found a use for Maurer.

Later on Pohl made him inspector of SS Commercial Enterprises. It was then that Maurer became acquainted with the concentration camps and became quite interested in the prisoners working for SS enterprises. He saw the peculiarities of the Kommandants and the camp officers, and the negative attitude concerning these enterprises. Most of the older Kommandants and camp officers believed that the prisoners were being treated too well and that the managers of these factories learned too much from the prisoners about what went on in the camps. These old-timers played many a trick on these managers by suddenly pulling out the most capable and expert prisoners. They were instead put to work in the fields or were kept in the camp. In their place they sent completely incompetent workers. Maurer proceeded without mercy against these ploys and supplied Pohl with many useful reports. In order to stop this practice, Pohl took Maurer's suggestion and appointed all camp Kommandants as directors of the SS factories in which their prisoners worked. They now received a large monthly increase in pay, depending on the size of their operation, and later they would receive a percentage of the net profits also. With this one move he made the Kommandants pay more attention to these war factories. They now watched their subordinates more closely and tried to convince them of the necessity of these factories. Maurer was also the one who convinced Pohl to reward the prisoners by introducing bonuses. Later in 1944, Maurer followed Pohl's idea by creating a prisoner pay scale by which prisoners could earn a pay check according to the amount of work performed. However, the prisoner pay scale never was put into effect.

When the Inspectorate of Concentration Camps was merged with Economic Headquarters, Maurer became director of D II, Deployment of Prisoner Labor. Maurer now proceeded to completely reorganize this office. In every camp he established a work deployment office, which was responsible to him, and was instructed in detail to make certain the prisoners were deployed in the most important war factories. They also had to set up files and list all the civilian occupations of the prisoners. They had the strictest orders to make certain that each prisoner was working at what he was most capable. Most of the camp officers, duty officers, and Kommando leaders tried to sabotage what the work deployment officers were trying to do because, for their self-glorification, *they* wanted to be the ones to give the orders where prisoners should work. In the beginning there was a lot of friction but Maurer proceeded mercilessly when he learned about what was happening.

Maurer was very energetic, alert, and clear-sighted. He immediately saw if something was out of order in the camps, and he either called this to the Kommandant's attention or reported it to Pohl.

Maurer enjoyed Pohl's complete confidence. While Glucks liked to cover up any unpleasantness, Maurer did the opposite and brought it to Pohl's attention.

After Liebehenschel was transferred, Maurer became Glucks's deputy.

By doing this, Glucks literally and figuratively gave Maurer the position of inspector of concentration camps. Glucks gradually relinquished almost all the important matters to Maurer. For appearances' sake only did Glucks still call himself the inspector of the concentration camps. From then on everything was viewed from the standpoint of the prisoner deployment for war production, which was most important to Himmler. It was only natural that everything was geared to that.

I knew Maurer from Dachau and Sachsenhausen. But we didn't get to know each other well until my time as Kommandant of Auschwitz. We always understood each other and we worked well together. Through Maurer I was able to get a lot of information to Pohl, which I could never do through Glucks. We had the same opinion about almost all questions concerning the camp and the prisoners. We disagreed only about selecting the able-bodied Jews for work. Maurer wanted to have as many Jews as possible work, even those who were only there for a short time. I wanted to select only the best and the strongest because of all the reasons I have already mentioned. We never reached an agreement on these questions. Later, the consequences of Maurer's viewpoints could clearly be seen, but he never wanted to admit it.

Maurer saw Auschwitz develop from the beginning and on each of his visits I pointed out the terrible conditions. He also saw them and he made sure Pohl knew' about all of this; but it was no use.

Maurer always argued that the prisoners should be well-treated. When he inspected the arms factories, he often talked directly to the prisoners about their housing, food and how they were being treated. All of this actually harmed the prisoners rather than helped them because the Kapos always lurked in the background. Maurer was very busy with his main duty, which was prisoner deployment for the war effort. He didn't rest and made no allowances when it came to that. He made a lot of official trips. In one place he straightened out the deployment of prisoners, in another he made sure that after a factory was started that it was running well. He straightened out the problems between the factory managers and the work Kommando leaders. In another place he took care of the complaints about the way prisoners worked or from the prisoners themselves as to how they were being treated by the management of the plant. He handled hundreds of things!

There were constant requests from the War Ministry and the Todt Organization for new prisoners. This was the eternal cry to Auschwitz: transport more Jews.

Maurer truly had his hands full with work, but it was never too much for him, and in spite of all his activities nothing disturbed his composure.

His constant requests to be sent to the front lines became a reality with Kammler's help. He became administrative officer for Kammler's "V" Division from January 1945 until April 1945. This later became an artillery corps.

During the air raids on the "V" factories near Buchenwald, Maurer lost his wife and four children when a direct hit destroyed the bunker they were in at the SS settlement where they were living. Shortly before that his apartment in Berlin had also been destroyed by bombs.

Maurer always had a great understanding about prisoner problems even though he only looked at them from the point of view of work deployment. He would never admit that he *decisively* contributed to the deterioration of Auschwitz and the other camps by his overzealousness in selecting Jews for work. And yet, that's the way it was!

XI/46 H.

Möckel

SS *Lieutenant Colonel Karl Mockel was Burger's successor as director of the Auschwitz site.* Mockel comes from Saxony. He was an early member of the Nazi Party and had a very low number, 110.

In the early days before Hitler came to power he was working in the Main Administration of the SS in the regiment and the sector of his home area. In 1933 he came to Munich, where he worked for the SS chief administrator. This office later became the Economic Headquarters and Meckel was working in many of the different offices until 1941. After the various headquarters offices were formed by POW, Meckel became chief of the W III office, which included all food factories and similar plants. His special assignment was to take over and enlarge the mineral spring distribution centers. Because of the war there was an unforeseen boom in the need for mineral water. The front lines and the military hospitals needed large amounts. Meckel became an expert in this area. The war also caused a rapid growth of all food industries and the building of new bread and meat factories in Germany and in the occupied countries in order to supply the Waffen SS. Mockel was very busy with administering the many factories but he managed all this through his administrative techniques. On his own initiative he really never achieved anything noteworthy. He wasn't capable of that. Even though he was a hard worker, he loved to be pushed to do more. Mockel was a quiet, somewhat comfortable man who let everything pile up before he would start to work and take care of things. He was also very headstrong and did not want anyone telling him his business.

That's why he didn't get along with POW, who thought Meckel was too slow and had no zest in his work. From the very beginning of the war Mockel wanted a front line position or a job in any administrative post in the Waffen SS.

The POW factories were directed by officers of the General SS. But Pohl always refused to transfer him. Finally, in 1941, after a huge argument, POW approved Meckel's transfer to the Waffen SS. However, Mockel had to give up his rank. He was an SS Oberführer [between a colonel and a general] in the General SS. Now he had to start as an ordinary SS private again and go through basic training in the reserves. Meckel was in the administration of the Waffen SS. Gradually he was promoted and used in the SS reserve battalion. In the spring of 1943 he came to Auschwitz. Because of the food factories, Meckel became familiar with the administration of a concentration camp, especially one the size of Auschwitz, but it was not easy for him. Mentally he was somewhat on the slow side when he had to do things that were new to him. This is the reason it took him such a long time to get used to the way of doing things in Auschwitz.

He carried out his duties fairly well and he worked as hard as possible to do the right thing for everyone. But the conditions in Auschwitz demanded more. As a comrade, I helped him where his duties affected me, because personally he was too good-hearted. But Meckel didn't show any progress. He had little help from his ever-increasing staff, even though he did have a few good men. Since he himself was oblivious to almost everything, he was cheated and deceived at every turn.

Meckel had a young wife and did not have a good marriage. He therefore started to drink more and more, and was useless for days. Working under Liebehenschel everything became worse as both of them tried to drown their problems in alcohol. Most of the work was done by Meckel's deputy, Captain Polenz, who did the best he could. Under Meckel's administration nothing substantial was done about the constantly worsening conditions in Auschwitz. When the Garrison Administration became independent and was changed into the Central Administration, Meckel made it his special task to ensure that the independence of his office was preserved. But he was unable to really take care of all that needed to be done. His subordinates muddled their way through at their own discretion and were happy that they had such a good boss.

XI/46 Höss

Müller

SS Major General and Lieutenant General of the Police Muller was the chief of Bureau IV of the State Security Main Bureau and deputy of the chief of the State Security Police and of the Secret Service.

Muller was an officer during World War I, and afterward, when Hitler came to power, was transferred to the Bavarian Political Police and served under Best, who took him to Berlin in the Gestapo Headquarters. He soon became a leading figure in this office under Heydrich and finally became the chief of the Berlin office himself. Muller was a policeman by nature. He didn't join the police until Hitler came to power and was taken relatively late into the SS. His specialist knowledge in police work, his continued experience in an executive position, and his talents came in handy in the development and improvement   of Gestapo Headquarters. He was also influential in organizing the Gestapo.

Muller always remained in the background. He did not like to be connected to any events or actions. Yet, he was the one who organized and led all of the important police actions and made certain they were carried out.

After Heydrich's death he became the leading figure in the Security Headquarters. Kaltenbrunner was only the chief and occupied himself primarily with the SD [Security Service].

Muller was always well-informed about all the important political occurrences in Germany. He had many undercover agents in all possible government positions, mainly in the economic sector. He kept in touch with his agents only through intermediaries. He was a master in camouflaging his work.

Muller visited the concentration camps only a few times, but not all of them. Nevertheless, he was always well-informed about all of them. It wasn't for nothing that each chief of the Political Department was also a member of the Stapo [state police].

Eicke and Muller understood each other very well, even as far back to the time when Eicke was Kommandant of Dachau.

It was never learned what Muller's views were concerning the concentration camps and the prisoners. All his remarks concerning these questions always started with, "Himmler wishes that . . ." or "Himmler ordered . . ." It was never possible to find out what *his* views were.

When I was adjutant at Sachsenhausen, then Kommandant of Auschwitz, and later director of inspections, I had to conduct business with him very often. But I never experienced him saying even once that, "I'm deciding that . . ." or "I order this . . ." or "I want. . . ." He always covered himself and hid behind Himmler or the chief of the Security Police or the Secret Service, even though everyone who knew the situation realized that he was the one making the decisions and that Himmler and Kaltenbrunner depended completely upon him in all matters concerning prisoners. Mullerdecided who was sent into the camps and who would be released. He was the only one who decided on executions, as far as those ordered by the Security Headquarters. In important cases he presented the execution orders to Himmler for his signature.

He had numerous and very sensitive cases of the special prisoners precisely in his memory. He knew exact data about every single one of these countless prisoners and he knew where they were kept and their weaknesses.

Muller was an incredible, versatile, and tenacious worker. He made very few official trips, but we could always reach him, even on Sundays or holidays, either in his office or at home.

He had two adjutants and two secretaries whom he kept busy by alternating them in day and night shifts. Every inquiry was always promptly answered by him, mostly by telegram, "because he always had to ask Himmler for his decision first!"

From Eichmann and Gunther, who worked more intensly with him than I did, I learned that Muller made all the important decisions concerning the roundups of the Jews, even though he let Eichmann have a pretty free hand.

As I have stated before, he was well-informed about all the concentration camps, including Auschwitz, which he personally never saw. He knew all the details, whether it concerned Birkenau, or the crematories, or the number of prisoners, or the death figures. He knew the facts so exactly that I was often astounded.

All of my personal complaints to him to slow down the roundups in order to ease the terrible conditions were always unsuccessful because he always hid behind Himmler's order, "The ordered roundups are to be carried out ruthlessly and without consideration!" I tried everything with him to convince him, but it was useless, although I got a lot accomplished through him where I had never succeeded with the others. Especially later, when I was director of inspections, he relied on my judgment a great deal. Today I believe that those who were higher up did not want to alleviate the terrible conditions in Auschwitz in order to increase the number of deaths in a "cold way" rather than by the gas chambers.

Muller had the power to stop the roundups or at least slow them down. He would also have been able to convince Himmler. He did not do it; although he knew the exact consequences. It just was not wanted. This is the way I see it today. At that time I was unable to understand the behavior at headquarters.

Muller told me repeatedly, "Himmler is of the opinion that the discharge of prisoners during wartime must be refused because of security and political reasons. That's why discharge petitions have to be limited to an absolute minimum and only considered in special cases." Muller also said, "Himmler issued orders that all prisoners of foreign nationality categorically must be denied discharge for the duration of the war!"

"Himmler wants foreign prisoners executed for even the smallest attempt at sabotage in order to intimidate the other prisoners!"

After reading the above it isn't hard to guess who was behind these orders and wishes.

All in all, one can say that Muller was the real hand behind all the consequences caused by SS Headquarters, or rather their executives.

Personally Muller was a correct person, very obliging and full of camaraderie. He never acted like a boss or insisted on rank, and yet, it was never possible to become friendly with him. This was confirmed again and again by his coworkers, who had been with him for years.

Muller was the ice-cold executive and organizer of all the necessary measures ordered by Himmler for the security of Germany.

11/46 Höss

Palitzsch

SS *Master Sergeant Palitzsch* was also from Saxony. In 1933 he came via the "political preparedness group" in Dresden to the concentration camp Sachsenburg guard troops. In 1936 he was transferred to Sachsenhausen to carry out the duties of a block leader. I came to know him in that position when I came to Sachsenhausen as adjutant in 1938. I never noticed Palitzsch in the Kommandant's staff. Camp Commander Sauer, Officer of the Day Schilti and later Eisfeld really bragged about Palitzsch and his skillful manner and his devotion to duty. After Schilti's transfer, Palitzsch became the duty officer and held that post even when I was protective custody camp commander. Palitzsch performed his duty to everyone's satisfaction. And yet, I could never rid myself of the feeling that in secret he tortured the prisoners. I often stalked him and also asked many people about him, but I could never get enough evidence to take action against him. The strange thing was that the prisoners did not like to talk about him and always tried to evade answering. The block leader and Kommando leaders who had come from Sachsenhausen were old hands, so there were very few outsiders. This clique had been educated by Eicke, Loritz, and Koch and had learned their trade well. Each one covered for the other. The prisoners also knew them from their years in the camp. The Kapos were trusted by them and obeyed them instantly.

I have no personal knowledge, nor have I ever heard, that Palitzsch was involved in any atrocities in Sachsenhausen. I do not doubt that he beat prisoners. In any case he was cunning enough never to get caught. He had received from the previously mentioned camp Kommandants an "outstanding education."

When Auschwitz first began he was recommended to me by Loritz and transferred from Sachsenhausen with thirty professional criminals he himself had selected. In one way I was glad that I got Palitzsch, an experienced duty officer who at least had an idea about protective custody camps, was devoted to duty, and knew how to handle prisoners. But from the beginning I always had the feeling that Palitzsch was lying to me and that he was two-faced. My feelings did not deceive me. Soon enough he was in league with Fritzsch and the second camp commander, Meier, and became very involved in their activities. From Meier he got the final polish in perfecting all the possible foul deeds. Meier was also one of those "warmly recommended" by Glucks, Meier

312

had been in Buchenwald, where he could not have remained a minute longer because of his loathsome behavior. He was one of the creatures of Koch, who participated in all kinds of truly disgusting things, a true gangster.

Meier was only at Auschwitz a few months when I succeeded in uncovering enough evidence to find him guilty of serious black marketeering and was able to hand him over to the SS court. Glucks was really angry with me about this, because he thought that he would have to give an accounting of this to Himmler. Meier had constantly maintained that he was a relative of Himmler, thereby preventing many of his superiors from taking steps against him.

Meier, Palitzsch, and a prisoner of the same name [different spelling] who was a tailor, made some illegal transactions with money, valuables and textiles. Meier obtained these by confiscating them from Auschwitz *in my name*. But I didn't learn this until 1944, after Palitzsch had been seized by the SS court. This information came from Meyer [the tailor], after he was caught and brought back from his escape from the camp. As it turned out, Meyer had been aided in his escape by Palitzsch and two NCOs in the camp administration because they were afraid their illegal dealings would be discovered. Meyer had threatened to expose them if they didn't let him escape. About this Meier, Palitzsch, Meyer trio one could write a fascinating gangster novel. Meier's replacement was Seidler. Seidler, like Palitzsch, was already known from Sachsenburg and had also been at Sachsenhausen for several years. Even though Seidler wasn't a creature in the same sense of his predecessor, he was nevertheless of the same makeup as Fritzsch and Palitzsch in the way they treated prisoners. He too was very good at hiding his mistakes from me.

No one could beat Palitzsch in his devotion to duty. He was always at his post and could be found everywhere. He was well-informed about everything, in fact, better than the camp commander. You could trust him with the most difficult jobs. Because of his shrewd spy system, which watched over the Kapos and block elders, he was the true boss with the prisoners. His strength came from playing one against the other. The most notorious officials were under his protection and when their actions became obvious they had to spend time in the punishment company and like it. Palitzsch didn't forget about them and got them out again on time. Those who knew too much or actually didn't want to continue playing along suffered accidents at work with deadly results or they died of spotted fever. The "immortal" camp elder,

[Bruno] Brodniewitz, was the master conductor of Palitzsch's schemes.

Palitzsch was shrewd enough never to expose himself in any way. He had learned the lessons from his vast experience. Besides that, he was always covered by Fritzsch, Seidler and Aumeier. After the Meier affair, I chased after him like the devil. He not only guessed it but he knew, and covered himself all the more.

In the three-and-a-half years he was under my command I could not catch him, even though I took many risks and spent a lot of time trying to. It was absolutely impossible to learn anything from the prisoners themselves.

I couldn't even get anything out of the prisoners who had been transferred to other camps. The fear of the consequences was too great. The captured Meyer blabbed only when he knew for certain that Palitzsch was under arrest.

To an outsider this seems unbelievable. And yet, whoever has been a prisoner in Auschwitz or was more acquainted with the circumstances there knew what powerPalitzsch had and which roll he played.

Palitzsch was always present at executions, and he probably performed the most killings by shooting in the back of the neck. The many times that I watched him, I could never discover even the slightest emotion or desire to do that. Calmly, composed, without any haste, his face without expression, he carried out his deadly and horrible work. And it was the same when he was on duty at the gas chambers. I could not detect even a trace of sadism. His face was always expressionless and showed no movement. Psychologically he was hardened to such a degree that he could kill without stopping and without giving it a thought.

Palitzsch was also one of those who was directly involved with the exterminations who never came to me in a quiet hour and poured his heart out about these horrible events.

After his wife died of typhus in 1942 he lost even the last of his inner stability, the last of his inhibitions. He started to drink excessively and was constantly involved with women. Women constantly came and went from his quarters. Most of them were female guards. Before all this I had never heard anything about him concerning women. This is probably how he came to have an affair with a Latvian Jewess in Birkenau. This caused his arrest. I had warned Schwarzhuber long before of his escapades, and had pointed out Palitzsch's weaknesses. Schwarzhuber also had been after him for quite some time. After Palitzsch was arrested all his filthy deeds gradually came to light. As far back as 1940 he had stolen money, valuables, material, clothing, etc. from the Jews in Auschwitz and the newly admitted Polish prisoners. Later he stole uncounted amounts during the Jewish roundups. But he had become very selective and took only the valuable items.

Even after he was arrested, no exact facts were ever learned about his activities in the camps concerning the mistreatment of the prisoners. The prisoners avoided testifying because they were afraid of the Kapos and the block elders. Whether Palitzsch killed prisoners on his own accord and by his own choice could never really be learned, but it was nevertheless believed to be so. He was careful enough never to create any troublesome accomplices. He didn't even need to mistreat or kill the prisoners himself. He had enough compliant creatures among the prisoners who gladly did these things for him. By doing this they gained all kinds of advantages at the cost of their fellow prisoners. The life or well-being of their fellow prisoners meant nothing to them as long as *they* had it good!

It is mainly Palitzsch's fault that there were such depraved violations and inhuman mistreatment of the prisoners. As duty officer he was in a position to prevent most of it, but to the contrary, he wanted this to happen in order to feed his hunger for power. It was also his doing that allowed the Kapos to rule, which caused such a disaster in Auschwitz. All this suited him perfectly since he wanted to hold power over everything. In his alcoholic dazes he bragged often enough that *he* was the most powerful person in Auschwitz and that *he* controlled everything.

Whether Fritzsch, Seidler, and Aumeier had become dependent upon him because of all the violations, I have no knowledge, but it is very possible that he deliberately got them to play into his hands. No means was too evil to strengthen his power. He behaved in the same manner toward his SS comrades. If he didn't like one of the subordinates, or if they hindered his plans, he managed to find a suitable occasion to let him "stumble" and thus removed him from his command.

I repeatedly tried to get rid of Palitzsch by showing Glucks the reasons for my suspicions. He paid no attention to me whatsoever. If I didn't have *clear proof* in my hands, he would not transfer him. I was told to watch him more closely and that I also should be able to cope with the noncommissioned officers.

I had gotten to know many people during my long time in all the services, but Palitzsch was the most cunning and slippery creature that I have ever gotten to know and experience in the many concentration camps.

He literally walked over bodies to satisfy his hunger for power.

XL/46 H.

Pohl

The head of the SS *Economic and Administrative Headquarters was* SS *Lieutenant General Oswald Pohl.*

I first became acquainted with Pohl during my service in Dachau, which began on December 1, 1934.

Pohl came from Kiel and was a paymaster in the navy. He was an early Party member and also a member of the navy SA. In1934 Himmler transferred him and appointed him chief of the administration of the Federal Command of the SS.

While this office never played a role under his predecessor, Pohl managed in the shortest time to make himself indispensable to Himmler. His office became feared and Pohl understood how to become all-powerful.

His auditors were specially selected by him and were responsible to him only and backed by him. All of the men and officers working in administration offices were deeply afraid of Pohl's men. Pohl had achieved his purpose with these auditors, since it kept the administration of the SS clean and trustworthy. All the crooks in the administration were caught and eliminated.

Under Pohl's predecessors the higher SS officers were quite independent in money matters and ruled as they saw fit. Pohl managed to convince Himmler that all money matters would need Pohl's approval and would be subject to his scrutiny. This caused a great deal of resentment and *excitement,* but Pohl succeeded with his well-known energy and thereby won tremendous influence over all units in the SS. Even the most obstinate and pigheaded among the higher SS officers, like Sepp-Dietrich and Eicke, had to swallow their arrogance and beg Pohl for money, especially when it dealt with extra budgetary expenditures.

Every unit in the SS had an exactly figured yearly budget which had to be adhered to with the utmost accuracy. Pohl's bloodhounds found every penny which had been spent over or under the budget.

Pohl's main job from the very beginning was to make the SS *totally financially independent from the government and the Party, by creating factories and plants operated by the SS. This was to ensure that Himmler would have total freedom of action with all of his plans.*

This was a task with a far-reaching goal and Pohl was convinced that it was possible to accomplish it. He worked continuously to make this a reality. Almost all of the industrial SS factories were created by his initiative. Beginning with the DA W [Deutsche Ausrüstungswerke-German war factories], porcelain manufacturing in Allach, the combined manufacturing of the stone quarries, brick-making plants, cement factories called the DEST[Deutsche Erd und Steinwerke], and the clothing factories. Included in the W III Bureau were the German food industries. They consisted of the combined bakeries and meat-processing plants, food wholesale warehouses and cafeterias, the numerous mineral water distributors, the agricultural and forestry enterprises, the print shops, and finally the book publishers. All these represent quite an economic power. And this was just the beginning.

Pohl had already begun economic plans of such enormous sweep that they would even eclipse anything I. G. Farben had accomplished. Pohl's energy would have probably accomplished that too.

For the research and experimental labs alone, Himmler needed vast sums of money. Pohl had always managed to find them for him. Himmler was always very generous in authorizing money for special purposes, and Pohl financed everything. It was easy for him because all the economic enterprises created a tremendous *profit,* in spite of the new investments which were constantly being made. The Waffen SS, the concentration camps, the SS Headquarters, the police, and later on some other service branches of the SS were all financed by the Reich government. Major General Frank, Pohl's administrative adjutant, carried out the negotiations on Pohl's order. Frank was also his budget representative and his deputy.

These budget negotiations with the federal finance minister were wars of power of the first order, because without federal means it wasn't even possible to outfit and set up even one *new* SS company. Frank was clever and tough and succeeded with all his demands, often after weeks of negotiations. He was trained by Pohl and Pohl stood by him all the way.

Later Frank took over the entire administration of the police, which had completely atrophied, and reorganized it. After the attempt on Hitler's life, Frank became the chief administrator of the armed forces, while Pohl stood behind all the scenes and directed all the moves.

Frank and Homer, who later was to become chief of Bureau B, were Pohl's closest coworkers and confidants. Since 1934 only those two could dare oppose Pohl in critical situations and state *their* opinions regardless of the consequences.

During the early years after Hitler's assumption of power, Himmler, his staff, and the SS administration were located in Munich. Pohl lived in Dachau in the vicinity of the concentration camp. Consequently, he was in touch with the concentration camp and the prisoners. This is how he got to know what the needs of a concentration camp were and about the inmates from the ground up. Because of his great interest in the development of the industrial factories in the Dachau Concentration Camp, he was very often present in the camp. On Sundays he loved to walk around and visited all the installations of the entire camp. He intentionally avoided, however, setting foot in the actual camp itself, so as not to give Eicke an opportunity to have cause to complain to Himmler. There was a great deal of friction between Pohl and Eicke because both were brutal men. Their attitudes conflicted over the service area, jurisdiction, the treatment of prisoners that is, shelter, provisions, clothing and work in the factories.

As long as I have known Pohl, even up to Germany's collapse, he always had the same attitude about the prisoner question. He believed that a prisoner who was housed in a good, warm place, was well-fed and clothed would work hard on his own. Punishments were to be administered only in extreme cases.

On Pohl's initiative herb gardens were developed, because Pohl was an enthusiastic disciple of the health food theory. All sorts of spices and herbs were grown in these herb gardens. The goal was to dissuade the German people from using health-damaging foreign spices and artificial medicines and to switch to the use of harmless, good-tasting German spices and natural herbs for illnesses.

The SS and police were obliged to use all these spices. During the war almost all of the armed forces obtained these spices from Dachau.

It was in these herb gardens that Pohl found the opportunity to talk to the prisoners about why they were arrested and about life in the camp. This is how he always knew what was happening in Dachau. Even in the later years he still returned almost once a month to the herb gardens in Dachau, where he also lived when he had business in Munich or near the camp.

Pohl persistently supported the release of prisoners whom he knew, if he believed they were wrongfully arrested, or if the sentence seemed too long. This was a major cause of the unresolvable disagreement between him and Eicke. This later carried to SS Headquarters and even to Kaltenbrunner. In some of the worst cases, Pohl was not afraid to go directly to Himmler himself and ask him. This is something that he normally never did. He was unsuccessful for the most part because Himmler adhered strictly to the judgment of the headquarters staff in questions of release. During the time I was in the Department of Inspections, I had the task of trying to persuade the headquarters staff to Pohl's demands, or rather, remind them of their duty. He always set short deadlines and became very indignant if the demanded releases did not happen at the given deadline. Yes, even in the most hopeless cases, as with the Nuremburg Communists, he never gave up. In a few cases he was able to get a prisoner a conditional release, i.e., the prisoner had to work under guard in one of the SS factories attached to the concentration camp, but as a free civilian employee. This form of release proved successful in the later years of the war. There were very few relapses.

In 1941 the concentration camps were incorporated into Group VIIof the SS Economic Headquarters and came under Pohl's command.

Pohl was precisely informed about every concentration camp because all the factories in the system provided a network of information available through the factory directors, the inspectors-Maurer was one of themthe bureau chiefs and the directors of Departments A, B C, and W.

When the concentration camps came under Pohl's control, he immediately started to reform them according to his philosophy. A few camp Kommandants had to go at first. These were men who either didn't obey Pohl's orders or, as in Loritz's case, were no longer tolerable.

Pohl's principle demands were: treat the prisoners decently; stop the arbitrary and high-handed treatment by subordinate SS soldiers; improve the food wherever possible; get warm clothing for the prisoners in the cold seasons; provide adequate housing and improve all the sanitary conditions.

All these improvements were supposed to maintain prisoner fitness, so that they would be able to perform the work demanded of them.

However, the effects of the war were stronger than his desires. The poor and arbitrary treatment of prisoners was a direct result of the shortage of qualified and dependable officers and noncommissioned officers in the protective custody camps and the labor camps. Other reasons were the enormous growth and spread of the camps and work areas, which made the supervision of the guard personnel almost impossible because of the sheer size of the place, in addition to the month-to-month deterioration of the guard troops. Conditions became increasingly severe because of the continuous rationing of the food supply. It also didn't help when Pohl appointed a nutrition inspector, a professor by the name of Schenk, who despite all his knowledge and ability, could not increase the rations. Of course, there were small improvements by increasing the raw vegetables, but improvements were mostly in theory only. All his plans were for nothing, however, when the next decrease in rations took place. The textile shortage also brought about cuts and more cuts for the prisoners. The mandatory clothing quota could not be met as far back as 1940. Not even using the clothing and footwear from the extermination of the Jews could sufficiently improve the clothing shortage. Adequate housing was defeated by over- crowding in all the camps, the shortage of building materials, and last but not least, the total stoppage of housing construction.

Even the best construction foreman would not have been in a position to keep up with the speed of the increasing numbers making the camps ever larger, not to mention the impossibility of keeping up with improving and enlarging the sanitary facilities.

Pohl continuously inspected a large number of work camps. He saw the terrible conditions and tried everywhere to help and improve things. If he saw that the conditions were caused by the officers or the noncommissioned officers, he ruthlessly proceeded against them without considering the person or his merits. Most of the time his inspections were unannounced and were very thorough. He didn't let anyone lead him around. He wanted to see everything for himself. Without considering the time, his person or his meals, he rushed from one place to another. He had a fabulous memory. Once he quoted a number he never forgot it. He could also remember what he saw during the previous inspection and could always recall it. The orders and directives he had given were always in his memory. There were severe consequences for those who made mistakes or were guilty of negligence and got caught.

After Dachau he kept a special eye on Auschwitz. He committed all his energy to building up and expanding Auschwitz. Kammler often said to me that Pohl started all conferences in Berlin with the question, "How far are we with Auschwitz?" The Raw Material Bureau of the SS had an extensive me filled with demands, replacement orders, and mostly letters from Pohl, all concerning Auschwitz. I was probably the only SS officer in the entire S8 who had extensive and full powers to purchase anything needed for Auschwitz.

Later, when I was director of inspections, Pohl ordered me again and again into the concentration and labor camps where he had discovered grievances and abuses he had been unable to clear up. I had to search for the guilty parties and try to alleviate the worst conditions.

But because the basic cause was not eliminated by Himmler, all efforts to improve conditions were hopeless from the beginning!

One side of Pohl was that of a cold, sober calculator, a numbers man who demanded from his subordinates the greatest sense of conscientiousness of duty and work performance. He pursued violations and negligence in an inhumanly hard way and insisted on having his will and his wishes done without question. Woe to him who dared to cross him and his plans. Pohl didn't rest until his adversary was removed or destroyed.

The other side of Pohl was one of a great comrade, helpful with those who got into trouble without it being his fault. He was very soft, considerate, and thoughtful where women were concerned. He placed great value on proper treatment of the female guards, radio operators and other female civil employees. He wanted them treated politely and preferentially. He was particularly concerned about the bereaved families of the S8 soldiers who died or were killed in the war and supported them to the fullest. They could turn to him. The SS officer who failed to do his duty in this area or was rudely negligent was forever finished with Pohl.

He never missed noticing those who worked hard and used their brains.

He was grateful for all good ideas, improvements, and suggestions on how he could take action or improve things. Those who distinguished themselves by good performances could come to him anytime with their requests and wishes. He always helped them as far as his power could.

Pohl was very moody and often went from one extreme to another.

It was not advisable to contradict him when he was in a bad mood and this led to serious rebuffs. When he was in a good mood, you could tell him anything, even the absolute worst and most troublesome problem and he never took offense. It wasn't easy to spend anything but a brief time in his presence. Adjutants were changed often and very suddenly.

Pohl loved to make a show of himself and let one feel his position of power. His uniform was markedly plain and he wore no medals whatsoever. Only after he was awarded the Iron Cross and the Knight's Cross with Distinguished Service Medal did he wear them and only because Himmler ordered him.

In spite of being over fifty years old, he was extremely vigorous, lively, and incredibly tough. It was no pleasure to have to go on an official trip with him.

His relationship with Himmler was strange. Pohl was held in the highest regard by Himmler. Every letter and even the telegrams were always signed:

"Your faithful H. Himmler." And yet, Pohl never went to Himmler unless he was summoned.

Pohl looked at every wish of Himmler, and there were many, as an order! I have never heard Pohl make a disparaging remark about any of Himmler's orders. An order from Himmler was for Pohl something chiseled into stone, a fact, and had to be carried out regardless of the consequences that might occur. Pohl didn't care for it when a Himmler order which often was unclear was guessed about or mention was made that this order could not be carried out. Particularly Kammler and Glucks, who both had very loose tongues and who generally presumed a lot with Pohl, were often clearly reprimanded.

Pohl was, in spite of his authority, the most willing and obedient executor of all the wishes and plans of the leader of the SS, Heinrich Himmler.

Pohl's first marriage ended in divorce in Dachau. His first wife could not handle his rise to power. He had one son and two daughters from this marriage. His son served in the Waffen SS with great distinction. He was wounded several times and an excellent leader. The daughters were both married to SS officers and had several children. Pohl's second marriage was to the widow of an officer who had fallen in World War I. From his second marriage Pohl had two children. He lived on a grand scale on an SS estate near Ravensbrück. He definitely did *not* enrich himself personally as far as I got to know him in the ten years of our acquaintance. But he did not ignore the privileges which his position brought him.

In the middle of April, when Germany was about to be divided in two separate parts, on Himmler's orders, Pohl went with the rest of the SS staff to Dachau. Only a few liaison officers remained in Berlin.

His wife owned a house in the Bavarian Alps and she and his family had driven there a short while before.

Administrative Group D still had radio contact with Pohl until Oranienburg was evacuated. After that I heard nothing about him.

SCHWARZ

SS *Captain Heinrich Schwarz* came from Munich and was a book printer. He was an early member of the Nazi Party. When the war started he was drafted into the Waffen SS and at first served with the troops and only later in the concentration camp Mauthausen. From there he came to Auschwitz in 1941 as a work Kommando leader. Schwarz was a typically hot-tempered person, very easily excited and quick to anger; however, he never acted without thinking. He was very conscientious and dependable. When he received an order, he carried it out to the last letter. He followed my orders willing and attentively. With Schwarz I never had the least suspicion that he would fool me or go behind me back. Because of his eagerness to serve me, he was often laughed at by the other officers of the camp. They also did not like him because he took his duties seriously. He was unrelenting toward those who worked sluggishly. Schwarz was a tireless worker; nothing was too much for him. He was always alert and ready for duty. I could give him the most difficult task and not worry. He carried out everything in a conscientious manner.

As work Kommando leader he had a very difficult job. Schwarz was subordinate to Maurer of D II and Maurer truly gave him a hard time.

There were continuous changes in orders; often the new orders were the direct opposite of the old ones and superseded directives from D II. Schwarz's job was to see that every prisoner work at the job he had been

323

expert at in civilian life. The prisoners changed their expertise so that they could get better jobs, or for some other reason *they* felt was important. Schwarz had his particular frustration with prisoner transferred to other camps. The final count was never right because some prisoners always became ill or were kept back in the protective custody camp for whatever reasons. The prisoners who were on standby for these transports had professions different than the ones needed, so they were useless. When the transports finally started rolling, the complaints then began from the Kommandants and the labor camp leaders of the receiving camp; either the prisoners weren't strong enough, or couldn't perform the assigned work, or didn't have the necessary skills in the profession they said they had in civilian life. The letters Schwarz received from D II about these complaints were devastating and demoralizing. These letters were filled with words such as: undependable and incompetent. Maurer did this purposely to "liven up the work Kommando leader," as he called it.

Because Schwarz was so conscientious, these criticisms often caused him great despair, although I told him time and again that D II doesn't really mean it seriously. He did not take my advice, and he never lost his dread and timidity of Maurer's letters even to the end. This was all the more strange because otherwise he was very tough.

Schwarz never found a way to deal with those under his command.

Since he was a hard worker, he demanded the same performance from them. In addition, Schwarz had a great number of useless and incompetent men to work with. There was no chance for exchanging them for someone else because most of the time the replacements weren't any better.

Schwarz was interested in being a comrade, but he never covered up for their violations or carelessness. This brought him in continuous conflict with the camp commander and the troops. They were just as cautious with him as they were with me.

He was very strict with the prisoners; he demanded a great deal as far as the amount of work was concerned, but I always had the impression that he was fair. He did not tolerate their unreasonable actions.

A major part of his work was providing the guard details for the construction of the subcamps. The factories caused a great deal of aggravation to him, at least until they started operating and until the plant managers learned how to handle the prisoners. There were constant problems with the

Kommando leaders. How often they had to be transferred! There were constant incidents with the guard details, either with our own SS or those sent over from the army, navy, or air force.

In spite of the different tasks, Schwarz supervised everything and he always knew what was going on. If he was deceived by those under him or if his directives were not followed correctly, it happened only because no one could watch over his men for twenty-four hours and he didn't have enough dependable SS soldiers. Schwarz did his best to try to prevent the terrible conditions and to clear up the deplorable state of affairs.

Schwarz was my faithful helper who took a lot of work off my shoulders. Even during the extermination of the Jews, I could relax when Schwarz was on duty. Because he was attentive, he usually did not miss anything. I also don't believe that Schwarz was ever guilty of being overbearing or ever issued any directives using my name.

As leader of the work Kommandos, he tried to be fair with their many demands according to the importance of the project. He made his judgments on what he saw; if he had doubts, he asked me to make a decision. He often had serious arguments with the construction bosses and the farm people outside the camp. When Schwarz became Kommandant of Auschwitz III [Monowitz-the Buna synthetic rubber factory], his areas of responsibility basically remained the same. The only difference was that he was rid of the labor details, but he still had to create new labor camps. The difficulties increased in the factories because only a few factory managers really understood how to handle prisoners and only a few old-time prisoners knew what the work was all about. Schwarz always stubbornly demanded that the prisoners be treated decently, be given good food, and have adequate shelter. He moved quickly and often drastically against those responsible when there were legitimate complaints, and he didn't rest until the grievance was remedied. He was unable to act against the general day-to-day problems, but he tried to increase the rations and achieve a substantial improvement in the food supply.

After evacuating Auschswitz he took Hartjenstein's place in Natzweiler, which in turn had to be evacuated. It consisted mainly of labor camps in Baden and Württemberg.

Conditions in the labor camps hastily erected by the Todt Organization were not much better than those in Birkenau. In addition, Kommandant

Hartjenstein did not make any substantial improvements in the six months he was there. The prisoners of these camps were almost exclusively Jews from Auschwitz. During an inspection trip in January 1945 that Pohl had ordered, I saw mostly sick and dying prisoners. As the American advance increased in April and May of 1945, Schwarz was ordered to pull back with his wretched survivors from the labor camps to the concentration camp at Dachau.

Looking at the whole picture, Schwarz was one of the few capable officers in Auschwitz.

XI/46

Sell

When the war started, SS *First Lieutenant Sell* was drafted into the SS reserves of the Death's Head Division.

Sell was ordered from the women's camp at Ravensbrück to Auschwitz by Maurer. He was sent there to lighten Schwarz's burden. I cannot remember when this happened. He was supposed to take care of the correspondence, the files of the labor operations and handle all the reports so that Schwarz could spend more time with the labor camps.

Sell was a very transparent person. He was tired and slow, had difficulty comprehending the situation and was neglectful in all his work, which constantly aggravated Schwarz. Schwarz could never depend on him and had to check everything Sell did. He pushed most of his work onto the prisoners, even the items stamped "secret state matter." He often worked against what Schwarz wanted concerning the labor operations because he did not agree with the way Schwarz was doing things. He made a great many promises to many of the factories which could never be fulfilled. I also suspect that he took bribes. He also had to be on duty for twenty-four hours at the gas chambers just like the other officers of the protective custody camp. He always had quarrels with the doctors on duty because he tried to make "selections of his own." I always suspected that Sell stole valuables from the personal belongings of the Jews who had been exterminated. Even though I kept a very close watch on him, I could never catch him doing it. The special commission of the SS Court investigated him but without any results. His mood dictated how he treated the prisoners.

His "pet labor service," prisoners working directly for him, were under his special protection and were able to commit the worst cases of graft and profiteering. This racketeering really became worse when Sell himself took command of the labor assignments after Auschwitz was divided into three camps-each with its own Kommandant. Using the money and valuables from the racketeering, the shrewd and experienced prisoners were always able to get easy jobs. Schwarz tried and tried to stop this, but Sell just continued the black market labor in secrecy. Sell especially liked to occupy himself with the women's camp by obliging the female guards and the female prisoners who were his favorites. He actually preferred the female prisoners and put them into "elevated positions." He paid little or no attention to the main body of prisoners and how they were deployed. He graciously allowed the female guards or even the female prisoners to take care of them. Even though Maurer made him personally responsible for the transports to the labor camps in Germany, Sell didn't really trouble himself about this.

When I was still there, Maurer wanted to get rid of him and his replacement was already in Auschwitz. But I had to have his replacement arrested after just a few days when I caught him taking valuables from the Jews in Canada at Birkenau. The replacement was sentenced to death.

Because of this Sell remained at his post with no one to replace him.

Nevertheless, Maurer constantly kept an eye on Sell and treated him quite harshly. Sell, however, had a thick skin and really didn't pay any attention to this. Sell led a loose lifestyle during his off-duty hours-many women and even more alcohol! Naturally this affected his work. None of his subordinates paid any attention to him. He tried to make himself liked by his fellow officers by behaving obscenely, but the decent and reasonable ones refused to have anything to do with him!

Sell caused more damage than good to Auschwitz!

XI46 H.

Thomsen

SS *Major Thomsen* was the director of the Polish section of IV, D II of SS Headquarters.

In 1940-41 Thomsen was with the director of security in Krakow, then in 1942 he was with the inspector of the Security Police and Secret Service in Breslau. From there he came to SS Headquarters and was appointed director of the Polish section.

While he was in Krakow and Breslau, he came to Auschwitz many times.

When I was director of inspections, I often had to negotiate with him about escapes, captures, executions, inductions, transfers, and transporting pregnant Polish women from the police jails and concentration camps to Ravensbrück and from there to the abortion clinic. Furthermore, there were releases, death cases, shipping the personal effects of prisoners who had died, and other things to be handled.

Muller, who was director of Department IV at SS Headquarters, and Eichmann liked to give their reports verbally about the things I just listed. He nevertheless referred all matters which pertained to the Polish section to Thomsen. I had the impression that Muller was not well-informed about the General Government since his attention was on other areas of his duties. I remember further that all execution orders sent to Poland with a few exceptions were signed by Thomsen. The execution orders for other sections were always signed: Muller.

I cannot explain the exceptional treatment of the Polish section, especially because Thomsen was not outstanding in any way.

I want to add to this, that the general opinion at SS Headquarters was that the total annihilation of the Polish intelligentsia would also destroy the resistance movement. Thomsen was an ardent defender of this theory.

Jan 47 Höss

Wirths

SS *Major Dr. Edward Wirths* was the garrison doctor of Auschwitz from 1942 up to the evacuation. Before the war Wirths had a sizable country practice as a general practitioner in the countryside of Baden. In the beginning of the war he was drafted into the Waffen SS and was posted to the front lines with various units. He developed a heart problem when he overworked himself in Finland and could no longer be used at the front. This is how he ended up in Auschwitz. Wirths was an excellent doctor with a very strong sense of duty. He was also conscientious and very careful. He had an extensive knowledge in all fields of medicine and was always studying to increase his knowledge and abilities. And yet he was very soft and good-hearted; he needed a strong person to lean on. He followed each order and directive to the letter. When he was in doubt, he always checked to verify the order. Because of this, he always had me confirm the directives of Grabner's political section about executions before he carried them out. This constantly aggravated Grabner, who took great offense at this. Wirths very often complained to me that he couldn't reconcile the ordered killings [by injection of phenol into the heart] with his medical conscience and was suffering terribly from this. He constantly requested a change of duty assignments from Dr. Lolling and even the surgeon general. But all requests went for nothing. I often had to bolster his fortitude by pointing out the hard necessity of the orders issued by Himmler. The entire program of exterminating the Jews bothered his conscience; he had a lot of scruples about it. He often came to me and we discussed this confidentially as he poured out his heart to me.

Because he was so conscientious and careful, he conducted experiments with the Zyclon B gas and the phenol used for injections in order to make it easier on the victims. These experiments often caused him such mental anguish that I forbade him to continue them. Except for a few doctors, he really didn't get any help from his subordinates. First of all, there were too few doctors in Auschwitz; secondly most of these were nearly useless, that is, often unbearable because of their behavior or because of their deficiencies. As in all departments, the lack of personnel was chronic. Almost all the medical care given to the prisoners was done by prisoner doctors who practiced under the supervision of SS doctors. Their work was outstanding in part, and valuable, but often fatal. The hospital was the crowning glory for the Kapos and block leaders. Because of the confusion that exists in a large medical facility, it was impossible to surprise them with inspections.

It was almost impossible to keep the "V" people [those used for medical experiments] in the hospital. The prisoners who were informed preferred to keep silent! Wirths often reported to me about his attempts to alleviate the terrible conditions and how he failed miserably. It was impossible to prove any of the outrageous actions the prisoner doctors committed, especially during the mass dying, when the epidemics raged through the camps. Wirths also took great care to get information from those who had been severely beaten about who had done it, but without results. The fear of the all-powerful and all-knowing *real* power in the camp was just too great.

Wirths considered it his first duty to watch over the sanitary installations, to improve them, and to use all his power to rid the camp of the terrible conditions in them. Wirths was always warring with the building director because he constantly pushed for improvements and the building of new facilities. When he learned of mistakes, he was relentless and did not rest until bad conditions were cleared away.

In his monthly medical reports to D III Medical Headquarters and to the surgeon general, Wirths described down to the smallest detail the exact state of health, the situation of the hygienic and sanitary facilities, and the terrible conditions that had appeared. He did this in a clear style and with unsparing openness.

In every one of these reports Wirths begged for help to alleviate this catastrophe, which later would be labeled a horrible general health condition of the camp. Everyone who read these reports could form a realistic picture of these conditions. He did the same in verbal reports to D III and to the surgeon general. When an epidemic broke out, there had to be special reports. The high numbers of dead caused him to think about this situation; he would fire off reports and quote the reasons which led to the disaster. He was so explicit about what had happened that even I felt that these reports seemed to be exaggerated. But I allowed him to do as he liked. No noticeable help ever came to Auschwitz because of these reports. But no superior in headquarters who was involved in this section remained ignorant about the catastrophic conditions in Auschwitz, and no one at headquarters could ever maintain that he didn't know about the conditions at Auschwitz.

Wirths often despaired over this "hear no evil" attitude of his superiors.

Despite this he believed that someday they would finally take drastic action. I let him believe this, but we lost all hope after Himmler's visit in the summer of 1942. Wirths did everything he could to correct the worst conditions. He had some good ideas which were valuable. But by the time they could be carried out, they were obsolete and without value because of the increasing overcrowding.

I believe Wirths was a good and loyal helper, a good advisor in all aspects in his sphere of duty. Even Lolling admitted, which was something he didn't like to do, that Wirths was the best doctor in all the concentration camps.

In all my ten years of service in the concentration camps, I have never found a better doctor.

He was always proper in his dealings with the prisoners and tried to be fair and just to them.

Wirths was often too good-hearted and most of all too gullible. He was often taken advantage of because of his good heart, especially by the female prisoners, often to his disadvantage. He showed real partiality to the prisoners who were doctors; in fact, I often had the impression he treated them as colleagues. As I remarked, this caused quite a few problems in the camp.

As far as I know, the cancer research he conducted along with his brother and the few surgical operations in this area did not harm the prisoners. The results of this research were for the whole medical profession and of great unique significance.

After the evacuation of Auschwitz, Wirths first came to Mittelbau, then to Bergen-Belsen, and finally to Neuengammen. His heart condition became so bad because of working at Auschwitz that he almost became unfit for duty. His hearing also deteriorated rapidly. He had a happy marriage and had four children.

Wirths was a good comrade and was very much liked by his fellow man. He helped everyone who came to him, even the SS families. Everyone had the greatest confidence in him.

Höss

Night and Fog and Meerschaum

Night and Fog and Meerschaum were code names for Security Police actions against resistance movements in the occupied countries of the West, such as Norway, Denmark, Holland, Belgium, and France. These actions were closely connected with the completion of the fortifications of the "Atlantic Wall" and the preparations to defend against the threatening invasion.

The arrested were first brought to Natzweiler; later they were also brought to Sachsenhausen, Buchenwald, and Stutthof.

These so-called N-N prisoners were to be kept separate from the other prisoners and were not allowed to write letters or postcards. They were to be kept in one place for the duration. For the purpose of intimidation, their families were to know nothing of their whereabouts. Inquiries from the Red Cross were to be answered in an evasive manner. The separation from the other prisoners also served to keep the names a secret. The N-N prisoners were only allowed to be inside the actual camp. If they went to work, they did so in a very tight formation, went only to one place, and were more closely guarded. Escapes were to be avoided at all costs.

Krakow, Nov. 1946

Rudolf Höss

Lebensborn

Lebensborn was one of Himmler's ideas. The Lebensborn [fountain of life] program was a duly registered organization whose goal was to infuse and increase the German nation with as much clean hereditary blood as possible. According to Himmler, this idea had to become a reality:

1) The greatest expansion of the Lebensborn program was to take place through advertisement among the circles of people who possessed the prerequisites of the goal. This was to create a wide, ideal, and material basis as large as possible for the work of Lebensborn.

In spite of all the efforts of the Party and the state to change from a nation with too few children into a nation of many children, this idea had just not taken hold in the general public. The birth rate, however, had increased noticeably after diligent propaganda and subtle pressures of the organizations of the Party. More was accomplished through financial help such as loans to families and child bonuses. But the numbers were far off the minimum demand necessary to ensure the continuation of the German people, which was that each family would have to have at least four children just to fill the great shortage that existed, and ensure every available healthy blood strain be preserved. The unwed mother, the child out of wedlock, was still despised as it always was. Against this disrespect and all the disadvantages that arose from it, all means should be employed and used to eradicate it. Thousands of children remained unborn because unmarried women were afraid of the disgrace.

2) Through very skillful covert requests to all healthy men with healthy

wives, they were asked to produce as many children as possible within the marriage and outside of it. At the beginning of the war, Himmler gave notice to all SS and police members in which he demanded almost openly to reproduce with any unmarried woman who was willing to bear children because of the expected loss of blood in the coming war. A decree from the government allowed any child of a fallen soldier to take on his name if the parents were not married or even engaged. It was enough to have the written statement of the father that he would answer for the expected child.

3) Countless homes for expectant mothers and kindergartens were created.

The homes for expectant mothers were equipped with all the best; mothers could start preparing for the birth from the fifth month on. For unmarried women who expected a child from an SS or police member the stay at that home was free of any cost to her. Married women paid according to the income of their husbands, and these costs were relatively low.

After childbirth and after they had fully recuperated, the unmarried women could give their children to the kindergarten and go back to their jobs.

They could visit their children at any time, and if they so desired, take the children with them to live. Room and board for the children in the kindergarten was calculated according to their mother's financial means.

They also had the choice of giving the child to childless families for them to raise or to adopt outright. By the time the war started there were already six such homes.

By building a great number of these homes, the material aspect of the problem was to be solved.

The means for them were to come from a widespread membership circle, from contributions from the business firms of the SS, and finally from donations and stipends.

Thus, for example, every SS officer was obligated to be a member of Lebensbom. His membership dues were figured according to his income and, if married, according to the number of children for which he was financially responsible. Officers active in the Waffen SS and those in high positions had their dues deducted from their pay. SS families who had no children, and who after medical examination found they could not have children, were called upon by Himmler to accept one or more children from the Lebensbom, depending on their financial situation, and either raise them or adopt them. SS officers over thirty who weren't married yet received a demand from Himmler to marry within a certain time limit, usually one year. If they didn't comply they lost any further chance for promotion. They were put on ice.

Himmler reserved the decision to make any promotion from SS Major on up. Family circumstances and the number of children often were the things that decided in their favor with him.

According to Himmler's wish, SS families were to be the model and example for other German families in the creation of large families. Every healthy SS family was supposed to have at least five children.

Large, healthy families were helped in every way by Himmler, whether it was through stipends or generous gifts or tuition for schools.

Furthermore, he promoted extramarital procreation of children, especially by the members of the Waffen SS units. By using "whisper propaganda" in these units the "will to have children" was to be awakened. The SS was to have the task of breaking the moral ban on unwed mothers.

The newspaper of the SS, Black Corps, discussed this theme in long articles clearly and unequivocally long before the war, and, despite press censorship, created fights about its views.

Friendly foreign countries published cartoons and commented: "Himmler wants breeding establishments for Nordic men-the German woman is to be only a birth machine," etc.

Despite the many attacks, particularly from the churches, which tried to show contempt toward Lebensbom, Himmler's goal, slowly but surely, took on substance.

Krakow, Jan. 47. Höss

The Nürnberg Interviews

Höss awaiting execution

Rudolf Höss at Nürnberg
April 8, 1946

A forty-six-year-old man, Rudolf Höss, in the C wing in isolation. He sat with both feet in a tub of cold water, his hands clasped in his lap, rubbing them together. He said he had had frostbite for two weeks and that soaking his feet in the cold water relieved the aching.

I remarked that it hadn't been cold here, how did they get frostbite?

"I was in Schleswig-Holstein, barefooted in a cell. When the British captured me. I was naked and they just threw a couple of blankets around me and took me to prison. They didn't give me any shoes or socks."

I asked when he was arrested.

"On March 11, 1946."

Tell me about it, I said.

"I was hiding after I had been discharged under a false name as a navy sailor. I worked on a farm in Schleswig-Holstein."

I asked how the authorities found out who he was.

He said, "As far as I know, they questioned my family, who live in Schleswig, and my oldest son, age sixteen, must have given them my address."

Why didn't you give yourself up before? I queried.

"I thought I could get away with it."

What was your official position? I asked.

"As of November 1943 I was head of a branch of the Economics and Administrative Main Office in Berlin. Our office was actually in Oranienburg. This office was formerly called Rossbach Freikorps, which was stationed in the Baltic states, the Ruhr, and in Upper Silesia. Officially the Freikorps was not paid for by the government, but unofficially it was financed by the government and by industry. The Rossbach Freikorps consisted of three thousand men. There were innumerable Freikorps, from company to regimental strengths."

After 1921 he became an apprentice agriculturalist on an estate in Silesia and Schleswig-Holstein. He worked there until 1923, when he was imprisoned, "because of the murder of a man who had given Leo Schlageter to the French; Schlageter was one of the leaders of the active resistance against the French in 1923." You murdered the man who gave up Schlageter? "Yes, I was one of four men who clubbed him to death." Why? "This man had been a member of the Rossbach Freikorps and then stole some money and made illegal dealings and took off. Then in May 1923 he reappeared in Mecklenburg in order to get some people in my school to work for the French. His name was Walter Kadow. He was an unemployed German teacher about twenty-five years old."

How long were you in prison? "I was sentenced to ten years' hard labor, but was released after five years." How is it that you didn't receive a longer sentence since it was murder? "It was not seen as murder by the court, at least not as a plain murder. It was considered death as a result of an argument. It happened in a restaurant where we met. The other three men received twelve-, ten-, and eight-year prison terms. I was in prison in Brandenburg on the Havel near Berlin. I was released from prison in 1928. There was a political amnesty when all people who were Communists or belonged to the rightist parties were released. It was the so-called Hindenburg amnesty. My crime was called a political murder." What is the difference to you between a political murder and any other murder? "There is a difference. If you kill to take money or rob, it is plain murder, but if you kill because of political reasons, that is a political murder." Do you mean that it is all right to kill your political opponents? "No, I only mean the emotions which lead to such things are different, that is, the causes vary." But in both cases, it is murder? "Yes."

From 1928 to 1934 he returned to work on various farms and estates in Mecklenburg, Brandenburg, and so forth. He described his duties as being mainly "inspector of estates."

Concerning his political activity, he said that he had been a National Socialist since 1922, but participated in no political activity between 1928 and 1934. He had attended party meetings but never held any office. In 1934 he joined the SS because the owner of the estate for which he worked wanted to establish an SS horse stable, and "I was an ex-cavalryman." Once while on an inspection tour in Stettin, "Himmler met me and asked me if I wanted to take the position of supervisor of a concentration camp. I agreed." How did you happen to be in Stettin? "There was a general inspection of the SS there and I was leading an SS cavalry group."

Höss said that while he was commandant of Auschwitz, soap was not manufactured from human fat.

"We cut the hair from women after they had been exterminated in the gas chambers. The hair was then sent to factories, where it was woven into special fittings for gaskets."

Was this hair also from men and children?

"No, in 1943 I received the first orders to do it. We cut the hair only from women and only after they were dead."

Did you supervise gas chamber murders?

"Yes, I had the whole supervision of that business. I was often, but not always, present when the gas chambers were being used."

You must be a hard man.

"You become hard when you carry out such orders."

It seems to me you must be hard to begin with.

"Well, you certainly can't have soft feelings, whether it is shooting of people or killing them in gas chambers."

People were shot at Auschwitz also?

"Not Jews, but Poles of the resistance movement were shot. This was done under orders of Rudolf Mildner."

Were you a friend of Mildner?

"He often came to Auschwitz."

Did he have his court at Auschwitz?

"After the Poles were sentenced, after the party district administrator signed the death sentences, then they came to Auschwitz to Mildner's court and were told that they were sentenced to death. This amounted to about sixty or seventy men per month."

How many months was Mildner there?

"Mildner came in 1941 and left in 1943. I would estimate about 1,500 men were sentenced to death by Mildner's court."

April 9, 1946

Höss was sitting on his bed when I entered with Mr. Triest, the interpreter. He came to stiff attention and kept standing until I invited him to sit down. He said that his aching feet were somewhat relieved but that he still occasionally put them in a tub of cold water for temporary relief.

"I am going to court tomorrow or the next day, I was told this morning. I am going to be a witness for Kaltenbrunner." He has a somber but apprehensive and vacuous facial expression. He said: "Did I give you a report of the actual proceedings?" I told him to tell me whatever came to his mind. He said, "Auschwitz was originally thought of as a quarantine camp for Poles from the General Government. Poles were originally scheduled to come to a concentration camp in the Reich itself, and Auschwitz was originally meant to be only a transient quarantine station where prisoners would be held for a few weeks to determine whether they had illnesses which were contagious, such as typhus or fleck fever.

"The actual spot where the camp was is near a little city near Auschwitz. Originally it was the site of artillery barracks for the Polish army. I had the order to cultivate and work the surrounding farms with internees. This was a hard job because all of the surrounding territory was often flooded and quite run-down.

"Until 1918 Auschwitz was part of Austria and Silesia. Then it became Polish. It was on the Galician border. It is sixty kilometers from Krakow. But Auschwitz was not part of the General Government, it was considered part of the newly created province of Upper Silesia.

"I arrived at Auschwitz in May 1940 and I brought with me a cadre of thirty internees from the Sachsenhausen concentration camp, where I had been the first adjutant and then camp commandant. Auschwitz was just an empty couple of barracks when I arrived.

"The Polish concentration camp inmates began arriving from the General Government and other Polish territory. Auschwitz at that time became a camp for people who had participated in the Polish resistance movement. Very few were executed during the first year - only those that were sentenced to death by the Gestapo and SS corps." About how many would you say were executed? "I don't know. A few hundred or maybe more." How were they executed? "By shooting. "The camp was run-down and I supervised the rebuilding of houses and barracks and prepared it for twenty thousand internees, but in the first few months we received only two thousand to three thousand men.

"In the spring of 1941, Himmler arrived on an inspection tour. He ordered me to enlarge the camp to the greatest possible extent, and party district administrator Fritz Bracht, who was present and who was responsible for the area, was ordered to put at my disposal the entire territory, which was about twenty thousand morgen, or five thousand hectares. In the camp itself, I was ordered to erect several large workshops such as carpentry and machine shops.

"Then I was ordered to dry out the swamps and erect model farms and build up agriculture as much as possible. I was ordered to construct a prisoner-of-war camp to accommodate 100,000 in a neighborhood three kilometers from the original camp, called Birkenau. The population in that territory, consisting of about seven villages, was evacuated and sent to the town of Auschwitz. Those that could be employed in factories or the railroad stayed in Auschwitz, but the others, who were only farmers, went to work for the General Government elsewhere.

"The 100,000 prisoners of war for the camp at Birkenau, the POW camp, never arrived, and that project was later discarded.

"In the summer of 1941, I was called to Berlin to see Himmler.' I was given the order to erect extermination camps. I can almost give you Himmler's actual words, which were to the effect: 'The Fuhrer has ordered the final solution to the Jewish problem. Those of us in the SS must execute these plans. This is a hard job, but if the act is not carried out at once, instead of us exterminating the Jews, the Jews will exterminate the Germans at a later date.

"That was Himmler's explanation. Then he explained to me why he selected Auschwitz. There were extermination camps already in the East but they were incapable of carrying out a large-scale action of extermination. Himmler could not give me the exact number, but he said that at the proper time Eichmann would get in touch with me and tell me more about it. He would keep me informed about incoming transports and like matters.

"I was ordered by Himmler to submit precise plans as to my ideas on how the extermination program should be executed in Auschwitz. I was supposed to inspect a camp in the East, namely Treblinka, and to learn from the mistakes committed there.

"A few weeks later, Eichmann visited me in Auschwitz and told me that the first transports from the General Government and Slovakia were to be expected. He added that this action should not be delayed in any way so that no technical difficulties would arise and that the schedules of transports should be maintained at all costs.

"Meanwhile, I had inspected the extermination camp of Treblinka in the General Government, which was located on the Bug River. Treblinka was a few barracks and a railroad line side track, which had formerly been a sand quarry. I inspected the extermination chambers there. These chambers were built of wood and cement; each was about the size of this cell [approximately eight feet by eleven feet], but the ceilings were lower than in this cell. Along the side of the extermination chambers, motors from old tanks or trucks were set up, and the gases of the motors, the exhaust, was directed into the cells, and this is how the people were exterminated."

How many people at a time?

"I couldn't tell you exactly but I estimated that in each chamber, which was about the size of this cell, but not as high, about two hundred people were shoved in at one time - pressed into the cell very close together."

Men, women and children?

"Yes, but they were brought into the cells separately, that is, the men were exterminated in the same chambers but at different intervals."

You have this cell to yourself and it is not very large, therefore, two hundred people would have to be packed like sardines.

"Yes, the door had to be jammed shut and the people pressed very close together, standing up."

How many chambers were there at Treblinka?

"There were ten such chambers, each made of stone and cement. There were no peek holes, just big doors covered with metal sheeting. The authorities at Treblinka would leave the people to be exterminated in these chambers with the motors running for one hour after they had started the motors, and then they opened the doors again. By that time all were dead. I don't know how long it really took for the gas to kill them."

How did they remove the bodies?

"They were removed by other internees. At first they were placed in mass graves in the sand quarries, and later when I inspected they had just started burning the corpses in open sand quarries or ditches and had begun to excavate the mass graves and burn those that had been buried." How long did you stay in Treblinka?

"Only a few hours, then I went back to Auschwitz.

"Then the first transports arrived in Auschwitz.

"I had two old farmhouses somewhat removed from the camp which I had converted into gas chambers. I had the walls between the rooms removed and the outer walls cemented to make them leak-proof. The first transport that arrived from the General Government was brought there. They were killed with Zyklon B gas."

How many people at a time were exterminated in each farmhouse?

Höss stared at the floor and thought for several moments. He shifted his eyes from me to the floor to Mr. Triest, and finally after about thirty seconds of silence, said: "In each farmhouse eighteen hundred to two thousand persons could be gassed at one time. The two farmhouses were separated by a distance of six hundred to eight hundred meters. They were completely closed off from the outside by woods and fences."

How often were these buildings used?

"Well, it was like this. These transports didn't come daily; sometimes two or three trains arrived on a single day, every train containing two thousand people, but there were periods when no transports arrived for three to six weeks."

How long were these people kept at Auschwitz?

"No time at all. A side track went to Birkenau and unloaded, and there the selection was made. Those who were able to work were sifted from those unable to work."

What criteria for selection were used?

"Well, we had two SS doctors and they sat at tables, and the people from the transports got off the train and walked by these doctors. These people were fully clothed; they just walked by and the doctors judged by their looks, age, and strength."

Out of the transport of two thousand, approximately how many were saved for work?

"In all of those years, I figured an average of twenty to thirty percent of the people were able to work."

And then what happened?

"Those not able to work were marched to the farmhouses. These were a good kilometer from the side track. There they were made to undress. At first they had to undress in the open, where we had erected walls made of straw and branches of trees that kept them from onlookers. After a while we built barracks. We had big signs, all of which read 'To Disinfection' or 'Baths.' That was in order to give the people the impression that they would merely receive a bath or be disinfected, in order not to have any technical difficulty in the extermination processes.

"And the internees whom we used as interpreters and general helpers in those stations instructed the people that they should take care of their clothing when they laid it on the ground in neat piles so that they should be able to find their clothes when they came out of the bath or disinfecting room. These internees helped quiet all of the people by answering their questions in a reassuring manner and telling them they would only be bathed in those houses.

"Then the people were brought to the chambers and the internees who accompanied them went along with the people into the extermination chambers so that the people would be quiet, since they saw the attendants go inside themselves. It was so done that all of the chambers were filled up at the same time. At the last moment, when the chambers were filled, the internees who worked for us slipped out, the doors were jammed shut, and the Zyklon B gas was thrown through small openings."

Was there any panic among the people prior to their murder? "Yes, sometimes, but we worked it smoothly, more smoothly as time went on. The men were always exterminated in a separate chamber, and the women and children together in the same chamber."

At what age, for example, did you distinguish between a child and a grown-up, that is, between a boy and a man?

"I can't say. We judged by the looks of the boys - you know, some are grown-up at fifteen years, others at seventeen. We judged mainly by stature."

Do you mean that all of those executed were unfit to work?

"Not exactly, but one can assume that the majority of those exterminated were not able to work."

Why?

"Well, the doctors who checked on the people fully clothed when they filed out of the transports also were present when the people whom they had selected for extermination were undressed, and they often remarked that their quick selection at the railroad siding was accurate because with few exceptions the people who had been selected for extermination were not capable of much work."

I don't understand. You said that the doctors who made the selections sat at the railroad siding and the people filed past fully clothed?

"Yes, but what I mean is that the doctors said such things later, when they were present at the undressing, right next to the gas chambers, out in the open. They would say that their selection generally had been accurate."

How long did it take for Zyklon B to work?

"After all of the observations done all of those years, I feel that it depended upon the weather, the wind, the temperature; and as a matter of fact, the effectiveness of the gas itself was not always the same. Usually it took from three to fifteen minutes to extinguish all these people, that is, for no sign of life anymore. In the farmhouses we had no peek holes so that sometimes when we opened the doors after a considerable period of time had elapsed, there were still some signs of life. Later on, in the newly erected crematory and gas chambers, which I designed, we had peek holes so that we could ascertain when these people were all dead.

"After a half hour, the farmhouse doors were opened. There were two doors, one on each end, and the room was aired. The workers were equipped with gas masks and they dragged the corpses out of the rooms and placed them at first in large mass graves.

"I believed that crematoriums could be erected fast and so wanted to burn the corpses in the mass graves in the crematory, but when I saw that the crematory could not be erected fast enough to keep up with the ever-increasing numbers exterminated, we started to burn the corpses in open ditches like in Treblinka. A layer of wood, then a layer of corpses, another layer of corpses, et cetera. To start the fire, we used a bundle of straw dipped in gasoline. The fire was usually started with about five layers of wood and five layers of corpses. When the fire was going strong, the fresh corpses which came from the gas chambers could merely be thrown on the fire and would burn by themselves.

"In 1942 the great crematoriums were completed and the whole process was then done in the new buildings. New railroad tracks led to the crematorium. The people were selected as before, with the only exception that the ones unable to work went to the crematory instead of being marched to the farmhouses. It was a large, modern building; there were undressing rooms and gas chambers underground, and crematory above ground, but all in the same building. There were four gas chambers underground; two large ones each accommodating two thousand people and two smaller ones each accommodating sixteen hundred people. The gas chambers were built like a shower installation, with shower outlets, water pipes, a few plumbing fixtures, and a modern electrical ventilation system so that after the gassing, the room could be aired by means of the electrical ventilation apparatus. The corpses were brought by elevators to the crematory above. There were five double stoves.

"Burning two thousand people took about twenty-four hours in the five stoves. Usually we could manage to cremate only about seventeen hundred to eighteen hundred. We were thus always behind in our cremating because as you can see it was much easier to exterminate by gas than to cremate, which took so much more time and labor.

"When the act was in progress, two or three transports came daily, each with about two thousand people. Those were the times that were hardest because we had to exterminate them at once and the facilities for burning even with the new crematories could not keep up with the extermination."

How many were killed in this way?

"I can't give the exact number. In the first place, all files on these people had been destroyed. There was no record or names, and even numbers were only roughly estimated. In about 1945 Eichmann had to submit a report to Himmler, because Eichmann was the only one who had to save the numbers for Himmler. Eichmann told me before he went to Himmler that in Auschwitz alone 2.5 million people were killed by gassing. It is quite impossible to give an exact figure."

Do you think the figure might have been higher, perhaps as high as 3 million or 4 million?

"No, I think 2.5 million is too high, but I have no proof. None of the people exterminated were registered, only those who went to work were registered in the camp."

Were those who were selected to work, instead of being killed, exterminated later if they were Jews?

"No, only there were some who died a natural death, like an illness, for example."

Did many die of sickness?

"Yes, there were constant epidemics of typhus as a result of the crowded camps and the lack of sanitary installations, which could not be built as fast as people came in.

"I reckon in all of those years in all of the epidemics, approximately half a million people died as a result of sickness."

How many people went through Auschwitz?

"That is impossible to say. I have no idea how many went through the camp. I know that in the years 1943-44 we had 144,000 internees in the camp who worked there. Most of the newly arrived people able to work were transported away from Auschwitz, and I don't know what happened to them."

I have heard that the gold was taken out of the teeth of those exterminated.

"Yes, after the bodies were taken from the gas chambers, since early in 1942, orders were received from higher headquarters to remove all gold from the teeth and send it to the Finance Department. From there it was sent to the treasurer, I believe."

Who did this removal of gold from the teeth of the dead?

"Internees, mostly dentists who worked there. We usually saved doctors, dentists, and nurses from the gas chambers in order to use them in technical positions."

How many Germans were there in Auschwitz on your staff?

"Do you mean including the guards?"

Yes.

"Well, in 1943, about December, when I left, there were 3,500 guards and about 500 men on the administrative staff, and that included those who supervised the agriculture section, the testing laboratories, the supervision of the extermination chambers, crematories, et cetera."

How could the Germans not know of these affairs if at Auschwitz alone 3,500 Germans worked at it?

"I can't answer that because there is no doubt that it was widely known among many people, but certain precautions were taken. For instance, it was not carried in the newspapers; we used the same train crews for the transportation; and almost everyone who worked in Auschwitz had to make a sworn statement not to talk."

Can you explain more about these 3,500 Germans who worked at Auschwitz?

"Until 1939, that is until the outbreak of the war, concentration camps were staffed by the SS Death's Heads units. When war broke out, Eichmann, who was inspector of concentration camps, took them in one division for combat. The guards were replaced by older people from the General SS. In the later years, that is from 1941 on, we used many so-called ethnic Germans, from Hungary, Galicia, for example, who had to serve there.

"In 1943 and 1944 the large units of the army, navy, and air corps were transferred to the SS to supervise work in war factories, armament production, and the like. For example, in an armament factory that worked for the navy and that used internees for labor - in such a case, the navy had to supply its own guard personnel. The same was true for the army and air force, because there were not enough guard units in the SS. The army, navy, or air force personnel that were used as guards later on were transferred to the SS."

What happened to you after December 1943, when you left Auschwitz?

"I went to the headquarters in Oranienburg to work for the inspector of concentration camps. Auschwitz had become so big it had to be divided into three camps, called Auschwitz 1, 2, and 3. Or they could be labeled 'Auschwitz' itself; 'Birkenau,' which would be Auschwitz 2; and 'Monowitz,' which would be Auschwitz 3. In Monowitz were all of the work labor camps that belonged to Auschwitz. The figure 140,000 which I gave you before takes into consideration only those who worked in Auschwitz and not the transient internees, who were either liquidated or sent on to other places.

"I went to Oranienburg in December 1943. My immediate supervisor was Lieutenant General Richard Glücks. My job was chief of Office 1, the so-called political section. My work included the complete supervision of all concentration camps, the administrations, releases, punishments, exterminations, all dealings with the RSHA, all files of internees - in short, everything that went on in the concentration camps."

From the time you left Auschwitz until the end of the war, how many people were exterminated there?

"The figure 2.5 million takes care of 1944."

Were there any exterminated in 1945?

"No, at the end of 1944 the whole thing stopped. It was forbidden by Himmler."

What happened to the transports that arrived in 1945?

"Hardly any transports arrived in 1945, and the only people who came were those able to work."

Why did the exterminations stop? Was it because there were no more Jews to exterminate?

"In November 1944 I was with Eichmann in Budapest and he told me that there were negotiations going on between Himmler and representatives of the Jews in Switzerland through various middlemen and that from then on exterminations would have to stop immediately'"

When do you figure the last exterminations occurred? Höss thinks and rubs his hands together. He finally says: "I am not sure, but I think in

October 1944."

What sort of man in your estimation was Eichmann?

"Eichmann is thirty-four or thirty-five years old, a very active, adventurous man. He felt that this act against the Jews was necessary and was fully convinced of its necessity and correctness, as I was."

Do you know Bach-Zelewski?

"Yes, not officially, but in 1940 and 1941 Bach-Zelewski was the Higher SS and police chief in Austria. He was succeeded by Ernst Heinrich Schmauser.From then on I had nothing more to do with Bach-Zelewski."

Did Bach-Zelewski know of the extermination of the Jews?

"At the time he left Silesia the extermination program in Auschwitz had not begun, but in Russia there were *Einsatzkommandos*[action commandos] of Security Police in every district. There it surely happened, too. Because we never received any Jews from occupied Russia and I know for a fact that the Jews were rounded up and exterminated in Russia by these commandos."

Marital History:

Höss was married in 1929. His wife is now thirty- eight. They have five children, ranging from ages two and a half to sixteen years. He states that he was happily married during his four years in Auschwitz. His wife and children lived nearby in the city itself. He had no marital difficulties as a result of his work.

About the time of VE Day, Höss was with Lieutenant General Glücks in Flensburg. Himmler was also in Flensburg. "Himmler ordered us to go into hiding with the army or navy. I made some connection with a navy commander, a well-known submarine commander. He gave us navy papers and we were dressed as sailors and later discharged as navy men by the British in Schleswig-Holstein."

What happened to Glücks?

"I never saw him since Flensburg. He was quite sick and went to a navy hospital; I think he died there. The last time I saw Eichmann was in April 1945 in Oranienberg, when he told me that he was ordered to go to Prague. That was in the last days of the war. I never heard from him again. His family was in Prague."

Did you work near your family?

"I was seven kilometers away from my family in the navy camp until my discharge, then I went to a farm near the Danish border. I secured this job through the labor office. I worked there eight months before I was arrested."

Did you see your family during that eight months?

"No, my wife and oldest son knew where I was and communicated with me but I did not see them."

During the time you commanded Auschwitz, where did your family live?

"In Auschwitz."

What did your wife say or think about what went on under your command?

"My wife only learned about it in 1942. Whenever an SS man or guard talked to her or there was mention of these things, she declined to believe it. I myself didn't tell her when she asked me; I answered something else. In 1942 she heard a remark made by party district administrator Bracht of Upper Silesia, who referred to the extermination program, and then she believed it. After that she asked me about it and I told her."

What was her reaction?

"She was very upset and thought it cruel and terrible. I explained it to her the same way Himmler explained it to me. Because of this explanation she was satisfied and we didn't talk about it anymore. However, from that time forth she frequently remarked that it would be better if I obtained another position and we left Auschwitz."

Höss's children are as follows: boy age sixteen; girl age thirteen; girl age twelve; boy age eight; girl age two and a half. All are living and well.

Didn't it bother you to kill children of the same ages as your own?

"It was not easy for me or other military SS men but we were convinced by the orders and the necessity of these orders.

"If I had not had direct orders plus reasons for the orders, I would have been unable to carry them through on my own initiative - to send thousands, millions of people to death."

Do you feel guilty, or merely a soldier who has done his duty? "Up until the capitulation of Germany I believed I carried out orders correctly and acted in the right manner. But after the capitulation, when I read newspaper reports of the trials, et cetera, I came to the conclusion that the necessity for extermination of the Jews was not as they told me - now I am guilty, as are all of the others, and I have to take the consequences."

What do you think your punishment should be?

"To be hanged."

Do you really, or do you think that there are others more guilty than you?

"There are others more guilty than me, particularly those who gave me the orders, which were wrong. But as I saw it in the trial in Belsen where SS men worked under the same orders as I had, I will have to face the same punishment."

Do you know Josef Kramer?

"Yes, I know him well. He was my first adjutant at Auschwitz, then he was in other camps. For a time, he was commander of Birkenau, which is Auschwitz 2. His last job was commandant of Belsen."

What sort of man was Kramer?

"He was a quiet, practical man but he lacked wide horizons, had no perspective or outlook, was not very active or elastic, and therefore I couldn't use him as adjutant. He could not conceive of things easily or use his own initiative. Even later when he was camp leader in Birkenau, he executed orders very precisely but he was not able to adapt himself to new situations or to change orders to fit existing conditions. He had to be led at all times and to be told precisely how to do things."

Was Kramer a sadist in your opinion?

"No."

In your own opinion, are you a sadist?

"No, I never struck any internee in the entire time I was commandant. Whenever I found guards who were guilty of treating internees too harshly, I tried to exchange them for other guards."

Who invented gas chambers?

"They developed out of the situation. The courts brought in a lot of people who had to be shot. I always objected to having to use the same men for firing squadrons over and over again. During that period one day my camp leader, Karl Fritzsch, came to me and asked me whether I could try to execute people with Zyklon B gas. Until that time Zyklon B was used only to disinfect barracks which were full of insects, fleas, et cetera. I tried it out on some people sentenced to death in the cell prison and that is how it developed. I didn't want any more shootings, so we used gas chambers instead."

How many concentration camps in Germany or outside of it had gas chambers?

"Mauthausen, Dachau, Auschwitz, and in the east, Treblinka; in Russia, they used gas wagons."

What about Majdanek?

"They had temporary gas chambers but that camp came under the Security Police - the *Einsatzkommando* and Security Police. In Lublin there was a concentration camp which came under our inspection and supervision but it was not an extermination camp. Majdanek was near the city of Lublin and was an extermination camp under the direction of Lieutenant General Globocnik, who was the SS and political leader of Lublin."

April 11, 1946

Höss was sitting on his cot rather transfixed in facial expression with his hands clasped together, cracking his knuckles; he wore shoes today. I asked *him* how he felt and he said, "Good." He then went on to say that his feet still ached at times, which he attributed to frostbite incurred three weeks ago. Asked to describe this pain or discomfort in detail, he seemed unable to do so except to state that it was an aching beneath the skin. He took his shoes off and I examined *his* feet, which were not abnormal, of good color, and with no particular sensory disturbances as far as pinprick, light touch, or deep pressure are concerned.

I asked *him* today what he had been thinking about, and he had the usual puzzled, apathetic expression and gazed from me to the wall and back to Mr. Triest, the translator, in a doleful manner, and then answered, "I haven't been thinking of anything particular. The prison psychologist, Dr. Gilbert, asked me to write a short biography of my early life, and I have done so." He had beside him a few sheets of pencil-written material which he had just composed. He asked whether I would like to see this composition which he had almost completed. I did so and I hastily glanced over it. I asked him to tell me in his own words what he had written. "Just what I told you in the last few days and also something we began yesterday about my father and mother and sisters. It is hard to remember one's early life, and my life was a very good, happy childhood, only I wanted to be a soldier very early and I kept trying to run away from home to join the army. Many times I was taken off the transports on which I had hidden myself and returned to my mother."

Family History: "I come from a comfortable home. My father had been an army officer and later a merchant. I have two sisters, four and six years

352

younger than myself. My father died in 1914 and my mother in 1917."

Father: He died at the age of forty-two of a heart attack when the subject was fourteen years of age. As an officer in Africa, he had been shot with a poisoned arrow in the upper abdominal region, insofar as Höss can recall, and he never completely recovered from that wound. He also had recurrent attacks of blackwater fever, also contracted in Africa. He was retired from the army as a major after these illnesses and thereafter he engaged in business enterprises. Just exactly what business he worked at was vague but apparently he was an agent of some sort. At one time his father had been a teacher in the military school in Metz.

Mother: Died in 1917 at the age of thirty-nine. "I was in the field at the front at the time. When I returned my sisters told me that she had died of general sickness. She had always been sickly, never healthy." He was completely unable to depict the personalities of his mother and father except to say, "Both were very quiet, self-contained, very religious Catholic people. I can't remember any more, just that they lived well together and dedicated all of their love to the children. My parents wanted me to become a Catholic priest. Because of this I studied at the gymnasium."

Did you yourself ever want to become a priest? "No, I always wanted to become a soldier. In my childhood I might have been talked into becoming a missionary in Africa because my father told me much about the life of these missionaries there."

Siblings: Sister born in 1904; sister born in 1906. Both are married. The older has one child, the other has two children. The older sister is married to a carpenter, the younger one to a cement worker. Both brothers-in-law own their own businesses. Neither, so far as Höss knows, was a Nazi Party member, nor were his sisters. The husband of the older sister was never in the army, but the younger sister's husband was drafted, wounded soon thereafter, and retired to civilian life. When was the last time you saw your sisters, and how often do you see them? "Since I left home at the age of sixteen, I have seen my sisters very few times and have had little contact with them. Sometimes there is correspondence between us; once a year at birthdays, but nothing regularly. I saw my younger sister for the last time in 1937 and the older sister for the last time in 1941. The older one lives in Ludwigshaven and the younger one in Mannheim.

"I inspected the IG Farben factory in Ludwigshaven at that time, 1941, and so I dropped in and visited my sister." Did either of your sisters know of your occupation? "Yes, they knew I was in the SS and in charge of concentration camps, but of course they had no conception of the details of my work. Moreover, neither of them, being good housewives, had any idea of concentration camps, and I didn't talk much about them."

Adolescence: "I had little patience for school and was only an average student because I always had it in mind to quit school and join the army. In 1914 when the war broke out I had a very strong impulse to be a soldier but I was too young. I tried to smuggle myself to the front with troop transports but I was always caught and brought home. In 1916 when I was working as a helper in a hospital- all schoolboys were used in army hospitals part-time - I met a cavalry captain in the hospital who knew my father. He had served in the same regiment as my father. I talked him into taking me with him into his squadron.

"At the end of the school term in early summer, I pretended to be going to visit my grandparents in the Black Forest. That was the usual thing for me to do during the summer vacations, and so my parents did not become suspicious. But that year, instead of visiting my grandparents, I actually went to the garrison of the captain of cavalry. He was organizing a unit to be sent to Turkey - the Asiatic Corps. I was trained hurriedly and two weeks later left for Turkey. It was only after my departure that I wrote my mother of my whereabouts, because I was afraid if they knew where I was in Germany, they would have me returned."

Why did you want to leave home so urgently?

"I had a good life at home but I wanted to become a soldier, that is the only reason."

Was your father a companion to you as a child?

"A companion? What do you mean?"

A friend - that is, was he easily approachable and very friendly to you?

"Now that you mention it, I can hardly answer that question because it is so long ago and he died when I was fourteen. Most of the time he was away from home. No, I shouldn't say most of the time, but a good deal of it, and when he was at home he was a good father, but he was, like myself., so busy.

He did not have much time to play games or other things with us, if that is what you mean."

Further attempts to get a picture of his father or of his mother were fruitless. It would seem, however, that the mother was a chronic invalid, sufferer from illnesses which are either unknown to the subject or were possibly psychosomatic. This is all so vague that a conclusion about it cannot be made. The only certain thing that can be said in regard to Höss's relationship to his mother is that it was not an intimate one and that at her death he was left quite unaffected and not at all surprised, since she had always been, as Höss says, "sickly and unhealthy."

"Then I served in the field in the Freikorps after my army career. Is there anything else you want me to tell you?"

Of your five children, who is your favorite?

"There is no difference, all five are alike."

Do you love them?

"Of course, my only concern now is not my own fate, because I know I shall hang, but the welfare of my wife and children." The latter expression of concern was made with the same apathetic appearance and lack of expression as previously.

Regarding the disciplining of your children, what did you do?

"I hardly did it, my wife took care of it. Only rarely did I take care of disciplining, and that was with the older children. Maybe I hit them lightly two or three times if they were bad. There was never any occasion for punishing the children; they were never bad and always well behaved. My wife is a very energetic mother in bringing up the children."

What do you mean by energetic?

"Well, she treated them with love, but in their whole education and upbringing they were taught to obey immediately."

How many servants did you have in your home at Auschwitz?

"Until 1940, I had just one girl servant, whom I obtained from the Labor Service. These girls had to serve a year of compulsory service in a home plus a half year with a family with children. It was part of the labor movement. After 1940 when I lived in Auschwitz, I had two women internees who worked for us. These women belonged to a religious sect, the Jehovah's Witnesses. Whenever they circulated pamphlets or participated in active ways in that sect, they were placed in concentration camps. The two women who worked for me in my home were over fifty. These women from the Jehovah's Witnesses, when physically fit, were put into families with children in order to make them forget their religious sects. They lived in my house, were free to go shopping, wore civilian clothes. Of course, they had to remain in the house at night and could not go around visiting."

How did you meet your wife?

"When I was released from prison in 1928 I went to an organization which was called the Union of Young People, people who wanted to be sent from the city to the country in order to learn farming and eventually become farmers themselves. My wife was also a member of this union and I met her on an estate where she was a helper in the household of the estate owner. But she was never a servant girl."

How old was she and how long did you court her?

"She was twenty years old when I met her and I knew her three months before we married."

Have you ever had any difficulties sexually?

"None. Such things were always very good. As a young man they were always very good, too. When I was seventeen I had my first sexual experience with a nurse in a hospital in Damascus. She was in her twenties, slightly older than myself Everything went fine."

Have you had any sexual experience since May 1945?

"No."

Any sexual desires?

"Well, no, first of all there was the hard work on the farm, and further the knowledge that I was sought after by the police."

Have you ever had any nervousness at any time?

"Yes, for example, in Auschwitz during my last year there, 1942, 1943, I had much to do. The exterminations were just a small part of my work. Every night the telephone would ring and I would be summoned somewhere. I was rundown not only because of the exterminations but because of the other work, too. My wife often complained that I spent too little time with my family and that I lived completely for my job. Only in 1943, after I went to Berlin, my doctors reported to my superiors that I had worked too hard and that I was run-down. I then had a six-week vacation toward the end of 1943. I spent that time alone in a hunting lodge in the mountains. My wife did not come along because she was in her last months of pregnancy with our last child and so she remained in our house in Auschwitz."

How did your nervousness manifest itself?

"I don't know, except that my efficiency suffered a little and I found that I was a little jumpy and more irritable than usual. Usually I am very calm an-self-possessed."

How do you feel at the present time - nervous, or self-composed? Höss seems to think for quite a while, stares at the floor, looks at me and then at the wall with his unblinking, wide, flat eyes. "I feel less nervous now than I did then."

What kind of house did you have in Auschwitz?

"I had a house which was located just before the gates of the camp. It originally belonged to the administrator of the Polish artillery. When I arrived in Auschwitz, the house was not quite finished. I had it fixed up, put in a garden around it. had ten rooms, not considering the baths and kitchens. But they were small rooms, nothing very large or fancy."

I asked him whether he subscribed to any religious belief.

"I left the church in 1922 and my wife left it in 1935." Why did you leave the church? "During my experiences at the front in Iraq and Palestine Ithought that there was a lot of humbug connected with the so-called holy places and that things were not done right, especially by the Catholic Church, of which I was a member. And that diverted me from my formerly rigid, strict Catholicism."

Just what humbug did you see and what in particular was wrong with the Catholic religion as you found it in Palestine and Iraq?

"I don't know, it is a long time ago and I was so busy since then I have had no time for thinking about religion, but all of this money that went to the church, well, it seemed to me that it was humbug."

Has there been any change in your religious attitude since your arrest?

"I wouldn't say a change, but for the first time I desire to see a Bible because I want to see what religion teaches a person. When I left home and was no longer under religious influence Iwas too young and inexperienced to really understand it."

Do you attend the Catholic services here?

"No."

Have you any desire to do so? You know that you can if you want to.

"That would be saying too much that I have a desire for religion. But now since I know that my life is over, I want to find an inner peace. Now I should like to find out whether what I have done in my life, not only at Auschwitz but before that, was not wrong. Maybe what I did and what I always considered to be the right thing was wrong, because I see, since the defeat in Germany in May 1945, that in the eyes of the church and in the eyes of the world culture and ideology these things were wrong." What do you think of your activities yourself? You mentioned you wanted to find inner peace. Do you feel some emotional disturbance? "Just that my feet ache and that I am more concerned with my family's welfare than with my own."

Does the fact that you put the phenomenal number of 2.5 million men, women, and children to death, not to mention your supervision of exterminations and excursions in all of the other camps that you supervised since 1943-does that fact not upset you a little at times?

"I thought I was doing the right thing, I was obeying orders, and now, of course, I see that it was unnecessary and wrong. But I don't know what you mean by being upset about these things because I didn't personally murder anybody. I was just the director of the extermination program in Auschwitz. It was Hitler who ordered it through Himmler and it was Eichmann who gave me the order regarding transports."

Do you ever have any thoughts of these executions, gassings, or burning of corpses - in other words, do such thoughts come upon you at times and in any way haunt you?

"No. I have no such fantasies."

What newspapers did you read during the last ten years?

"There were only the party papers, for instance, *Das Reich,* the weekly political paper published by Goebbels. I also read information circulars and magazines given out by the SS."

Did you ever read *Der Stürmer?*

"Occasionally I got hold of one, but I myself disapproved of it because it was too superficial, pornographic, and had too much propaganda in it. I don't think it was completely truthful, either."

That is an interesting observation: you murdered 2.5 million Jews but you disapprove of *Der Stürmer.*

"Oh yes, all people with any sense disapproved of *Der Stürmer.*"

Did you ever read the *Völkischer Beobachter?*

"Yes, I got it too, but I paid less attention to it than to the other periodi-

cals. I don't care much for daily newspapers."

Do you have any dreams of any sort?

"No, once in a while I dream but I can never remember the next morning what they are."

Do you ever have any nightmares?

"Never."

Is your wife a good cook? Do you have any preference in regard to the different types of food?

"No, I paid little attention to food - to the sorrow of my wife, who is a good cook. Food always played a minor role in my life."

Was your wife ever a party member?

"No, she was a member of the Women's Organization but was never active, had too much work to do in the home, bringing up the children."

Did you ever have any secretaries?

"No, in concentration camps we had no secretaries, only adjutants and military clerks." What was the highest rank in the SS you ever achieved?

"Lieutenant colonel."

Do you have any favorite sports or hobbies?

"Riding and hunting, to a certain extent, but I had little time for the latter because I was always so busy and tired out from my work."

CPSIA information can be obtained
at www.ICGtesting.com
Printed in the USA
FSHW010948210122
87835FS